The NEW COOK

Pamela Gwyther

This is a Parragon Publishing Book.
This edition published in 2002
Parragon Publishing, Queen Street House, 4 Queen Street, Bath BA1 1HE, UK

ISBN: 0-75258-777-3

Printed in Dubai

Designed and created by the Bridgewater Book Company Ltd.

Recipe Photography: Mark Wood, Ian Parsons
Home economists: Pamela Gwyther, Sara Hesketh

The publisher would like to thank Steamer Trading Cookshops
in Alfriston and Lewes, East Sussex, for the loan of kitchen utensils.

NOTE
This book uses imperial and metric measurements.
Follow the same units of measurement throughout; do not mix imperial and metric.
All spoon measurements are level: teaspoons are assumed to be 5 ml,
and tablespoons are assumed to be 15 ml. Unless otherwise stated,
milk is assumed to be full fat, eggs are large
and pepper is freshly ground black pepper.

Recipes using uncooked eggs should be
avoided by infants, the elderly, pregnant women, convalescents,
and anyone suffering from an illness.

AUTHOR'S ACKNOWLEDGMENTS
Thanks to family and friends for their support and encouragement,
and for eating and testing my recipes over the years. Particular thanks to
my husband, David Gwyther, for wine recommendations, to Mark Wood
for his photographic expertise, to Lorraine Turner for her professional editing,
and to my suppliers—butchers Andrew and Steve, and equipment suppliers
Kitchens of Bath and Kitchen Aids in London.

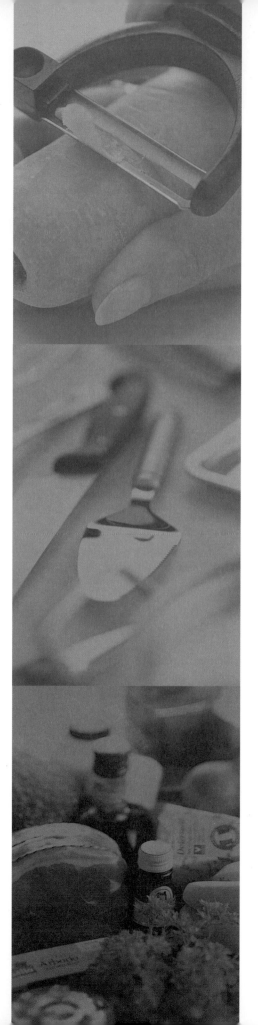

CONTENTS

Good eating

W e are what we eat. But what we eat has been changing over recent years, under a range of influences. Foreign travel has broadened our tastes. Economic pressures have made us more aware of the cost and quality of food—of its value, in financial and nutritional terms. Busier lifestyles have given us less time to shop and prepare meals. But supermarkets now have a wider range of fresh foods—meat, fish, fruit, and vegetables—and herbs and spices to add more exciting flavors. We can pull all these trends together under two keynotes of good eating: simplicity and healthiness.

SIMPLICITY

Today we are able to obtain raw materials at the peak of their quality, owing to better production practices and improved transportation around the world. We can therefore enjoy food at its simplest, not overworked or overcooked—indeed quite often raw or lightly cooked. This way we are getting the best of flavors and of food values, with much less effort.

If we choose food carefully, there is no need to spend hours preparing it. Long, slow, cooking processes still have their place for some occasions but the newer, quicker methods like stir-frying and griddling are ideal for busy people at the end of a working day. Slicing and grating vegetables means that we can eat them raw in salads or quickly pan-fried. They do not need peeling; carrots and other root vegetables can just be scrubbed. Meat and fish can be prepared by the butcher and fish store, so that we have ready-to-cook, smaller portions rather than a whole cuts or fish.

No longer do we have to disguise the poor cuts or "off" tastes of foods that are past their best, by smothering them with overpowerful sauces. Food now is served unadulterated, leaving natural flavors to be enjoyed in their own right. The only exception is adding handfuls of fresh, readily available herbs and flavorings from all over the world—parsley, cilantro, garlic, and ginger—to bring a whole new range of natural flavors to old favorites.

Keep a good pantry of basic materials for good, quick meals—rice, pasta, and lentils, oil, spices, a few cans of tomatoes and beans, and bouillon powder. These will quickly help to transform basic ingredients into delicious meals.

Cut down your consumption of red meat to reduce the chance of heart disease. If you do eat red meat, make sure it is lean and cooked by a healthy method, such as broiling. Eat more chicken and game because they are healthier options.

Eat fish at least three times a week. It is a good source of lean protein and the oily varieties give us essential fatty acids. All fish is very quick and easy to cook.

Eat at least five portions of vegetables, salads, and fruit a day. One portion is an average-size fruit like an orange, an apple, a pear, a medium banana, two smaller fruits like clementines or plums, a cupful of berries or grapes, or a large slice of melon or pineapple. A small glass of juice, about ⅔ cup, is a portion, but restrict juice to 1 glass per day. A small bowl of salad greens, tomatoes, cucumber, celery is a portion, or 2 tablespoons of vegetables such as peas, beans, spinach, sprouts, or cauliflower. The more fruits and vegetables you eat, however, the better.

Restrict excess fat in your diet, particularly saturated animal fats from meat and dairy products. Resist spreading butter too thickly on your bread and piling it on your vegetables. In some cooking, oil can take the place of butter. Try adding olive oil to your mashed potato and enjoying the flavor. Lower-fat cheeses are available, or stick to the normal ones and reduce the amount you eat. The same applies to yogurt and cream. Low-fat and skim milk are sensible options because they are lower in fat but still contain all the valuable nutrients of full-fat milk.

Hidden fat is the greatest enemy in prepared foods like cakes and snacks. Try to avoid these foods if possible, or read the label and try to choose lower-fat alternatives. Remember, though, that a low-fat diet is only a healthy option for those aged 5 and over—below this age a child needs easily accessible energy.

Eat more whole-grain cereals. Instead of white bread, eat whole-wheat and multigrain varieties and change to a high-fiber breakfast cereal or granola. Try whole-grain pasta and brown rice—the latter particularly has a nuttier flavor.

Drink at least 6¼ cups of water per day. You will feel healthier and your body will benefit. Limit tea and coffee because they contain caffeine, a stimulant that will keep your body in overdrive. Alcohol, in moderation, can lower the risk of fatal heart disease, but limit your intake to 1–2 units per day if you are a woman, and 2–3 units per day if you are a man. One unit is equivalent to a glass of wine, 1¼ cups of lager, or a jigger (2 tbsp) of spirits.

Always taste food at the table before you add extra salt. Restrict salt in cooked dishes and try to cook vegetables without any salt in the water. Too much salt can lead to high blood pressure.

Eating healthily will not stop you getting some diseases but it will affect how your body deals with them. A healthy diet will help you have a healthy life. In this country with so many people overweight, it really is time to question our eating habits and adjust them to be sure that we are getting the maximum benefits from good food.

LEFT Eating fresh, nutritious, simply cooked food is the best way to improve health and increase vitality.

BELOW To protect against heart disease, cut down on red meat and eat more fish, poultry, and vegetables instead.

Part 1
Nutrition and Techniques

BASIC NUTRITION

*I*n order to lead a healthy life we need to be sure that the body is receiving all the necessary nutrients to grow, maintain, and repair it. Food is utilized by the body to produce movement, warmth, growth, protection, repair, and reproduction. In order to do this efficiently, the body must have a good selection of foods that produce a balanced diet. We can break down the foods into five food groups: carbohydrates, proteins, fats, vitamins, and minerals. No one food contains a single nutrient; foods are a complex mixture of carbohydrates, proteins, and fats with very small amounts of vitamins and minerals, plus water. Water is a very important part of the diet because it makes up two-thirds of the total human body weight.

CARBOHYDRATES

This group includes all sugars, starches, and fiber. Sugars are referred to as simple carbohydrates because they have a simple structure and can be broken down by the body easily to give a rush of instant energy. Too much sugar is not good for the body, however, because it can increase the risk of diabetes, heart disease, obesity, and tooth decay.

Complex carbohydrates are present in whole-grains like corn, oats, and barley and in fresh fruit and vegetables. Their complex structure takes longer to break down in the body and provides a longer, steadier flow of energy in the bloodstream.

Fiber is not really a food because it cannot be digested by the human digestive system, but it is still very important in the diet because it provides bulk to assist the passage of the food through the intestines. In this way, a good intake of fiber helps to prevent constipation.

PROTEIN

Protein is essential for growth and repair of the body, and any excess can be used to provide energy. Proteins have a complex structure and are composed of amino acids. The ones that are necessary for the human body are called essential amino acids.

These are present in the correct ratio in animal proteins—in meat, fish, poultry, milk, cheese, and eggs—and are said to have a high biological value. Vegetable proteins, known as incomplete proteins, provide only some of the essential amino acids and therefore need to be eaten in mixtures that complement each other. But there is such a variety available that it is unlikely that people not eating any animal protein would suffer from a deficiency.

FATS

Oils and fats are present in the diet as the most concentrated form of energy. They are available as visible fats, such as butter, margarine, oils, and fat on meat, but also as invisible fat in cheese, cookies, cakes, chips, and nuts. Not all fats are bad. The baddies are the saturated fatty acids found in animal fats like butter and cheese and in animal products like sausages, bacon, pork, lamb, hamburgers, eggs, and full-fat milk. Saturated fats are thought to increase blood cholesterol levels and therefore to be responsible for heart disease. Polyunsaturated and monounsaturated fatty acids, on the other hand, are believed to reduce cholesterol levels; these are available in corn oil, olive oil, soy, and sunflower oils, and nut oils (not coconut).

VITAMINS

Vitamins help to regulate important body processes. Apart from vitamin D, all the vitamins must be supplied in the diet because the body is unable to manufacture them.

Vitamins fall into two groups, water-soluble and fat-soluble. Water-soluble vitamins include B1, B2, B6, and B12 and vitamin C; the fat-soluble vitamins include A, D, E, and K. If a vitamin is not present in the diet, then specific symptoms of deficiency will be observed. For example, lack of vitamin C results in scurvy. Vitamins may be taken as supplements but

they are expensive and if you have a well-balanced diet they should be unnecessary.

MINERALS

Minerals are inorganic elements needed by the body in very small amounts. They perform three main functions:

- Important constituents of bones and teeth (calcium, phosphorus, and magnesium)
- Present as soluble salts in body fluids (sodium, chloride, magnesium, potassium, and phosphorus)
- Aiding the process of releasing energy (iron, phosphorus, and zinc)

Trace elements are also needed, such as copper, fluoride, selenium, iodine, manganese, chromium, and cobalt, but in smaller amounts.

A well-balanced diet should provide all of these elements, particularly a diet rich in fruit, nuts, grains, and leafy greens. Supplements are widely available but they should always be used with discretion.

WATER

The most essential part of any diet is to drink at least eight glasses of water every day. Water is needed in the body for transporting nutrients, for digestion, for circulation, for body heat regulation, and excretion. No matter how healthy your diet, if you are not drinking enough water, the body will not function properly and you will feel lethargic and under par.

Sensible, healthy eating requires a good balance of food, which is low in saturated fats and simple carbohydrates. A reasonable amount of protein, vitamins, and minerals, plus plenty of fiber and water, will ensure that the body continues to function correctly.

PREPARATION TECHNIQUES

*D*o not be daunted by all the different food preparation techniques and descriptions. The range of definitions given here will be all you will need.

BAKING BLIND
This means baking pastry cases without a filling so that the pastry is well cooked and crisp. The quiche pan or pie dish is lined with pie dough or sweet pastry and then lined with baking parchment or foil, which is then weighed down with baking beans (actual dried beans or you can buy ceramic or metal ones) to prevent the pastry from bubbling up while cooking. The beans and foil are then removed and the pie shell cooked for a while longer to dry it thoroughly.

BEATING
This term refers to mixing food to make it lighter by incorporating air. You can use a fork, a wooden spoon, or an electric mixer for beating. It is most often used for eggs, for an omelet, and for making a cake, beating together the butter and sugar (this is also known as creaming). It is also used to beat a sauce or a custard, not to incorporate air but to make the consistency smooth and remove any lumps.

BLENDING
Blending means combining ingredients together, usually with a spoon. You can blend cornstarch and water, for example, to a smooth paste before using to thicken soups and stews. Blending also refers to mixing soups and purées in a blender to reduce to a smooth liquid and remove any lumps.

CRIMPING
This means to decorate the edges of a pie in order to ensure the edges are well sealed. This is done by pinching the pastry with a finger and thumb of one hand and pressing with the first finger of the other hand, giving a fluted edge. Crimping is also used purely decoratively on shortbread or plate pies.

CUTTING
Cutting is a basic technique used to prepare meat, fruit, and vegetables. Using a knife correctly is an important step in preparing food. Food that is correctly prepared will cook more evenly and have a more attractive appearance. A good knife and a firm board are essential. Make sure the knife is sharp because blunt knives cause accidents. Use the correct knife for the task, for example a bread knife for bread and a serrated knife for tomatoes.

CHOPPING
This is one step on from cutting. The food is divided into small pieces by more than one cut. To chop an onion, for example, you halve the onion from the top down through the stem and root, then you place the flat side of one half down on the board, and cut the onion from root to stem into fine slices. Then you turn the knife and slice through the onion the other way making sure that you have even pieces. Chopping herbs is another important skill. Hold the tip of the blade down with one hand and raise the handle of the knife up and down with your other hand as you chop into the herb, moving from left to right and back again so that you work all over the food.

Chopping can be done roughly or finely: roughly means pieces of food about ½ inch/1 cm, whereas finely means much smaller pieces. It is important to chop all the pieces to an even size. Sometimes a recipe might ask for food to be diced: this means pieces not only of the same size but of a regular shape; for example, diced cucumber should be small cubes.

CRUSHING
This technique is used for crushing herbs or garlic. To crush garlic, simply press down on the garlic using the flat side of a knife blade. Crushing is also used for making cookie crumbs for cheesecakes or flan shells. To make cookie crumbs, simply put the cookies in a large plastic bag, cover the end, and then crush with a rolling pin until they are reduced to crumbs. You can also crush garlic cloves with a garlic press or a heavy knife.

DREDGING
Dredging means sprinkling dough with flour before rolling it out. The board and the rolling pin should be lightly floured to

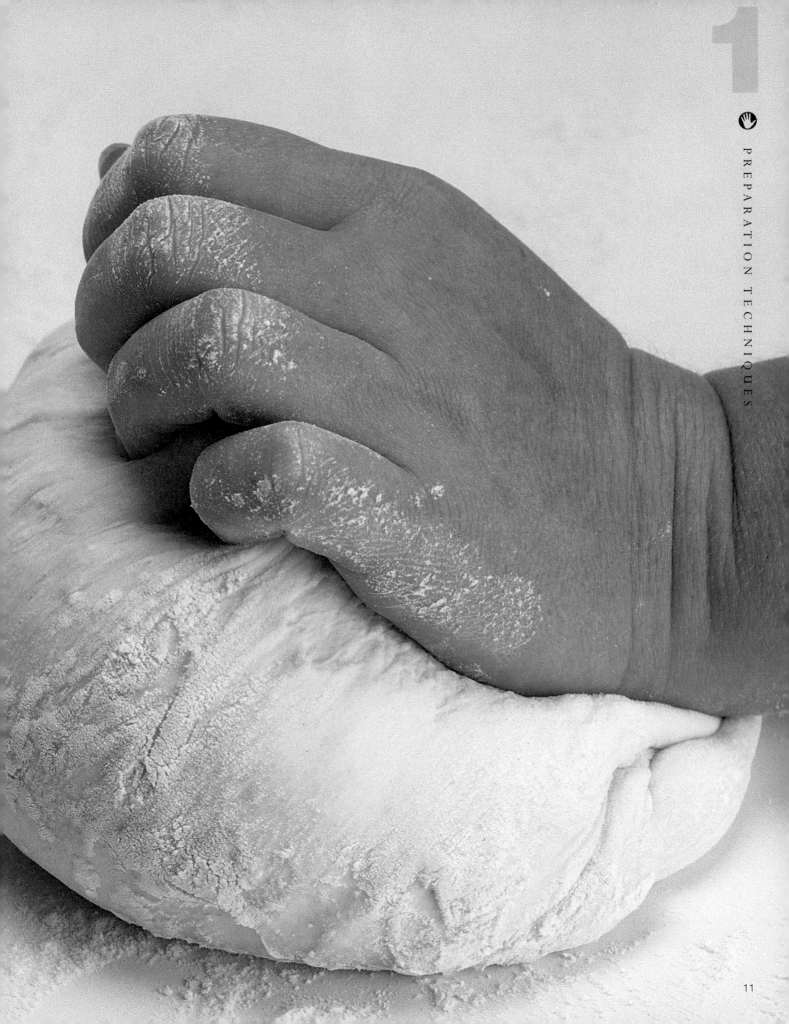

prevent the pastry from sticking. The term can also be used for sugar and unsweetened cocoa powder, as dredging a cake with confectioners' sugar. These days it is fashionable to dredge a plate with sugar or cocoa powder before serving a dessert.

FOLDING IN

The term used to describe how to incorporate flour into a cake mixture. It is a gentle movement, made with a metal spoon or a plastic spatula to cut through the mixture in a figure eight movement, enabling the flour to combine without losing the air already incorporated. The same term applies to meringues and soufflés.

GLAZING

A glaze is a finish given to pastry and bread before baking. It can be simply milk, or beaten egg, or a water and sugar glaze.

Savory pies are usually brushed with egg before baking to give them a rich, golden-brown, glossy finish. Sweet pastry products are often brushed with water and then sprinkled with superfine sugar to give them a crisp, crunchy finish. Breads and rolls can have either a savory (egg) finish or a sweet (sugar) glaze.

You can also glaze a ham. In this case the ham is partly cooked and the skin then removed, and a coating of sugar and mustard spread on. The ham is then baked further until golden and crisp in appearance.

GRATING

A grater is used to shred food into small particles. The two most common uses are for cheese and for citrus fruit peel. A box grater is useful because it has different-size surfaces and can produce medium and fine gratings. A food processor can grate food very quickly and is useful if you have a large quantity to prepare.

GRINDING

Grinding means reducing foods to a powder or very small particles for use in recipes. For example, you can grind spices in a mortar with a pestle until you have achieved the required texture. An electric coffee grinder will do the job quicker but you may get too fine a result. You will also need to keep it separate for the job because other flavors will ruin the coffee. A food processor will grind nuts and chocolate satisfactorily.

Grinding also means chopping food, such as lean beef, pork, lamb, chicken, or turkey, very finely. It is best done with a hand or electric meat grinder. A food processor can also be used to grind food.

KNEADING

This technique is used in breadmaking. The dough is kneaded to develop the gluten in the flour so that it will hold its shape when risen. The dough is pummeled on a lightly floured board until it is smooth and elastic. Kneading involves a particular technique that uses the heal of the hand to pull and stretch the dough, which can be quite therapeutic. Kneading can also be done in a free-standing mixer using a dough hook.

MARINATING

This involves allowing food to soak in a marinade, which will tenderize it and add flavor. Marinating is used for meat, poultry, and game. The meat is covered with a mixture of oil, wine or vinegar, and some added flavorings like garlic and herbs. The food can be marinated for a few hours or a few days. During the cooking, the marinade can be used to baste the food.

MASHING

This usually refers to potatoes and other root vegetables. Cooked vegetables are mashed, using a fork, a potato masher, or an electric hand mixer. This makes them smooth and light and other flavors can be incorporated at the same time, for example, herbs, garlic, and mustard. The addition of butter or cream makes them more luxurious.

PEELING

This is the removal of any unwanted peel from fruit and vegetables. Thick peel, such as orange rind, will require a sharp knife, but for vegetables with a thin skin, such as a potato, it is better to use a vegetable peeler because you will have less waste.

PUNCHING DOWN

This is the term for knocking the air out of the bread dough after its first rising. It involves literally punching the air out of

the dough and then gently kneading for 1 minute. The dough is then gently shaped before a second, usually fairly brief rising or "proving" in a warm place.

RUBBING IN

This is a method of cake making where the fat is rubbed into the flour. The same technique is also used for pastry and breadmaking. The fat is rubbed into the flour using the tips of the fingers, lifting the flour high out of the bowl so that the air will be trapped in the mixture. This technique makes the mixture lighter and achieves better results.

SCORING

A method of making light cuts on the surface of food to help it cook more quickly, to reduce fat, and also to make the food's appearance more attractive, for example, scoring duck breasts before broiling.

STRAINING

This is a method of rubbing cooked food through a strainer to form a purée. The food is pushed through the strainer using a wooden spoon. Straining can also refer to straining vegetables after cooking to remove the cooking water.

SIFTING

This is the same as straining (see above) but refers to dry ingredients, for example sugar and flour, to remove lumps and to add air to the mixture. With these finer ingredients, however, there is no need to push them through with a wooden spoon.

TENDERIZING

The technique of beating raw meat with a rolling pin or a meat mallet to soften the fibers and make the meat more tender before frying or broiling. This method is useful for steak that is not of the finest quality.

TRUSSING

This is the technique used for poultry and game whereby the bird is pulled into shape and then held with skewers or by string to maintain its shape during cooking. It is particularly useful if the bird has been stuffed because it prevents the stuffing from falling out.

WHISKING

This is another method used to incorporate air, but it is usually used for a lighter mixture, for example egg whites or cream. To make the task easier and more efficient, you really need an electric mixer for whisking. However, a wire whisk used in a large mixing bowl with lots of energy can perform the task adequately. Indeed, many chefs prefer to use their balloon whisks and a copper bowl for meringues.

COOKING METHODS

*A*gain, do not be daunted by the variety of the cooking techniques. Enjoy experimenting, particularly with some of the increasingly popular and healthier techniques like stir-frying and griddling. Here is all you need to know.

BAKING

This is the term used for cooking food in the oven by dry heat, for example, a baked potato or baked custard. It is also the process for preparing baked goods, such as cakes, cookies, and bread.

BASTING

The process of moistening meat, fish, or poultry while roasting in the oven. The cooking juices and fat are spooned over the food to keep it moist, to add flavor, and to improve the appearance of the finished dish. If the pan becomes too dry, then a little liquid, either stock or wine, can be added to the juices. Roasting vegetables are basted with oil so that they are well coated and will crisp evenly, and fried eggs are basted with hot oil to make sure the tops of the eggs are set.

BLANCHING

Blanching used to mean "to whiten" and was used to whiten veal and variety meats. Today there are two more usual meanings. The first is to immerse food in boiling water for a few seconds and then into cold water in order to remove their skins, for example tomatoes, nuts, and peaches. The other is in preparing vegetables for freezing. You immerse the vegetables in boiling water for a short period to destroy enzymes that will spoil the flavor and texture of the vegetables, and then into cold water to stop the cooking process. Blanching also helps to preserve the color of vegetables.

BOILING

This is cooking food in a liquid (water, stock, or milk) at 212°F/100°C (known as boiling point). The main foods cooked in this way are eggs, vegetables, rice, and pasta. Although sometimes fish and meat are placed in boiling liquids, the heat is then reduced, and the food is simmered only. Continued boiling would render these foods lacking in flavor, shrunken in size, and of poor texture.

BRAISING

A long, slow, moist method of cooking used for cuts of meat, poultry, and game that are too tough to roast. Braised food is usually cooked in one piece and the amount of liquid used is quite small. The food is browned in oil and then cooked with vegetables in a casserole with a close-fitting lid. The dish can then be cooked on the stovetop or in a low oven.

BROILING

A very quick and easy method of cooking, which is also very healthy. The food is cooked by radiant heat, which makes sure that the outside of the food is well cooked and browned while the inside remains moist. The food must be tender and of good quality, for example steak, chops, chicken, burgers, sausages, and whole fish like trout and fish cutlets and fillets like salmon and cod. Vegetables, such as mushrooms, bell peppers, tomatoes, and onions are also suitable for broiling. The broiler must be preheated and the food brushed with oil to give a little protection from the fierce heat. Cooking on the barbecue is the outdoor equivalent of broiling and is suitable for all the above foods although it produces a more smoky flavor.

CASSEROLING

Another, more modern name for braising, taken from the name of the cooking vessel—an ovenproof casserole dish with a tight-fitting lid (this is often flameproof and can be used for the initial browning process, which cuts down on the dish washing). The food is often served from the casserole dish at the table. Casseroling also includes stews, in which the pieces of food are often cut into small pieces and more liquid is used.

FRYING

The process of cooking food in hot fat. There are three main ways to fry food: pan-frying or sautéing, shallow-fat frying, and deep-fat frying. Frying gives the food a delicious golden-brown color and a wonderful flavor.

PAN-FRYING

A more modern method of cooking, pan-frying is devised to cook food quickly and easily in a healthier way that uses very little fat. Some naturally fatty foods, such as bacon and sausages, can be dry-fried because they contain enough of their own fat to be sure that they will not burn. Small cuts of meat, poultry, and fish are cooked at a high temperature in a very little fat (half vegetable oil and half butter are ideal for this because the oil allows the fat to reach a high temperature without burning and the butter adds the flavor). The food is added to the hot skillet, either with or without a little hot fat, and cooked on one side; the heat quickly seals the food and keeps it moist and tender. It is then turned over and cooked on the other side until cooked through. The food is then removed from the skillet to a warm plate and a sauce can be made with the cooking juices and a dash of wine or stock. Pan-fried food is served immediately.

SHALLOW-FAT FRYING

This method is used for coated foods, for example fish cakes and crumbed fish, or scallops of meat and chicken, which are coated with flour or bread crumbs. Use a vegetable oil, such as corn oil, in a shallow skillet and allow enough oil to prevent the food from sticking. The thicker the food, the more oil you will need. Heat the skillet and the oil to a high temperature and add the food: the oil will seal the food and hence will not allow it to absorb too much fat. Once cooked on one side, turn the food over and cook on the other side. Remove it from the skillet with a metal spatula or a slotted spoon, shake it gently to remove excess oil, and drain on paper towels, which will absorb any remaining fat. Serve while still hot.

DEEP-FAT FRYING

With this method, food is cooked while completely immersed in hot fat. The choice of fat is important because you need an oil that can be heated to a high temperature without smoking. Corn oil and soybean oil both have high smoke points—in other words, they smoke at a higher temperature—and are good for deep-frying. However, peanut oil is the best: it has one of the highest smoke points.

Foods need a protective coating when they are deep-fried and popular coverings are bread crumbs or batter. The most usual foods to deep-fry are French fries, shellfish, fish, and chicken. For this method, you need a deep, heavy pan and a wire basket to lift the food out. It is quite a dangerous method of cooking because a very high temperature is needed and many housefires are caused by deep-fat pans catching fire. A better method is to have an electric deep-fryer, which is thermostatically controlled so it is safer and easier to use.

GRIDDLING

A griddle was once a flat metal plate used on the stovetop to cook cakes and cookies. Nowadays, the expression "to griddle" refers to a ridged griddle pan rather like a skillet—it has a ridged surface, which gives the food attractive brown stripes. This equipment has become popular because it is used by many television chefs. It does produce very appetizing food and is a healthy way of cooking because the food needs only a light brushing of oil. Griddling is suitable for thin steaks, chicken, salmon fillets, squid and shellfish, and for vegetables such as eggplant, zucchini, bell peppers, fennel, and onions.

POACHING

A gentle method of cooking food in a liquid at simmering point (see *Simmering*, below). Poaching is suitable for small pieces of fish, for example steaks or fillets, particularly for smoked fish like haddock and cod because the liquid absorbs some of the flavor and can then be used to make a sauce. Whole chickens can be poached so that the meat is succulent and tender and the well-flavored stock can be used for soups. Whole fish like salmon can be poached to serve whole (see pages 118–19). Poached eggs are simple to cook if you use very fresh eggs. Fruit also lends itself to poaching because the long, slow cooking tenderizes the fruit without losing its shape and you have a well-flavored juice to serve with it.

SIMMERING

A method of cooking in liquid like boiling, but simmering is done at a lower temperature, just below boiling point. It is easy to control because you can judge it by eye. Boiling liquid has large bubbles and the surface is very agitated, but liquid at simmering point just has a gentle stream of small bubbles hardly breaking the surface. The simmering method is suitable for vegetables, chicken, fish, and fruit.

STEAMING

This technique involves cooking food in the steam of boiling water, either in direct contact or indirectly. Steaming is an

economical method of cooking because more than one item can be cooked at a time. It is also a healthy method of cooking because there is no immersion in water and therefore very little loss of nutrients.

The most usual foods to be cooked by steaming are vegetables; often potatoes are boiled in a pan and a steamer is set over the top and other vegetables cooked in the steam. You can buy 1–2 tiered steamers, which will fit over your pan and enable you to cook more than one vegetable at a time. The firmer vegetable should be in the base of the steamer and the more tender one at the top (where it is slightly cooler). The whole steamer is covered with a lid until the vegetables are tender and cooked through.

Bamboo steamers are now very popular and inexpensive. They can be used for fish, poultry, and vegetables. Just bring a small amount of water to the boil in a pan or a wok and stack up the steamers containing the food.

Another sort of steamer is the small, folding metal steamer. It is quite small and so not very difficult to store and will fit inside any pan. Bring 1 inch/2.5 cm of water to a boil in a pan and place the steamer and the vegetables in the pan, cover with the pan lid, and steam until tender.

Steaming is also used for desserts. The dessert bowl, well covered, is placed in the pan, on a trivet if you have one. The pan is filled halfway up with boiling water and the dessert is steamed for the correct time, checking the water level from time to time. Steaming produces a lighter, softer dessert than one that is baked.

ROASTING

This is a method of cooking food in the oven, like baking, but it is usually used for meat, poultry, and vegetables (nowadays we roast fish as well). Roasting often requires added fat to protect the food and moisten it while it is cooked at a relatively high temperature. Roasted meats are cooked in a fairly shallow roasting pan to allow the air to circulate and the surface of the meat to brown. Large, tender cuts of meat and tender poultry and game are suitable for roasting. If you are in any doubt about the tenderness of the meat, braise or casserole it instead. The cooking juices can be used to make a gravy to accompany the meat.

The most popular roast vegetable is the potato, but we can now roast all sorts of vegetables—parsnips, squashes, turnips, fennel, onions, garlic, carrots, sweet potatoes, tomatoes, bell peppers, and eggplant—giving them a delicious flavor.

SAUTÉING

This method is similar to frying, but sautéing usually means "moving" the food at the same time. The most common use of this method is preparing onions for stews or casseroles. You fry the onions in a little oil in a frying pan (or a sauté pan, which is slightly deeper) but you keep them moving because they are

finely chopped and need to be kept moving to prevent them from burning in the hot pan. It is this technique that has evolved as stir-frying.

STEWING

This long, slow method of cooking is very like braising, that is to say, cooking in a liquid. It is used for tougher cuts of meat, older chickens, and game. In a stew the meat is usually cut up into small pieces and cooked in a large quantity of liquid. The liquid usually needs to be thickened or reduced before serving with the meat. Stewed fruit is often still referred to, but quite often the term "poached" is now used instead. This is particularly so when the fruit is left whole, as in poached peaches. The term "stewed apple," when the fruit is broken down to form a purée, is still used.

STIR-FRYING

This is a very quick way of cooking small pieces of food in a healthy and appetizing way. It has become a very popular way to cook because it is seen regularly on television programs and also the availability of woks (see page 30) has become widespread. Stir-frying means sautéing a variety of foods together at a high temperature. In order to achieve this you need to prepare the meat or fish and the vegetables in advance. Make sure all the pieces are the same size so that they will cook evenly. If you do not have a wok, a large skillet will suffice. Make sure everything is prepared before you start to cook because it takes very little time once started. Heat a little oil in the pan and make sure it is really hot before cooking. Cook only small quantities at a time because you need the food to fry and not to steam. In fact, I think stir-frying should be done for only 1–2 people at a time—any more and some of you will not have fresh, hot food.

The most successful foods cooked in this way are thin strips of beef or pork, strips of chicken breast portions, shrimp, scallops, slices of salmon, flounder, or monkfish, and lots of vegetables that are popular in Chinese cooking such as bok choy, Chinese cabbage (see page 163), cabbage, mushrooms, bell peppers, and scallions. Noodles are often added toward the end of the cooking time. Since this method of cooking mainly comes from Asia, suitable flavors are added, for example ginger, soy sauce, and sesame oil.

KITCHEN HYGIENE

When preparing food, it is necessary to be absolutely rigorous about hygiene. Improper food handling is responsible for many outbreaks of food poisoning, the incidence of which is on the increase. Special care needs to be taken when you are preparing food for vulnerable groups, particularly young children, pregnant women, sick people and convalescents, and elderly people. Here are some basic rules.

Buying

Always buy from a reputable source where you have confidence in their food handling techniques. Buy the freshest foods and the best quality possible.

Storing

Keep food for as short a time as possible before cooking or serving, and make sure that it is stored at a safe temperature. A refrigerator should operate at below 41°F/5°C, so keep a thermometer in the refrigerator and check it from time to time to be sure it is working satisfactorily. Adjust the thermostat when necessary.

Cover all food with plastic wrap in the refrigerator so that one food may not contaminate another. Be specially aware of any meat products, which might leak blood onto other foods.

Check "use by" dates on packs of food before cooking.

Thaw frozen food thoroughly before cooking. Thaw it overnight in the refrigerator rather than at room temperature.

Preparing

Carefully wash any foods that need cleaning and dry well with paper towels—this is more hygienic than using a cloth.

Wash your own hands frequently with soap when preparing food. Use a separate hand towel, not a dishtowel.

Keep counters clean and use different cutting boards for cooked and uncooked foods, particularly meats. Wash them well and then rinse with diluted bleach between each use. Wash knives and other kitchen utensils in hot water and soap between each use.

Keep dish cloths clean and make sure that you change them often. Keep trash bins covered and empty them frequently, disinfecting regularly.

Cooking

Make sure food is cooked thoroughly and serve it piping hot as soon as practicable.

When cooked food needs to be kept, make sure it is cooled quickly, covered, and placed in the refrigerator as soon as possible. It is when food is kept at room temperature that food-poisoning bacteria multiply, so avoid keeping foods for long periods at this temperature.

Only reheat food once; if it is not used up then, throw it away. It is safer than risking illness. However, never reheat a marinade, especially one used for marinating meat.

Part 2
Before you cook

UTENSILS

*B*efore you begin to cook, you need to consider the utensils you will need. Everyone has a favorite tool for a particular job but there are a few basics you really need.

KNIVES

These are the most important things in the kitchen. With a good knife you can do most of the tasks you need to prepare basic ingredients. They come in all shapes and sizes and are made from different materials; do be prepared to spend in order to buy the best you can. A good knife will really last a lifetime. You do not need all the knives below: a cook's knife, a serrated knife, and a small vegetable knife would be a good start, and then add any of the others when you feel you need them.

Care, safety, and sharpening
Good quality knives are made from high-quality steel, which is virtually stainless. It is important that they are kept in a safe place, away from children, and also to protect their sharp edges. A knife block is ideal and keeps them always handy for use. A knife roll can also be used but the knives are not so easily accessible.

A sharp knife is safer than a blunt one, so always make sure that the blade is sharpened regularly, either using a steel or a simple pull-through sharpener. It is a pity that the days of the knife grinder are gone, those men who sharpened knives on a revolving stone were very useful. If you have a friendly butcher, he might be persuaded to sharpen your knives for you.

Small
vegetable knife

Serrated knife

Cheese knife

Grapefruit knife

Canelle knife

Small vegetable knife

A very small knife, usually only 2–4 inches/5–10 cm long, used for peeling small vegetables and fruit. Traditionally this was used by chefs for "turning" vegetables, that is, shaping them into even-size small cigar shapes; not really necessary in this day and age. This knife could also be used for filleting meat and fish: work as near to the bone or skin as possible, taking care not to tear the flesh.

Serrated knife

This is an all-purpose knife, the one you reach for when you need to do a quick job like slicing tomatoes and preparing fruit.

Cheese knife

This is really a serving knife for the table. It has a straight, one-sided, serrated edge for cutting through the cheese and has a curved forked tip for serving the pieces.

Grapefruit knife

This is a very flexible knife with a curved, double serrated blade used to cut the flesh from a grapefruit or an orange. If you eat a lot of fruit for breakfast this might be useful. Skill is required in order not to waste too much of

the fruit or vegetable. Again practice makes perfect. Luckily there are special peelers available (see page 24).

Canelle knife

This is used as a decorating tool for lemons and other citrus fruit by gouging out thin slices of peel, which can then be used for garnish or to make the sliced fruit look more attractive. It can also be used on cucumbers in the same way.

Cook's knife

This is the most important knife in the kitchen. They come in a range of sizes: choose one that feels comfortable. I have small hands and therefore am happy with an 8 inch/20 cm blade. Chefs tend to use enormous bladed knives, but for home use one of 8–12 inches/ 20–30 cm is more suitable. There should be enough space under the handle for the knuckles to sit comfortably and allow you to chop without hitting your hand on the chopping surface. Slicing and chopping are the most usual tasks for this knife. Make sure you keep it razor-sharp and look after it when it is not in use by keeping it in a protective cover or in a knife block.

The main use of the cook's knife is to chop. The point of the knife is held down with the left hand, and then the knife handle is raised and lowered with the other hand, using enough pressure to cut through the food, repeatedly working in an arc from left to right and back again. A little practice and you will be very proficient and prepare finely chopped ingredients in no time. It is also useful for slicing and shredding. The cook's knife is also used for crushing, using the thick end of the blade on its side. For example, place a clove of garlic under the knife and bring the blade down firmly with enough pressure to crush the clove.

Bread knife

This is a long knife with a serrated blade, which is suitable for cutting through the crust and soft body of a loaf of bread. The art of cutting wafer-thin sandwiches is something our grandmothers were taught; unfortunately, with the wide use of sliced bread, this is now a lost art. However, we still need to cut through loaves when we want thick chunks for toast or for eating the wider range of different breads now available. A bread knife is also useful for

cutting and serving cakes. Choose a well-balanced knife with a strong, slightly flexible blade.

Carving knife

This knife usually comes with a carving fork. The knife is quite long, about 12–14 inches/ 30–35 cm, with a pointed blade that allows you to cut around the bone of a roast. The fork has long, straight prongs, which enable you to hold down the meat so you can carve. The knife must always be kept sharp so that it can slice through the meat to produce neat slices without tearing the flesh. Carving is a lost skill. The head of the household always carved the Sunday roast in front of the whole family, but unfortunately it is becoming less usual for families to eat together and so the skill, passed on from one generation to another, has gone. Using a sharp knife and a good fork will make the job easier.

Spatula

This is a long-bladed, flexible knife, which is often used to lift food from one place to another. It comes in various sizes. The smaller ones (4 inches/10 cm) are used for spreading butter, cream, and frosting.

Cook's knife

Bread knife

Carving knife

Palette knife

OTHER CUTTING TOOLS

Good cutting tools make life easier, although they are not
absolutely essential if you have a good set of kitchen knives.

Mandolin slicer

Cheese slicer

Lemon zester

Apple corer

Vegetable peeler

Scissors
These are the most versatile piece
of equipment in the kitchen. Not
only are they useful for cutting
rinds off bacon, they are
wonderful for snipping herbs into
a cup and scallions into salads.
They are also useful for trimming
pastry and meat. Make sure the
blades are fairly long and that the
handles are comfortable.

Vegetable peelers
These make the job of peeling firm
vegetables and fruit much quicker
and more efficient. There are two
main types, the traditional swivel-

bladed peeler, and the newer Y-
shaped peeler. The Y-shaped
peeler is very swift when peeling
long vegetables like parsnips and
carrots but tends to be more
cumbersome and can nick your
fingers when peeling smaller
vegetables and fruits. Choice is
personal, so try out a friend's
before buying.

Lemon zester
This popular little tool has a series
of small metal circles, which are
attached to a handle. You simply
scrape the tool down the side of a
lemon (or orange or lime) and you

have lovely fine lemon zest, which
is much more regular than if you
used a grater. The zest can then
be used for garnishing or
decorating food. Its use also
means that you get only the zest
and no pith.

Apple corer
This is a specialized tool but
because we eat a lot of apples in
this country it is probably worth
having. It is a cylindrical blade,
which you use vertically to cut
down through the fruit and
remove the whole core in one
piece. You then have a lovely

cavity to fill with sugar, butter, and
dried fruits before you bake the
fruit. It is also useful for pears.

Mezzaluna
This kitchen tool has become very
fashionable of late, owing to its
popularity with certain television
chefs. It is a useful item because
it chops herbs and vegetables
quickly. It has a blade shaped like
a half-moon, with a handle on
either side. You simply rock the
blade from side to side and cut
through the herbs using the whole
length of the blade. Some
varieties have two blades, which

Kitchen scissors

Pastry or
cookie cutters

Cherry pitter

Mezzaluna

make for even quicker chopping. Take care when storing because they are very sharp, and make sure you dry them well after use.

Egg slicer
A wonderful tool that slices hard-cooked eggs into even pieces. It consists of a series of wires held tightly on a frame, which cut through the whole egg to give perfect slices for use as a garnish or in sandwiches.

Cheese slicer
This allows you to slice cheese into very thin wafers, which is

useful for sandwiches and for arranging cheese attractively when making a salad. It works best on softer, waxy cheeses like Emmenthal or Swiss cheese.

Pastry or cookie cutters
These are available in a range of shapes and sizes, fluted and plain. The two most useful are the 3 inch/7.5 cm size for lining 2½ inch/6 cm patty pans for making jam tarts, and the 2½ inch/ 6 cm size, which are perfect for the tops of mince pies. Make sure you wash and dry them well after use to prevent them from rusting.

Mandolin slicer
The mandolin slicer is a flat piece of equipment with a slide that is pushed over a blade in order to cut vegetables into fine slices. It is a very good utensil to have in the kitchen if you tend to prepare a lot of vegetables. It allows you to slice vegetables into very thin, uniform slices quickly. There are three types available: wooden, metal, and plastic. They also come in a range of sophistication. Some have a range of blades, both straight and rippled, to give different effects. The cost varies tremendously so you need to

assess how much it would be useful to you and how often you would use it.

Cherry pitter
Another specialist tool but one that works particularly well. It is a simple device for removing pits from cherries. You put the fruit in the tiny bowl and squeeze the prong through the fruit. Out pops the pit and you have pitted cherries quickly. It is probably only worth buying if you have a passion for dishes containing cherries, but it can also be used on olives.

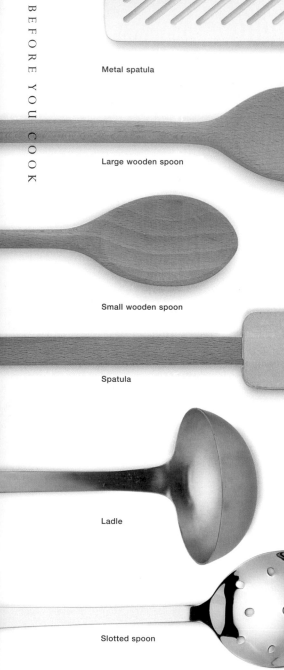

Metal spatula

Large wooden spoon

Small wooden spoon

Spatula

Ladle

Slotted spoon

Basting spoon

SPOONS AND SPATULAS

A small selection of spoons and spatulas is important, and adds character to your kitchen.

Wooden spoons

These handy utensils are traditional and still most useful in the kitchen. You need a selection of sizes and shapes: a small, short-handled spoon for stirring sauces—the ones with one squared edge are good because they reach into the corners of the pan to ensure even mixing, a large, flat spoon is useful for creaming butter and sugar together in cake making, and a spoon with a very long handle is necessary when making jam.

Wooden spatulas

These are flat with a squared-off end, and are useful for turning food while cooking, for example sausages. They are also handy for stirring to ensure even cooking, for example, when frying onions. They are particularly good when used in nonstick pans because they do not scratch the surface. I would recommend using flat spatulas for stirring savory foods and keep separate spoons for stirring sweet foods. In this way you will not run the risk of having onion-flavored desserts.

Plastic and rubber spatulas

These are used for mixing and folding in ingredients in a bowl when baking and can also be used to reach the bottom of a pitcher or blender to scrape out the last remnants of food. Care should be taken when using them in hot pans because they may not be completely heatproof.

Slotted spoon

A very useful tool for removing larger items from liquids, such as boiled and poached eggs. You can also use it for serving the meat and vegetables from a casserole before the sauce.

Ladle

You can buy ladles in various sizes. They are useful for serving soup and other sloppy foods. When making a risotto, you need a ladle to add the hot stock to the rice throughout the cooking process. A ladle is useful for straining soups and fruit purées: the shape enables it to squeeze the contents through a strainer quickly and easily.

Metal spatula

This tool is used for lifting and turning fish during poaching or frying, and is also useful for transferring biscuits and pastry items from hot cookie sheets. The flat, flexible, broad blade can be slipped under the food, which can then be moved easily.

Basting spoon

A large, metal spoon is useful for stirring, skimming, and basting. Try to find a good size, one that is larger than a tablespoon so that you can use it with large mixtures like your Christmas pudding. Also, if it has a good, long handle, it will be safer when basting large joints.

Measuring spoons

In baking where accuracy is important, these spoons can be a great help. They come in all shapes and sizes—usually ¼ teaspoon, ½ teaspoon, 1 teaspoon, and 1 tablespoon sizes linked together—and can be made from metal or plastic. They are particularly useful for raising agents, gelatin, and spices.

Measuring spoons

GRINDERS AND GRATERS

Not all of these items are essential: you can just buy them as you need them.

Rotary cheese grater
This is a handy little grater and works very well. It is at its best with medium cheeses like Cheddar. It is best to cut the cheese to the shape of the grater and put it in the container, press down with the lever, and turn the handle to grate the cheese. It produces a good, fine grate and is also useful for nuts and chocolate.

Box grater
This is the traditional all-purpose grater. It has four sides for different sized gratings: coarse for cheese and bread crumbs, fine for harder cheeses like Parmesan and lemon rind, a slicing side for potatoes, cucumbers, and other vegetables, and a very fine grater for nutmeg. It is easy to use but can be difficult to clean; an easy tip is to use a pastry brush so that you do not waste any food.

Nutmeg grater
This is specifically for grating nutmegs. Nutmeg is a spice that is much better when freshly grated because it loses its flavor very quickly. Nutmeg graters are small, but some types allow you to store the nutmegs inside.

Nutmeg grinder
These are newer and work on the same principle as a pepper mill. However, I have not had great success with them because they seem to be reluctant to grind well.

Garlic press
A garlic press is useful when you want to use only the puréed garlic flesh. The pressure squeezes the garlic clove through the fine holes in the press, resulting in a smooth purée. Garlic presses can be very awkward to wash, but they do keep your hands reasonably clean and fresh. If you do not have a garlic press, garlic can be crushed with a heavy knife quite easily.

Pestle and mortar
These popular tools have been used for centuries. They can be made of wood, glass, or ceramic. The mortar is the bowl and the pestle is the rounded stick, which is used to grind seeds and spices. They are very satisfactory to use and the flavor of freshly ground spices exceeds those bought ready-ground.

Salt and pepper mills
Pepper mills have been around for years, particularly in Italian restaurants where they are usually of enormous proportions. But they are really useful—there is nothing better than the flavor of freshly milled black pepper; the ready-ground stuff has no flavor, just the sneeze. The traditional wooden ones work well and use a screwing action, which gives a fine grind. Salt is not so important for grinding but a salt mill is good to have on the table for use with salads and vegetables. There are newer mills available now, which work by squeezing two arms together at the top. These have two advantages: they come in a variety of colors and they can be used with only one hand, which is helpful when you have messy hands during cooking.

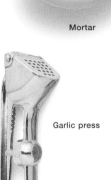

Mortar

Pestle

Garlic press

Salt and pepper mills

Nutmeg grinder

Bottle opener

Openers

Here are the most useful openers.

Bottle openers
Openers are needed to remove fixed bottle tops. They come in all shapes and sizes and are quite often incorporated with a corkscrew. Every kitchen will need one if only to open the beer!

Corkscrews
There are many sorts available, from the simplest to the most expensive. If you are fit and strong, then the simple ones will suffice. However, if you have poor strength in your hands or find opening bottles difficult, it will help to pay more for one of the lever-type openers. If you are a wine enthusiast, then a special opener that has a device for cutting the foil around the bottle might suit.

Can openers
These tools are essential in this day and age. We eat and drink quite a few things from cans and need to have a simple opener. Some are easier to use than others. One type takes off the rim of the can and leaves a sharp edge— beware. Make sure the opener has good handles that are easy to grip, and a firm and smooth action. You can buy electric can openers but it really does depend how much you will use it to justify the expense.

Combined corkscrew and bottle opener

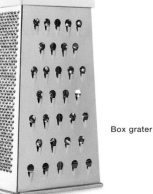

Can opener

Rotary cheese grater

Lemon wedge squeezer

Box grater

EQUIPMENT

BAKING

Once you learn to bake fresh bread and cakes for yourself, and experience the enjoyment of all the enticing smells and tastes, you will need to buy some basic equipment. Here are some suggestions for the most useful items.

Pastry boards
These are not always necessary if you have good kitchen counters. However, traditionally a large board made from wood was used to knead dough. It was also traditional to have a piece of marble on which to roll out pastry because of its cool qualities and its smooth surface, which allows the pastry to be moved around easily. If you are going to make pastry on a regular basis, it would be a sound investment to buy a specific board.

Rolling pins
In order to roll pastry well you need a heavy, smooth rolling pin. In emergencies a bottle can be used but it does not give an even rolling. Make sure the pin is of adequate length and has a smooth finish. Pins can be bought in a variety of materials: wood is traditional but you can buy metal and glass, which are cooler. Ceramic rolling pins used to be popular but seem to have gone out of fashion now. Rolling pins with handles have also become unpopular because they reduce the surface for rolling.

Pastry brushes
These brushes are useful for all sorts of jobs in the kitchen, such as brushing excess flour from the pastry and for glazing with egg or milk. They are also used for greasing pans and brushing oil on meat and poultry before and during cooking. They are available in all shapes and sizes and in various materials. Wood is traditional but plastic brushes are now available—make sure you

wash and dry them well or the bristles will start to fall out. Paint brushes are often used these days because they have a broad, flat brush, which covers the surface well. It is a good idea to have a very small one and a larger one for different tasks.

Baking beans
For years dried beans or rice have been used to weigh down waxed paper or baking foil. This technique is known as "baking blind," and enables you to cook pastry without a filling until it is crisp; the filling is then added later. Today you can buy ceramic and aluminum "beans," which have a good weight and will last forever.

Cookie sheets
A good, heavyweight cookie sheet is a must. It is not worth buying a cheap sheet because it will buckle in the oven and possibly spill the contents. Large cookie sheets should have only one upturned edge so that you can slip a large or delicate item on and off easily. Cookie sheets with an edge all around are especially useful when making things like sausage rolls because they prevent the fat spilling into the oven. Make sure the trays are not too big for the oven—leave a gap all around in order for the air to circulate properly.

Cake pans
You need to decide what types of cakes you are interested in making because there are so many shapes and sizes of pans available. Perhaps the best

Cookie sheet

Cake pan

Springform cake pan

Quiche pan

Pie dish

Muffin pans

starting point is two 8 inch/20 cm layer pans, which are at least 1 inch/2.5 cm deep. They can be used for both sponge cakes and layer cakes.

Loaf pans also come in many different sizes. I always use one 2 lb/900 g size and two 1 lb/450 g pans at the same time when making bread (it does not seem worth making a smaller amount of dough or having the oven on for less). They can also be used individually for tea breads and fruit terrines. Always buy the best quality you can afford: nonstick can be helpful but they still require a light coating of oil. Make sure you wash and dry them well before storing.

Muffin pans

A set of 12 patty pans or a muffin pan is useful for making small cakes, tarts, and muffins and also for individual Yorkshire puddings. If you are going to bake quite frequently, or if you might make mince pies for Christmas, a second tray is helpful so that you can assemble one batch while one tray is in the oven, making for more efficient working.

Quiche pans

Quiche pans or tart pans, call them what you will, these items are very useful for sweet and savory dishes. Always use steel pans, because those made from porcelain or glass do not allow the food to cook properly. Loose-based pans are the best because they allow you to remove the pan easily before serving; this is done by placing the flan on an upturned bowl and allowing the ring to fall to the surface. You can then transfer the flan on the base to a serving plate. An 8 inch/20 cm quiche pan is the most useful size but if you have a large family or frequently cook for six or more people, a 12 inch/30 cm pan would be helpful. Small, individual pans are also available and these can be used for brown bag lunches or picnics.

Pie dishes

Pie dishes need to be quite deep with a good rim so that the pastry will be supported. They come in a number of sizes, usually oval or round, and can be glazed ceramic or glass. Some are made from enamel and tend to be oblong in

shape. Larger ones need to be used with a pie funnel to support the pastry in the center.

Cooling rack

A cooling rack is particularly useful if you intend to bake bread and cakes. A rack allows the steam to escape from the baked items and prevents them from becoming too soggy. As soon as a cake is baked, turn it out of the pan onto a potholdered hand and then place it, base down, on the cooling rack. This way the attractive crust on the top is maintained. Cooling racks can usually be bought in rectangular or circular shapes.

Flour strainer

Sifting flour is important, not only to make sure there are no lumps but also to introduce air. A stainless steel strainer is best, of a medium size. It can also be used to strain vegetables but make sure it is always cleaned and well dried after use. Plastic versions are also available. A very small strainer is useful for sprinkling confectioners' sugar over cakes and desserts, or you could use a tea-strainer.

Flour dredger

A flour dredger makes it easier to sift flour onto a pastry board, dough, and rolling pin because it controls the amount of flour you use. I also find it useful for sprinkling flour into casseroles to prevent lumps from forming.

Mixing bowls

These bowls are available in stainless steel, copper, glass, plastic, and glazed ceramic. The choice is up to you. I have a large plastic bowl, which I have had for a very long time; it is particularly good because it has a rubber base, which keeps the bowl steady when mixing. A metal bowl is good for whisking egg whites because it keeps cool and the surface can be kept absolutely smooth and clean.

Bowls

You will need a variety of sizes for different tasks, such as beating eggs and whipping cream. A selection of small bowls is ideal for assembling your prepared ingredients before starting to cook. Some come with lids, which is an added advantage.

Cooling rack

Rolling pins

Heatproof bowl

Flour dredger

Baking beans

Mixing bowl

Pastry brushes

Roasting pans

Griddle pan

Steamer

COOKWARE

You can start with one or two of the following items to get you going, then add to your collection as your skills develop.

Milk pan
A nonstick milk pan is preferable because milk pans without a nonstick surface are devils to clean. A nonstick milk pan is also wonderful for making sauces and scrambled eggs. Buy one that is well balanced, has a good pouring lip and a solid handle. Always use a wooden spoon or wooden spatula in it. Since your milk pan is likely to be well used, always buy one of a good quality.

Lidded pans
A set in small/medium/large is the best way to buy these. This set will cover all your needs: the small one for poaching/boiling eggs, one or two medium ones for vegetables, and the large one for pasta, potatoes, and rice. Make sure the bases are solid and flat, the lids are well fitting, and the handles are comfortable and heat resistant. You can spend a small fortune on pans but you always get what you pay for in terms of quality and durability; good ones will last a lifetime. Choose from stainless steel, cast iron, or enamel.

Steamer
This can be used with a medium/large pan to allow food to be cooked on the same heat at the same time. A steamer is a perforated, pan-like container, which sits on top of a pan and allows the food to be cooked by steaming. It is particularly good for steaming green vegetables over boiling potatoes or rice. Not only is this more economical but the vegetables retain more of their nutritional value cooked this way.

You can buy a steamer to match your pans or you can buy a "universal" steamer with its own lid, which will fit a variety of pan sizes. A steamer is useful if you have limited stove space and want simply-cooked food.

Skillet
There are many uses for a skillet and your choice should depend on what you will use it for the most. If it is bacon and egg for one person, then a small pan will be sufficient, but if you want to cook larger quantities, you will need a larger one. Like other pans, skillets come in many materials but you must ensure that the base of your skillet is heavy and flat so that it has good contact with the heat. A lid may be useful to enable you to continue to cook at a slower rate after the initial frying. A heatproof handle may also be desirable if you want to "pan-fry" a piece of fish and then place it in the oven to finish off. You can also choose a nonstick skillet: opinions are divided as to whether they are of any benefit and whether they last long enough. I personally like a nonstick pan: it is easy to clean and allows the food to move around the pan without using too much oil and without fear of catching. However, treat it carefully so that the nonstick surface is not damaged.

Wok
These deep, rounded pans are very popular for stir-frying small pieces of food. They work best on a gas stove. A large skillet. can be used instead of a wok.

Individual soufflé dish

Omelet pan

If you make omelets regularly, you will need a pan that you use for nothing else (except perhaps crêpes), because if the pan is used for bacon or onions, it will make an omelet stick more easily. It should be a small pan, about 8 inches/20 cm in diameter, made from stainless steel or cast iron with a nonstick lining. Used carefully and treated well, your omelet pan should last forever.

Griddle

These are very popular at the moment. They are heavy, flat, cast-iron pans with a ridged surface to enable you to cook at a high heat. They produce attractive brown stripes on the food and help to develop a wonderful flavor. Griddles are available in circular or rectangular shapes—the rectangular ones are larger and fit over two burners and act rather like an indoor barbecue. The secret is to heat them to a very high temperature, oil the food well before placing it on the griddle, and then leave it alone, without moving the food, for 2–3 minutes to ensure even stripes.

Casseroles

Casserole dishes are for braising or stewing food. I find that if you try to cook in a pot on top of the stove the food always burns a little on the base of the pot. A heavy casserole is better because it will enable you to start the cooking on top and then put it in the oven for a long, slow cook. Casserole dishes are available in different materials and come in different sizes. You will need a good size so that you can cook a whole chicken, if necessary. Obviously your choice will depend on the size of your household, but a large casserole enables you to cook double quantities and freeze

half for another day. Make sure the casserole has a well-fitting lid and that the two handles are large enough and comfortable so that you can lift the pot easily.

Roasting pans

These are necessary for roasting meat, poultry, game, and vegetables. Choose one that is large enough to hold a large bird (for example a turkey) for all your household's needs and one or two smaller ones for when you need to cook only a couple of chicken pieces. Make sure the pans are a good, solid weight so that they will not twist in the oven and that they have deep sides to prevent too much splattering. A shallow pan is also very useful for roasting vegetables as an accompaniment. A large one must not be too big for the oven, so allow 2 inches/ 5 cm of space all around to be sure of good circulation of air.

Ramekins

Ramekins are small dishes used for cooking in the oven and on the stovetop. They are generally used for crème brûlée, crème caramel, and individual soufflés. They can also be used for baked eggs. They come in a range of materials, including white porcelain, glazed earthenware, and glass. They are useful for holding prepared ingredients before you start cooking and are also good for serving small portions of butter and jelly.

Soufflé dishes

Traditional soufflé dishes, made from white porcelain, are deep and straight-sided to allow a soufflé mixture to rise easily. They are available in a range of sizes, but the 7½ cup dish is the most useful and serves four people. A smaller one, 3¾ cups, is perfect for two people.

Pan

Milk pan

Skillet

Large pan with lid

Ramekins

Casserole dish

31

Colander

Imperial/metric kitchen scales

Measuring cup

Digital kitchen scales

Strainer

Citrus reamer

Balloon hand whisks

Double potato masher

Large kitchen tongs

Small kitchen tongs

OTHER KITCHEN TOOLS

Finally, here are some suggestions for additional things that will make life easier and make you look like a real professional.

Colander
This is necessary for draining cooked vegetables, pasta, and anything that has been cooked in water and needs straining. The best colanders you can buy are stainless steel, which are very robust and easy to clean. Make sure your colander is solid and stands on a firm base so that your hands are free to pour from the pan.

Strainer
This is sometimes necessary for draining finer ingredients such as rice. It is usually a good idea to keep a separate one for sifting dry ingredients such as flour and sugar, or, if you use the same one for draining and sifting, make sure it is completely dry before sifting.

Kitchen timer
A timer is essential in the kitchen. If you do not have one, you should go and buy one. There are many available, from simple to hi-tech, but make sure your timer is reliable and the ring is loud enough to hear above the radio.

Knife sharpener
In order to keep your knives sharp, you are going to need a sharpener. You can choose between a steel or a pull-through device to achieve a good edge. A steel is the professional way and takes a bit of practice but gives a sound result.

Measuring cup
This is important for liquid measurements when recipe quantities need to be exact. It can be bought in various materials, for example metal, plastic, and glass. Metal ones are difficult to read, however, and glass ones tend to be rather heavy and of course can be dropped and broken. The newer plastic ones, which are made from polypropylene, withstand boiling liquids and have very clear print, making it easy to see the measurements. A 5 cup size is the most useful.

Kitchen tongs
These are necessary for lifting hot food from the cooking utensil to the plate. They are also useful for turning food in a hot pan when cooking on the stovetop or the barbecue. They should be a good length and fit the hand easily. They are usually made from stainless steel so they are hard-wearing and do not discolor.

Citrus reamers
There are many occasions when you will need the juice of a lemon or an orange, so a reamer is a sensible piece of equipment to have. There are two different types. The first is a traditional reamer made of glass or plastic, used by pressing a half of the fruit down onto the raised section and twisting it until the juice runs into the lower part of the dish; small, raised pieces of glass prevent the seeds from joining the juice, or holes in the plastic variety allow the juice to drain through. The other type is a hand-held one, which you can use over a bowl or pan directly; these are available in wood and plastic. You simply use a screwing action into the halved fruit and the juice falls into the receptacle; the only problem with this one is that you might get the seeds as well.

Balloon hand whisk
There are many sizes available, from tiny (for whisking a mug of hot chocolate) through medium (for use in pans) and large (for whisking egg whites). Look for a good-quality, stainless steel whisk that will not discolor, and choose a size with a comfortable handle to suit your needs.

Potato masher
A masher is a valuable tool for making mashed vegetables, which are now very popular again.

Choose a strong-handled masher because it will need to do quite heavy work. A comfortable handle is essential because you will have to put quite a lot of pressure into breaking down the lumps to make a smooth mash. A masher is also useful for stewed apples.

Scales
For many recipes you can manage to do without scales by using measuring cups and spoons. However, when you want to cook more precise recipes, such as baked items, then the accuracy is important and you might like to consider some scales. There are many types around: some cost modest amounts and some cost a king's ransom. Personally I use balance scales with weights, in both metric and imperial. There are also spring scales available, which have a bowl on top of the dial; make sure the bowl is large enough to weigh out bulky items like flour and pasta and that the dial is clear and large enough to read. Electronic scales are very hi-tech, both in use and in design—the weights flash up on the digital display and you can choose to weigh in either imperial or metric. They are very accurate but you may need to replace the batteries from time to time.

Cutting boards
A good knife is only as good as its chopping surface. Wooden boards have always been the traditional ones to use because they "give" with the pressure of the blade and do not blunt it. A solid cutting board will cost you rather a lot but should last you a lifetime. Polyethylene cutting boards have become more popular because they can be sterilized and will even go in the dishwasher. They are probably a good idea for raw meat and poultry to make sure that everything is completely hygienic. Cutting boards are available in different colors, which are useful for ensuring you do not cut fruit on the same board on which you have just chopped garlic. In fact, a tiny board kept just for the purpose of chopping garlic is a very useful accessory.

Thermometers

Oven
An oven thermometer is useful if you are uncertain about your oven temperature, particularly if you are living or staying in a place where the stove is unfamiliar. This thermometer is not essential but it could prevent disasters.

Oven thermometer

Meat
This thermometer is useful for checking if a large piece of meat is cooked through. It is particularly good for beef, because the temperature will tell you if it is rare, medium, or well done.

Sugar
This is useful if you are making jelly, marmalade, or toffees. You can check the temperature during the process and ensure good setting.

Sugar thermometer

Refrigerator
This thermometer checks that your refrigerator and freezer are working at the correct temperatures. It might save unnecessary food wastage.

Kitchen timer

Cutting boards

Sharpening steel

ELECTRICAL EQUIPMENT

There is all sorts of electrical equipment for the kitchen but all are rather expensive and many are for specific tasks. If we ignore teakettles and toasters (they are not really "cook's equipment") we can pick out two or three that will help take the hard work out of some food preparation.

Blender

Standing mixer

Hand blender

Food processor

Hand mixer

This is an inexpensive tool but very worthwhile. It enables you to beat and whisk very quickly, saving time and energy. It consists of an electric motor in the hand section and has two rotary beaters, which turn at variable speeds to incorporate air into mixtures. The beaters can also be used in pans to break down lumps and make purées. The whisks just slip out and are reasonably easy to clean, even in a dishwasher.

Standing mixer

This is a traditional mixer, which has a large bowl and a range of three basic tools—a wire whisk, a beater, and a dough hook—so that mixtures can be whisked, beaten, and kneaded. It is a very useful piece of equipment if you want to bake cakes and bread in quite large quantities. Some models come with a blender attached so that all kitchen tasks can be accomplished with one machine. The drawback of this machine is its expense and its heavy weight. It also needs to be kept out on the counter to facilitate easy use. However, once bought, it should last for many years and will take a lot of the drudgery out of cooking.

Blender

These can be bought freestanding and are essential if you want to make puréed soups, milk shakes, and smoothies. They come in a range of prices and sizes, so choose one that will suit your needs.

Food processor

This machine performs many tasks, so it is really useful. It consists of a bowl placed on top of a high powered motor. It comes with one very sharp blade for general use, but also comes with slicing and grating disks. It can chop, grind, slice, grate, shred, mix, blend, make bread crumbs, and knead dough. It is so versatile and has so many uses that it is worthwhile considering despite the high cost. Choose one with an adequate-size bowl for your needs and make sure you store the blade carefully because it is extremely sharp.

CONVERSION CHARTS

OVEN TEMPERATURES

Celsius	Fahrenheit	Gas Mark	Oven Heat
110°	225°	¼	very cool
120°	250°	½	very cool
140°	275°	1	cool
150°	300°	2	cool
160°	325°	3	moderate
180°	350°	4	moderate
190°	375°	5	moderately hot
200°	400°	6	moderately hot
220°	425°	7	hot
230°	450°	8	very hot

SPOON MEASUREMENTS

1 teaspoon of liquid = 5 ml

1 tablespoon of liquid = 15 ml

OTHER MEASUREMENTS

Volume

Metric	Imperial
50 ml	2 fl oz
100 ml	3½ fl oz
150 ml	5 fl oz
200 ml	7 fl oz
300 ml	10 fl oz
450 ml	16 fl oz
500 ml	18 fl oz
600 ml	1 pint
700 ml	1¼ pints
850 ml	1½ pints
1 litre	1¾ pints
1.5 litres	2¾ pints
2.8 litres	5 pints
3 litres	5¼ pints

Weight

Metric	Imperial
5 g	⅛ oz
10 g	¼ oz
25 g	1 oz
50 g	2 oz
75 g	2¾ oz
85 g	3 oz
100 g	3½ oz
150 g	5½ oz
225 g	8 oz
300 g	10½ oz
450 g	1 lb
500 g	1lb 2 oz
1 kg	2 lb 4 oz
1.5 kg	3 lb 5 oz

Linear

Metric	Imperial
2 mm	1⁄16 inch
3 mm	⅛ inch
5 mm	¼ inch
8 mm	⅜ inch
1 cm	½ inch
2 cm	¾ inch
2.5 cm	1 inch
5 cm	2 inches
7.5 cm	3 inches
10 cm	4 inches
20 cm	8 inches
30 cm	1 foot
46 cm	1½ feet
50 cm	20 inches

THE PANTRY

While different lifestyles mean it is impossible to decide what everyone should have in their pantry, a basic range of essentials will at least enable you to enhance your meals and also to produce a few quick and simple dishes when time or fresh produce are in short supply. This will be particularly important for people with limited accommodation. If you have more space available, though, you can keep some really delicious and interesting ingredients for meals and to keep in reserve for an emergency.

FLOURS

Storage

Always buy flour in the quantities you need. If you are going to bake bread, buy flour in large bags, but if you hardly ever use flour, buy the smallest pack. Store it in the dark in an airtight container in a cool, dry place. White flour will keep for 6 months or more, but whole-grain flours should be used within a shorter period because they contain more oil and may turn rancid. Check packs for "use by" dates.

All-purpose flour

Cornstarch

All-purpose whole-wheat flour

Malted brown flour

Self-rising flour

Strong bread flour

All-purpose flour
This is useful for thickening casseroles, making sauces, coating food such as scallops of meat and chicken before cooking, and rolling out bought pastry.

Cornstarch
This flour provides a quick way to thicken sauces.

Whole-wheat flour
Whole-wheat flour is ideal for making bread and pastry.

Malted flour
This flour is used for breadmaking and crumbles.

Self-rising flour
Self-rising flour is used for baking cakes, cookies, and desserts.

Strong bread flour
This flour is used for breadmaking. It has a higher percentage of gluten, which gives the dough its elasticity. Bread flour can be white, brown, and whole-wheat.

SUGARS

Storage

Store sugars in airtight containers in a cool, dry place for up to 12 months. They may need sifting before use if slightly damp. Brown sugars may harden during storage; if so, place in a bowl and cover with a damp cloth for 2–3 hours or overnight. The sugar will absorb the moisture and will then be soft and usable.

Granulated sugar
This is the one sugar you need on a day-to-day basis. Use it to sweeten tea or coffee (if you take sugar). You can also use it on cereals and with fruits when they are too sharp. Granulated sugar is also useful for desserts and fruit crisps.

Superfine sugar
This is finer than granulated sugar and is better for cakes, cookies, and meringues. It dissolves quicker and is therefore used for syrups for fruit salad and for custards and sauces.

Confectioners' sugar
A very finely powdered sugar, used for making frostings and for sprinkling over cakes and desserts as decoration. It often turns lumpy in storage so it is essential to sift it before use.

Brown sugar
This is a moist sugar, which is available in varying shades depending on how much molasses is present. Light brown sugar is suitable for cakes and desserts, while flavorsome dark brown sugar (molasses sugar) is only suitable for rich cakes like Christmas cake or gingerbreads,

and dark puddings like toffee sponge where its pronounced flavor contributes to the overall taste. Dark brown sugar is also good where stickiness is desirable, such as in flapjacks and brownies, because its texture is more moist and heavier.

Raw brown sugar
This is a partly refined sugar, which has some percentage of molasses. It is used mainly for its texture—it has large, crunchy granules, which give cakes, cookies, and crisp toppings their characteristic appearance.

Preserving Sugar
This sugar is specifically designed for jelly-making. Its large crystals dissolve quickly, forming a clear jelly with a minimum of scum.

Sugar crystals
These are used to top baked items such as Bath buns. Brown crystals are also available, which are served with coffee as sweeteners.

Sugar lumps
These are available in white and brown. They are very decorative and are generally used for sweetening beverages.

Granulated sugar

Superfine sugar

Confectioners' sugar

Light brown sugar

Raw brown sugar

Preserving sugar

Dark molasses sugar

Crystallised sugar

White sugar lumps

Brown sugar lumps

OILS

Good oil is important for many kitchen tasks—for frying, brushing foods before broiling, baking, making salad dressings, and simply drizzling over food to flavor and garnish it.

Storage

Oils keep for 10–12 months if kept in a cool, dark place but sometimes will turn rancid. Check bottles for "use by" dates. Once opened, they will start to deteriorate. Buy specialty oils in small quantities.

Sunflower oil

A good, all-purpose oil, which can be used for all cooking methods. It is a light oil with very little flavor so it can also be used to make dressings (perhaps mixed with a little olive oil).

Olive oil

If you like salads, it is worth buying olive oil because dressings made with it are far superior owing to the wonderful flavor. You can also cook with olive oil but of course it is more expensive.

Extra-virgin olive oil

This is the best olive oil you can buy, but it is expensive. It varies in color from pale yellow to a rich green, often depending on its country of origin. Some people prefer Italian, others Greek; it depends on what kind of foods you eat. Experiment with small bottles and see which you prefer. Use it for salad dressings and pasta, and for drizzling over broiled vegetables (there is a wonderful Italian oil mixed with lemon flavor that is ideal for this).

Corn oil

A cheaper oil with quite a strong flavor, which some people do not like. It is suitable for deep-frying, so if you often cook fried foods, this is a good buy.

Soy oil

This oil is cheap and has a high smoke point (smokes at a very high temperature), so it is suitable for deep-frying. However, it has quite a strong flavor, which some people find unpleasant.

Peanut oil

A light oil, which is suitable for all types of cooking. It has a very mild flavor and is good for mayonnaise and dressings.

Sesame oil

This is a dark, nutty oil frequently used in Chinese and Thai cooking. It has a wonderful flavor and aroma—sweet and very pungent. If used alone, it will burn easily, so it is best mixed with sunflower oil for cooking. Alternatively, you can cook in olive oil and use the sesame oil to flavor the food just before serving, as I do. It also makes a superb dressing for Asian salads—just mix it with a little lemon juice and soy sauce.

Nut oils

Walnut oil and hazelnut oil have wonderful flavors for dressings. They are particularly good when served with a salad containing a few similar nuts. They can also be drizzled over vegetables and pasta and added to bread dough.

Nut oil

Corn oil

Basil-flavored olive oil

Olive oil

Extra-virgin olive oil

Sunflower oil

Vegetable oil

VINEGARS

Vinegars have many uses in cooking and there are many different ones in the shops. Each country has its own style, for example Britain has malt and apple vinegar, France has wine vinegars, Spain has sherry vinegar, and Italy has balsamic.

Storage

Keep vinegars in a dark, cool place for 6–12 months. Buy small bottles so that you can use them up at their best.

Balsamic vinegar

This vinegar is very popular now. It originated in Modena in Italy and is the richest of all the vinegars, with a deep brown color and a fruity sweet flavor. The best varieties are aged in oak barrels for up to 25 years, but can be very expensive. Good things are worth paying for, however, so treat yourself. Buy some on vacation in Italy if you can because it will be less expensive. Use it in dressings for salads with some interesting greens and sprinkle it over simple fish dishes, pasta, roasted vegetables, and soups. Plates can be garnished with small drops of this vinegar before arranging food on them—a neat "chef's" trick.

Apple vinegar

A light vinegar with a slightly fruity flavor, used for pickling fruits and making dressings like the white wine variety. It is also used in recipes with apples.

Flavored vinegars

There are many of these available, such as raspberry vinegar and walnut vinegar. However, unless you have a particular favorite, it is probably better to concentrate on a good olive oil. Fruit-flavored vinegars were very fashionable but quite often stayed in the pantry and lost their potency.

Malt vinegar

If you are a fish-and-fries fanatic or a pickle-and-chutney maker, this is the vinegar for you. Otherwise avoid it. The colorless variety is distilled and very strong (up to 12 percent acetic acid) and is used for pickling onions where the color needs to be preserved. The dark-brown vinegar (famous with British fish and French fries) is colored with caramel and used to make chutneys. Do not try to make a dressing with this.

Sherry vinegar

This is used in Spanish recipes and salad dressings. Gazpacho (a Spanish cold soup) has sherry vinegar in the recipe and the vinegar can be used in sauces and other soups. It has a smooth flavor and can be used in dressings for salads with more robust flavors.

Red wine vinegar

Red varieties can be used in the same ways as white ones, although they have a more robust flavor. You need to try some different brands to decide which is the one for you.

White wine vinegar

A good, all-round vinegar, which can be used for dressings and sprinkling over food. It is mild and has a good flavor.

White wine vinegar

Red wine vinegar

Malt vinegar

Balsamic vinegar

SAUCES

You can have many sauces in the pantry for use in cooking and for use at the table—the choice depends on which type of food you enjoy.

Storage

Buy only those sauces you will use regularly—especially the Asian varieties—or you will have a pantry full of out-of-date sauces. Keep them in a cool, dry, dark place; once opened, you might like to store them in the refrigerator. Check labels for information and "use by" dates.

Tomato ketchup

This is a favorite for almost everyone, and goes particularly well with sausages, burgers, fish sticks, and French fries.

Brown sauce

This sauce is good in sweet-and-sour sauces and goes very well with bacon and egg.

Worcestershire sauce

This very spicy sauce has been a favorite for many years. Add it to casserole dishes and soups for a fiery flavor. It is also used in a Bloody Mary (a vodka-tomato juice cocktail).

Soy sauce

This is a popular Chinese sauce. It is used with all Asian foods, both in cooking and at the table. It adds a salty flavor, which is typical of this type of food. Soy sauce comes in light and dark varieties: use the light one with shellfish and chicken, and the dark one with duck and meat.

Sweet chile sauce

This hot sauce made from chiles, vinegar, sugar, and salt, is traditionally used as a dipping sauce, although it is sometimes used in cooking. If the flavour is too strong for you, the sauce can be diluted with hot water.

Plum sauce

This is also traditional with Peking duck but it can be served with other dishes. It has a fruity flavor with a spicy overtone and is an instant dipping sauce for crab cakes, spring rolls, and wontons.

Oyster sauce

A thick, dark-brown sauce consisting of oysters and brine and heavily flavored with soy. It is used with all sorts of dishes—fish, vegetables, and meat—where it imparts an Asian flavor.

Thai fish sauce (*nam pla*)

This sauce is used in many recipes in Thai cooking. It is rather like soy sauce; it adds flavor but also brings out the flavor of the other ingredients.

Brown sauce   Sweet chile sauce   Oyster sauce   Dark soy sauce

Tomato ketchup   Plum sauce   Thai fish sauce

Worcestershire sauce

Long-grain brown rice

Round-grain rice

White rice

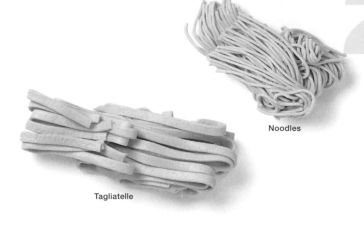

Tagliatelle

Noodles

RICE

A small range of different kinds of rice opens up a wide area of savory and sweet dishes. A good basic rice to have in your pantry is long-grain rice. For a wider choice, try basmati rice, risotto rice, round-grain rice, and brown rice. For more details see pages 181–2.

Storage
Store rice in airtight containers in a cool, dry place. Rice will keep for up to three years if stored correctly, so it is a good, long-term pantry item. If you have space and containers, it is a good idea to buy large packs because they are more economical (but only if you are going to use them).

PASTA

There are so many varieties of pasta available that you should stick to the ones you use regularly or you will end up with lots of half-empty packets. Spaghetti and macaroni are good basic pastas to have in your pantry. For a wider choice, try lasagne (sheets), cannelloni (tubes), fusilli (spirals), farfalle (bows), vermicelli (fine, hair-like pasta), tagliatelle (ribbons), conchiglie (shells), and stuffed pasta such as tortellini and ravioli. For more details see pages 180–1.

Storage
Dried pasta needs to be stored in a cool, dry place and will keep for around 18–24 months. The richer egg pastas will not keep so long as the plain varieties, so check labels for storage information. Fresh pasta should be stored in the refrigerator and eaten within 1–2 days.

NOODLES

Under this heading we are dealing with Asian noodles. They are fine noodles, which need only soaking in hot water or are quick to cook. Noodles in this category include egg noodles, rice noodles, cellophane noodles, and Japanese noodles. For more details see pages 181.

Storage
Keep fresh and dried noodles in a cool, dry place and use by the date on the packs.

Assorted dried pasta shapes

Spaghetti

Adzuki beans

Navy beans

Red lentils

Garbanzo beans

Red kidney beans

BEANS AND LENTILS

These are all known as legumes and are a good, economical source of protein. They are available dried and in cans. Using canned legumes cuts out the soaking and cooking time and makes them a useful, instant convenience food. Basic legumes to keep in your pantry include navy beans, garbanzo beans, and lentils. For a wider choice, try lima beans, cannellini beans, and red kidney beans. Other beans you might like to try include soybeans, pinto beans, borlotti beans, black-eye peas, black beans, and adzuki beans. They all have different shapes and colors and can be used to add bulk to casseroles, stews, and soups.

Storage
Buy dried beans and lentils in small quantities from a source that has a quick turnover. The longer you keep these dried legumes, the longer you will need to cook them because they toughen with age. Store in airtight containers in a cool, dry place for up to 1–2 years.

GRAINS

It is useful to have both couscous and polenta in your pantry because they are quick to cook and are a good staple to accompany any meat or fish dishes.
For further details see pages 182.

Storage
Keep grains in an airtight container in a cool, dry place for up to 18 months.

Couscous

Polenta

DRIED FRUITS

Many fruits are available dried and can be used in a variety of dishes. Dried fruits can also be eaten as a healthy snack food. Traditionally, dried fruits meant currants and raisins; then we had prunes, apricots, and dates. Nowadays we have dried pears, peaches, apples, figs, bananas, cherries, cranberries, blueberries, mangoes, papaya, and pineapples. All can be used in baking and savory dishes. They can also be added to granola for a tasty and nourishing breakfast.

Storage
Buy only what you need because the shelf life of dried fruits is only 6–8 months. It is useful to buy them from stores where you can weigh out the amount you need, rather than buying them in a certain-size packet. Store them in an airtight container in a cool, dry place.

Dried dates

Raisins

Almonds

NUTS

A few nuts are useful in the pantry to add texture to some dishes, but do not buy too many because they go rancid after only 2–3 months.

Storage

Nuts are best stored in a cool, dry place in an airtight container to prevent rancidity. Only buy small quantities when you know you will use them.

Cashew nuts

Walnuts
Walnuts are good in both salads and stuffings.

Almonds
These nuts are good for fruit crisps and salads and are also useful in baking.

Pine nuts
These are actually kernels of pine cones and are wonderful tossed in salads or rice dishes. Their flavor is improved if they are dry-fried or broiled until golden brown.

Cashew nuts
These sweet nuts have a soft, crunchy texture and are often used in Asian dishes and in some Indian cooking. Add them at the end of the cooking time for the best flavor.

Chestnuts
These are popular at Christmas time, both for stuffings and as an accompaniment to Brussels sprouts. They are also used in desserts, most often with chocolate. Chestnuts are available

whole (with skins that are difficult to remove), dried (which need soaking), vacuum-packed (which are very convenient), or canned. They are also available in purée form, both sweetened and unsweetened.

Hazelnuts
Hazelnuts are also sometimes known as cobnuts. They are small, round nuts, which are usually used in cakes, pastries, and desserts.

Peanuts
These are best bought roasted or salted and can be used in salads and stir-fries with rice and pasta. They can also be ground to form the basis of a satay sauce.

Pistachio nuts
These attractive nuts can be used in cooking or eaten as a snack. They are available salted in their shells (for snacks) and also unsalted and shelled, which are the most useful for cooking. They are also used in pâtés, stuffings, and as a colorful garnish.

Pine nuts

Pistachio nuts

Peanuts

Hazelnuts

Walnuts

Corn

Baked beans

Tuna

Anchovies

Artichoke hearts

Crab

Olives

Chopped tomatoes

Sardines

CANNED GOODS

Some essential foodstuffs come in cans and one or two delicacies are also available canned.

Storage

Cans have a long shelf life but it is easy to leave them at the back of the pantry and forget about them. Check them regularly and use them before their "use by" date.

Tomatoes

These are available whole or chopped. If you use them in casseroles, it will not matter if they are whole because they will cook down. However, if you want to make a quick pasta sauce, the chopped variety is better.

Baked beans

I cannot imagine many households having no use for this staple food. Baked beans are popular with adults and children of all ages: they make a healthy, quick meal or a useful addition to a simple food like sausages. They can be eaten hot for breakfast, lunch, or supper, and do try them cold for flavor.

Tuna

A can of tuna is another useful standby. It can be eaten simply with a salad or used to make a pasta or rice dish. Tuna is economical and full of protein, and is a versatile pantry item.

Corn

Canned corn is easier to store and use than frozen and it is very versatile. It can be added to soups and casseroles as well as being a vegetable in its own right.

Artichoke hearts

These are useful for salads and appetizers, and can be added to a platter of broiled vegetables.

Bamboo shoots

Bamboo shoots make a good addition to Chinese and other Asian dishes, especially stir-fries.

Water chestnuts

These are used in Chinese hot dishes and salads.

Coconut milk

This is a popular ingredient in all Thai recipes, and is a very quick and useful ingredient. Coconut milk can also be used for cooking rice and in desserts.

Red bell peppers

These are wonderful when you have no time to broil and peel peppers. They are ready to add to salads, soups, and casseroles.

Anchovies

These are used for pizzas, salads, and garnishes.

Crab

A useful extravagance for pasta and quiches. Buy the best quality possible. You can often get better value if you buy it abroad.

Sardines

These make a delicious snack served with lots of buttered toast, or as an instant pâté with butter and lemon juice.

Olives

There are a wide variety of olives available; some are flavored with herbs. Choose your favorites and keep them for nibbling and also for use in pastas and on pizzas.

Legumes

Canned legumes save lots of time in preparation and cooking (see page 42).

CONDIMENTS

Storage

Keep salt very dry because it tends to attract water and will solidify. Buy pepper as peppercorns and store in a cool, dry place. Dried mustard keeps well for 1–2 years in a cool, dry place. However, once jars of made mustard are open, you should keep them in the refrigerator. They will keep for 6–8 months. Buy small sizes unless you are addicted to them.

Salt

If you have only one type of salt, make sure it is sea salt. It has more flavor than ordinary table salt and not only flavors food but is a useful garnish. Buy it in flakes, which can easily be crushed with the fingers or in a mill at the table. If you are cooking for a large number of people, then cooking salt can be used to salt vegetable water and water for cooking pasta and rice. It is more economical—keep it by the stove.

Pepper

A wide range of peppers are available (see pages 54–55).

Mustards

Hot mustard powder

This has always been popular because it can be used in recipes as well as mixed to a paste with water to serve with steaks, beef, and ham. It has a strong, pungent flavor and quite a kick.

Dijon mustard

The traditional mustard of France is now gaining in popularity because it has a milder flavor than hot mustard and comes ready-mixed. It is delicious in ham sandwiches and is also good for glazing a ham roast. It can also be used wherever you might use any mustard.

Moutarde de Meaux

A whole-grain mustard, which is now also widely used outside its native France. It does not have the strong flavor of hot mustard, but it does have a wonderful texture, which makes it a good ingredient in sauces. Mustard sauce and mustard mayonnaise are made with this mustard. Try to buy a French brand.

Hot mustard

Moutarde de Meaux

Dijon mustard

OTHER ITEMS

Gelatin
This is used to set desserts, mousses, and soufflés. You can buy it in packets of granules or leaf gelatin. It should be stored in a dry place.

Poppy seeds
These very tiny, blue-black seeds are often used as garnish, in salads or in baking. They have a mild flavor and add a nice crunchy texture to food as well as an attractive color.

Sesame seeds
These seeds are best if they are lightly roasted before use, either under the broiler or dry-fried in a skillet. Sprinkle them on top of salads or add them to bread mixes and dressings.

Cocoa
Unsweetened cocoa powder is often used for baking and desserts, and can also be used for hot chocolate drinks. Keep it in a cool, dry place.

Sun-dried tomatoes
These can be snipped into salads and added to pasta sauces to give a vibrant flavor.

Pesto sauce
This is available in jars: red and green varieties are a good standby. Ready-made pesto is not so good as making your own, but it is a really useful item for making a quick pasta supper.

Bouillon cubes or powder
Different flavors (chicken, fish, meat, and vegetable) are useful when fresh stock is not available. The powder is very convenient because you can add very small amounts. You can now buy organic bouillon, which contains no artificial chemicals.

Syrup
This is mainly used for baking cookies and flapjacks and in treacle tarts and sauces. Sweet syrup is also delicious served with porridge.

Honey
Honey can be used as a sweetener in beverages, spread on toast, or spooned over yogurt. There are many flavors available and the runny type is probably the easiest to use.

Coffee
There are many types available: keep yours in an airtight container or in the freezer.

Tea
Keep your favorite varieties—leaves or teabags—in airtight jars.

Maple syrup

Honey

Red pesto sauce

Coffee beans

Sesame seeds

Sun-dried tomatoes

Tea leaves

Unsweetened cocoa powder

Bouillon cubes

REFRIGERATOR ESSENTIALS

Butter
Keep some butter not just for spreading, but for cooking too. Sweet varieties are available and are good for spreading on bread and also for baking cakes and sweet pastries.

Bread
There are many varieties available. A whole-wheat loaf will keep for a week if well wrapped in plastic.

Milk
Ideal for adding to beverages and pouring over cereals. It is also essential for white sauces. Low-fat milk is a good choice both for drinking and cooking. Milk keeps in the refrigerator for 4–7 days, but check the label for the "use by" date.

Crème fraîche
This keeps in the refrigerator for far longer than cream (up to 2 weeks) so it is a useful standby and it does not curdle when added to hot sauces.

Eggs
Keep half a dozen eggs ready for use. You can then make a speedy omelet or scrambled eggs on toast for a quick supper.

Cheese
Keep a small portion of Cheddar and a small portion of fresh Parmesan on standby in the refrigerator, both for nibbling and for cooking. Make sure you use the cheeses by the "use by" date on the packaging.

Bacon
This is a good standby for a quick sandwich or as the base of a pasta sauce.

Chocolate
If you have some good-quality chocolate, you will always have the perfect end to a meal (with a good coffee), or a little indulgence now and again. Try to choose chocolate that contains at least 70 percent cocoa solids.

Butter

Eggs

Cheese

Bread

Milk

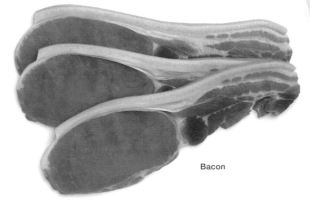

Bacon

Chocolate

FLAVORINGS, HERBS, AND SPICES

This is a range of the most popular flavorings you might need for your own cooking. You will not need them all to start with—your choice will depend on your own tastes. If you are a fan of curries, for example, you will need a range of spices, but if you prefer Italian flavors, then a good supply of herbs will be necessary.

FLAVORINGS

Capers
These small, green flowerbuds of the caper bush grow all around the Mediterranean. They are pickled in vinegar or preserved in oil, and are available in jars or cans. It is a good idea to rinse them before use. They have a sharp, sour flavor and are used in pizza toppings, pasta sauces, and the Italian "salsa verde," a strongly flavored sauce served with fish. Buy them in small jars and store in the refrigerator for up to 2–3 months once opened. Make sure they keep covered with the preserving liquid.

Juniper berries
These are the berry-like fruits of a tree of the Cyprus family. The berries are small, dark-purple and wrinkled, but have a wonderful flavor that is associated with gin. They are very good with game and pork, in stuffings, and also with cabbage, particularly red cabbage. The berries need to be crushed with a pestle and mortar

or the end of a rolling pin before use to allow the oils to escape. They are now available dried and they keep well for 1–2 years.

Garlic
An indispensable ingredient for many savory dishes. It keeps well in a dry, airy place.

Lemons
Lemons are one of the most popular flavorings in the kitchen. They can be used in sweet and savory dishes and in a variety of ways, either whole, sliced, cut into segments, just the juice, or just the grated rind, which has an intense flavor owing to its aromatic oils. Lemons are available all year round, so buy them regularly and store them in the refrigerator for up to 10 days. Once cut, cover the surface with plastic wrap to retain moisture. Freeze slices for use in drinks—a good way to use them up. If you are using the lemon zest, try to buy the unwaxed variety.

Garlic

Juniper berries

Lemon

Capers

HERBS

A wide variety of fresh herbs is now available in supermarkets so you can use them all year round. Alternatively, you can grow them in your yard or on a windowsill so that you can have them really fresh. It is always better to use fresh wherever possible, but you can now buy frozen herbs, which are a great improvement on the dried sort.

Buy herbs as you need them so that you use them as fresh as possible. Choose herbs with bright colors and no wilting leaves. If you are buying pot-grown herbs, water them carefully and keep them in a sunny position. Snip the herbs from the pot and allow them to grow on before cutting again. Packaged herbs are best kept in the refrigerator, either wrapped in a plastic bag or in a small container of water. Dried and frozen herbs are available and can be useful whenever the fresh is not obtainable: use 1 teaspoon of dried instead of 1 tablespoon of fresh or frozen.

Basil

A delicate herb, which can be very difficult to grow. It has a wonderful flavor and is particularly good with tomatoes and in Italian recipes. It is also an important ingredient in Thai cooking. It has a sweet, pungent flavor with a touch of anise seed. The leaves are very tender and bruise and discolor easily. They should therefore be torn carefully and added to dishes at the last moment to prevent loss of flavor. Use them in pasta dishes, pizzas, with fish, Italian cheeses, and salads, and particularly in tomato dishes and salad dressings.

Borage

A very pretty herb, which is easily grown. It is mainly used for drinks and soups because the leaves have a slightly cucumber flavor; the blue flowers are an attractive decoration. The herb can also be used in salads.

Bay leaves

These long, oval leaves from the bay tree are used in stocks and many meat dishes, particularly casseroles because the long, slow cooking allows the flavor to permeate the food. They can be used fresh or dried and are one of the ingredients in a bouquet garni. They can also be used to garnish finished pâtés or terrines.

Bouquet garni

This is the traditional collection of herbs tied together to flavor stocks and stews. It normally includes parsley stalks, thyme and rosemary sprigs, and a bay leaf.

Chervil

A very attractive herb with a subtle anise seed flavor. It can be used with fish, chicken, and cheese, and is particularly good with egg dishes such as omelets. It is also good in salads and its curly, delicate fronds make an excellent garnish.

Chives

Chives are very easy to grow and produce pretty purple flowers, which can be used for garnishing. It is a very useful herb: it is a member of the onion family and has a distinct flavor. Use it where a mild onion flavor is desired, with eggs, cheese, salads, soups, fish, and chicken. A quick sauce can be made by adding chives to sour cream to serve with vegetables or poached fish. Always snip the chives with scissors, rather than try to chop them, and sprinkle them over dishes just before serving.

Cilantro

A very popular herb today because it is not only used in Indian cooking but also in Chinese, Thai, South American, and Fusion cooking (Australian/Asian food flavors mixed together). Use this herb with fish, lamb, rice dishes, and stir-fries. It can also be used as a garnish—its bright green leaves add color to many dishes.

Dill

A very feathery herb, which is associated with fish. It has a pronounced anise seed flavor and has always been popular in Scandinavian countries. It is used in sauces and mayonnaise for serving with marinated salmon. It is also good with fish soups, potatoes, and cucumber. Since it is an attractive herb, it makes an ideal garnish.

Fennel

This herb is very like dill but is much stronger in color and flavor. Use it in the same way but when a more dominant flavor is required in sauces and stuffings for fish.

Marjoram

A Mediterranean herb that grows well elsewhere but may need some protection from frosts. Use it in European dishes, casseroles, pastas, and pizzas. It is also good with eggs, cheese, roasted vegetables, and salad dressings. The stalk is woody, so just use the leaves and chop them finely.

Mint

This is a traditional herb, which grows easily in any yard, in fact too well because the roots will take over everything, so plant it in

Basil

Mint

Rosemary

Oregano

Sage

a large pot instead. It is used in classic mint sauce as well as to flavor new potatoes. It is also delicious added to risottos, couscous, and salads and is widely used in Indian cuisine. When chopped with parsley, it makes a good garnish for root vegetables, and whole sprigs can be used to decorate desserts, particularly fruit and ice creams.

Oregano
Like marjoram but slightly stronger in flavor, oregano is used in Mediterranean dishes, particularly pasta sauces where robust flavors are required. The leaves are removed from the stems and chopped before adding to the dish. It is this herb that gives pizzas their characteristic flavor.

Parsley
This herb is very popular and is used all year round for garnishes and in stuffings and sauces. It is quite easy to grow but can be slow to germinate. There are two main varieties, curly parsley, which is mainly used for garnish, and the flat-leaf or Italian variety, which has a stronger flavor. Use parsley to flavor all fish dishes, stuff whole fish with a few stalks, and flavor sauces and butters with lots of freshly chopped leaves. Potatoes and other puréed vegetables are improved by the addition of parsley and so are mushrooms and onions. Sprinkle a handful over salads, too.

Rosemary
Another favorite Mediterranean herb, grown as a hardy bush, and available for use all year round. The spikes must be removed from the stalks and chopped very finely because some people find the spikes too hard and difficult to digest. Rosemary has a special compatibility with lamb and pork—its pungent flavor blends well with these meats. Greeks and Italians use this herb in their stronger dishes. Rosemary is particularly good with roasted foods and meat cooked on the barbecue, and the stronger stalks can be used as skewers for pieces of fish or meat.

Sage
A very strong, slightly musty-flavored herb, which can put people off if it is used in too great a quantity. The delicately colored gray-green leaves are chopped and used in stuffings and sauces. Sage is good with rich, fatty meats like goose and pork, and goes well with cheese and sausages. Sage and onion stuffing is the traditional accompaniment to goose. The herb also goes well with apples, tomatoes, potatoes, and some Italian dishes.

Tarragon
Tarragon has always been highly regarded by the French. It has a subtle flavor of vanilla and anise seed and its delicate leaves are used to flavor sauces like hollandaise, béarnaise, and tartare. It is good with fish, shellfish, chicken, veal, and egg dishes.

Thyme
Many varieties of thyme are available now. Common thyme is the most generally available, which can be very pungent so it should be used sparingly. Thyme is a small, woody plant with green-gray leaves, which need to be stripped from the stem before use. This herb is very good with all meats; roasts can be rubbed with the herb before cooking and casseroles benefit from its rich aroma during their long, slow cooking. Lemon thyme is less acerbic and has an additional lemon flavor, which is useful in stuffings, fish dishes, and salads.

Bay leaves

Thyme

Dill

Chives

Parsley

Tarragon

Cilantro

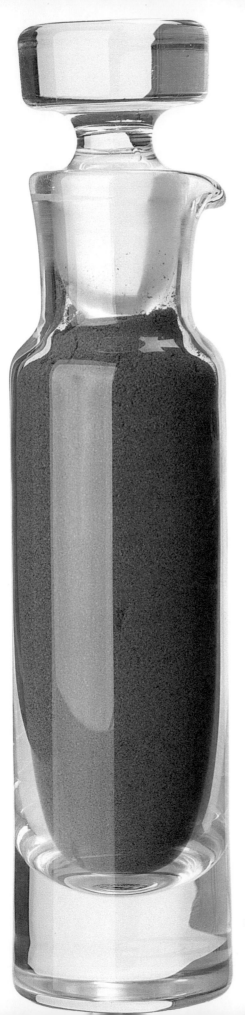

SPICES

There is a vast range of spices available nowadays. In fact it is confusing because there are so many. Here are some of the spices you might need to flavor some of the dishes in this book. It is a good idea to buy spices in small amounts because they tend to lose their flavor, especially the ready-ground ones. Store them in a cool, dry place out of the light and check from time to time the "use by" date to be sure you use them when they are at their best.

Allspice
This spice comes from the Caribbean and is available as red-brown berries or ready-ground. It is very aromatic and has a flavor of cloves, nutmeg, and cinnamon. Traditionally allspice is used in fruit cakes and Christmas puddings. It can also be used with chicken, beef, or pork, as in Caribbean cooking. Allspice is best bought whole because the ground spice loses its smell and flavor. It is best to grind it with a pestle and mortar when needed.

Apple pie spice
This is used for desserts and contains allspice, cinnamon, cloves, coriander, ginger, and nutmeg. It is useful if you only cook occasionally because it allows you to have the six spices in one jar. It can also be used in cookies, breads, and cakes.

Caraway seeds
These seeds are very popular and widely used in the countries of northern Europe. The seeds are used whole in casseroles, soups, vegetable dishes, and in baking. They have a warm, slightly bitter, almost medicinal flavor.

Cardamom
These are small, green pods, which contain tiny black seeds.

Chili powder

Cardamom

Cloves

Paprika

They have the most delicious aroma and flavor. Cardamom is an eastern spice and is used in curry dishes and also in some pastry and sweet recipes. It can be used to add spice to vegetable soups and purées. To use, crush the pods with a pestle and mortar, remove the dried pod, and add the seeds to the dish. Always buy whole cardamom pods—the ground variety is inferior.

Chili powder
This can sometimes be misleading because some brands have pure ground chiles but some contain a mixture of other spices, which reduces the intensity of the powder. The powder is usually made from a variety of chiles and can be very hot. You need to experiment to find the right amount to your taste. It is a good, red color and is used in curries but also in South American and Mexican dishes where a fiery taste is required.

Chinese five-spice powder
As the name suggests, this is a blend of five spices, which is used to flavor Chinese dishes. The mixture consists of cassia or cinnamon, cloves, fennel seeds, star anise, and Sichuan pepper. Use it in Chinese cooking, particularly vegetables, chicken, and duck.

Cinnamon
This is a very popular spice. It has a warm, sweet, spicy aroma, which permeates the whole house when used. It comes from the inner bark of a type of laurel tree and is bought as cinnamon sticks, which can be used to flavor sweet and savory dishes. Break off little pieces and remove before serving dishes such as poached fruits, Greek moussaka, or mulled wine. A cinnamon stick can also be used to stir hot chocolate to give added flavor. In some countries, cinnamon is used in baking, particularly in Christmas cakes and puddings. You need to buy cinnamon ready-ground because it is impossible to grind the cinnamon sticks.

Cloves
Cloves are the dried, unopened flowerbuds from an evergreen tree. They are used in Christmas baking, and to flavor bread sauce, mulled wine, pickles, and chutneys. Cloves can be used whole (always be sure that you remove them before serving because a whole clove tastes rather nasty) or ground, which is best done with a pestle and mortar. The flavor is very pungent, so care should be taken not to make the taste overwhelming.

Coriander seeds
Little brown coriander seeds from the cilantro plant have quite a different flavor from the leaves. The seeds have a warm orange flavor, and can be dry-fried before use to bring out their full scent. They are easily ground with a pestle and mortar and are best bought whole because their flavor fades rapidly once they are ground. This spice is one of the most important in Indian cooking. Ground coriander is used for curries, fish, meat, poultry, vegetables, and some baking.

Cumin seeds
This is a very important spice, and another essential ingredient in curries. Cumin is also important in the cooking of Mexico and North Africa. The narrow, brownish seeds are quite soft and easy to grind. Their aroma is strong and spicy with a bitter flavor. Use them in curries and meat casserole dishes, and also with rice. Dry-frying before use will enhance their flavor.

Curry powder/paste
This is a mixture of different spices blended together for ease of use. If you make a lot of curries, it is a good idea to prepare your own mixture in a larger quantity and use as needed. Indian curry powder usually contains coriander, cumin, fenugreek, black mustard, black pepper, turmeric, ginger, and red chiles. Commercial curry powder and pastes are available, and some are better than others. It is best to buy them from an authentic specialist Indian or Thai shop and try different brands until you find one that suits you.

Garam masala
Another Indian mix of spices, which is used to flavor curries, vegetable dishes, and rice. It is

Ground cinnamon

Garam masala

Coriander seeds

Cinnamon

often added at the end of the cooking time rather than at the beginning like curry powder. The mix includes bay leaves, black pepper, cloves, cinnamon, coriander, cumin, and green cardamom. It adds a more fragrant flavor to food rather than a hot sensation of chile. It is also available ready mixed.

Ginger

Ginger is a versatile spice. Fresh ginger root is easily obtainable; it has a fresh, spicy flavor and can be used chopped or grated. Preserved ginger in sugar syrup and is very sweet—it can be used in baking or served with ice-cream. Ground ginger is used in baking, particularly gingerbread, to which it gives its characteristic flavor and aroma.

Mace

Mace is the bright outer casing of the nutmeg and is used in its own right in cakes, desserts, and sauces. It tends to be stronger than nutmeg and should be used sparingly. Both mace and nutmeg have a warm, fragrant aroma. For baking, ground mace is best because whole mace is difficult to grind. Ground mace can also be used in pâtés and terrines.

Mustard

Mustard seeds are available in white, black, and brown varieties. The darker ones provide the heat and the pungency and the white ones the flavor. They can be bought whole and then you can grind them when needed. They are good roughly ground and mixed with potato for a slightly "curry" flavor. Alternatively, you can buy the ready-ground hot mustard powder and mix it with water before serving with meats and sausages. Mustard is also used in cheese dishes and to flavor sauces.

Nutmeg

This popular spice is used all year round, not just in desserts but in many savory dishes as well. It is available both whole and ground, but there is nothing like the freshly grated spice for flavor. Always keep a nutmeg close at hand with a small grater, so that you can add it to white sauces, pasta dishes, and vegetables. Nutmeg is also delicious grated on top of hot drinks.

Peppers

Cayenne: this is a very hot, pungent pepper, which is made from a particularly hot variety of chile. It has a distinctive color and flavor, but should be used with great care. A tiny pinch can add a hot fieriness to any dish. It is particularly good with cheese dishes, especially in biscuits and crackers. It can also be used in sauces and curries.

Paprika: this spice is made from dried, sweet, red bell peppers, which are ground to give a deep red spice. Paprika's color makes it an ideal garnish for savory dishes. It can be shaken over pale-colored food such as egg mayonnaise, or sprinkled on top of cauliflower cheese to add bite as well as color. Paprika is quite a mild spice and is always used in Hungarian dishes such as goulash. Buy this spice in small quantities because the flavor deteriorates rapidly.

Peppercorns: this is the most widely used spice—it is used every day in cooking and at the table. It is not confined to savory dishes either—a grating of black pepper is often encouraged with fruits such as strawberries and pineapple. Peppercorns have their own particular flavor and also the ability to improve other flavors. They are available in white and

Ginger root

Nutmeg

Paprika

Ground ginger

Cumin

Cayenne pepper

black. The white peppercorns are the kernels of fully ripened berries after the husks have been discarded, and the black ones are the whole green berries, which are picked while unripened and then dried until black. The outer layer of the peppercorn has the aromatic flavor. You can buy peppercorns either whole or ground. Freshly ground pepper is the only one to use for flavor and pungency; the ready-ground stuff is not worth buying.

Saffron

This is the most expensive spice. Saffron comes from the stigma of the autumn crocus. It is a bright yellow, and is used for its color as well as its subtle flavor. Saffron is used in soups, paellas, risottos, fish stews, cakes, and buns. You can buy it as tiny threads, which need to be crushed and soaked in a tablespoon of water before they are used.

Star anise

This attractive, star-shaped spice is really a fruit pod, and it is used extensively in Chinese cooking. It has a sweet, pungent, anise flavor and aroma and is used in both sweet and savory dishes.
It is good with chicken and duck and any stir-fries. It can also be used to flavor cakes and fruit compôtes. It is usually available whole, and must be removed from the dish before serving. It can also be ground with a pestle and mortar or in an electric grinder.

Turmeric

This is a brilliant, yellow-colored spice. Take care with it because it can stain clothes and utensils. It is widely used in Indian cooking, and comes from the ground root of a member of the ginger family. Its musky, earthy flavor is essential to curries. It is also useful as a cheaper substitute for saffron, purely for color, however, because

the flavors cannot be compared. Turmeric also adds color to rice dishes and to some breads and cakes as well.

Vanilla

The beans of the vanilla plant give us one of the most popular flavorings. The black beans are sliced and the seeds extracted for use in sauces, custards, ice-creams, and other desserts. The whole bean can be placed in a jar of sugar so that the sugar becomes flavored with vanilla. It is also available as vanilla extract: make sure you buy this and not vanilla "essence" or vanilla "flavoring," which are inferior.

Turmeric

Peppercorns

Vanilla beans

Part 3
Recipes

SOUPS

Soups have always been good staple fare, but are really back in fashion. We have supermarkets selling soup in cans and packets and the new, chilled, "fresh" varieties, which are very popular. They have introduced us to many new flavors and ingredients. At home we can make truly fresh soups using inexpensive ingredients and experiment with new flavors.

The base of a good soup is stock, so I have given two recipes for basic stock that can be easily made at home. You do not need to make stock, however. There are many brands of bouillon cubes and powder in the stores along with the new chilled stocks. The latter are quite expensive but can be useful when you want a particular flavor in a special soup. Some of the bouillon cubes have a very concentrated flavor and should be used in moderation. A good one to try is vegetable bouillon powder, which you can use by the spoonful and is excellent in vegetable, fish, and meat soups.

Stock can be made quite easily from simple ingredients but can be time consuming. The results do add flavor to dishes and, as you can freeze the stock, it is a worthwhile exercise. There are a few rules to remember when making stocks:

• Use the freshest ingredients: there is no point in spending time making stock unless you have fresh ingredients.
• When preparing the stock, make sure the water only simmers; rapid boiling will result in a cloudy stock (you can boil it at the end of the process after straining it).
• Always skim any scum from the top of the stock so that it will be clear.
• Make sure you strain the stock well through a fine strainer. This will make sure that you have a clearer, fresher soup.
• You can reduce the strained stock by boiling to make for a more concentrated flavor. It is also important if you are to freeze the stock so you have a smaller volume to store. Always check seasoning after reducing because this intensifies the saltiness.
• If you have time it is a good idea to let the stock cool, then you will be able to remove any excess fat from the surface, thus saving unwanted calories.

Making soup at home can be as simple or as complicated as you like. Start with good, fresh ingredients and prepare them carefully. Vegetables need to be peeled but try not to waste too much. The green parts of leeks, for example, are not often served as a vegetable but are invaluable for soups because they give a good color. Make sure all vegetables are cut to the same size so that they cook evenly.

Start by "sweating" the vegetables in a little butter or olive oil. Butter is preferable for some root vegetables because the flavor is better, but for health reasons you might like to use oil. Then add stock and simmer; do not overcook at this stage or the flavor may be spoilt.

If the soup requires blending, use a food processor or a blender. This way you will have a very smooth finish. If the recipe is quite rustic and you do not want too smooth a result, you can blend only half of the ingredients and then add the chunky vegetables. However, if you want a really smooth soup, you might want to blend it thoroughly and then strain it to make sure the consistency is correct. Thanks to blenders we do not need to add any additional flour to thicken soups, we can rely on the puréed vegetable matter to do the job.

Serving soups for every occasion

Serving soup correctly is very important. If it is to be served hot, make sure the dishes are hot and the soup is at the correct temperature; if cold, make sure that the dishes and the soup are chilled. Accompany the soup with some good bread and an appropriate garnish. A good handful of chopped herbs, a swirl of cream, a few chopped nuts, or a grating of cheese—all add color, flavor, and texture.

Soups can be delicate appetizers or robust, hearty meals, so here is a selection of recipes from across the whole spectrum: basic stocks, chilled smooth soups, puréed soups, and thick, chunky soups that can be served as a complete meal together with some fresh crusty bread.

BELOW Winter Bean and Lentil Soup

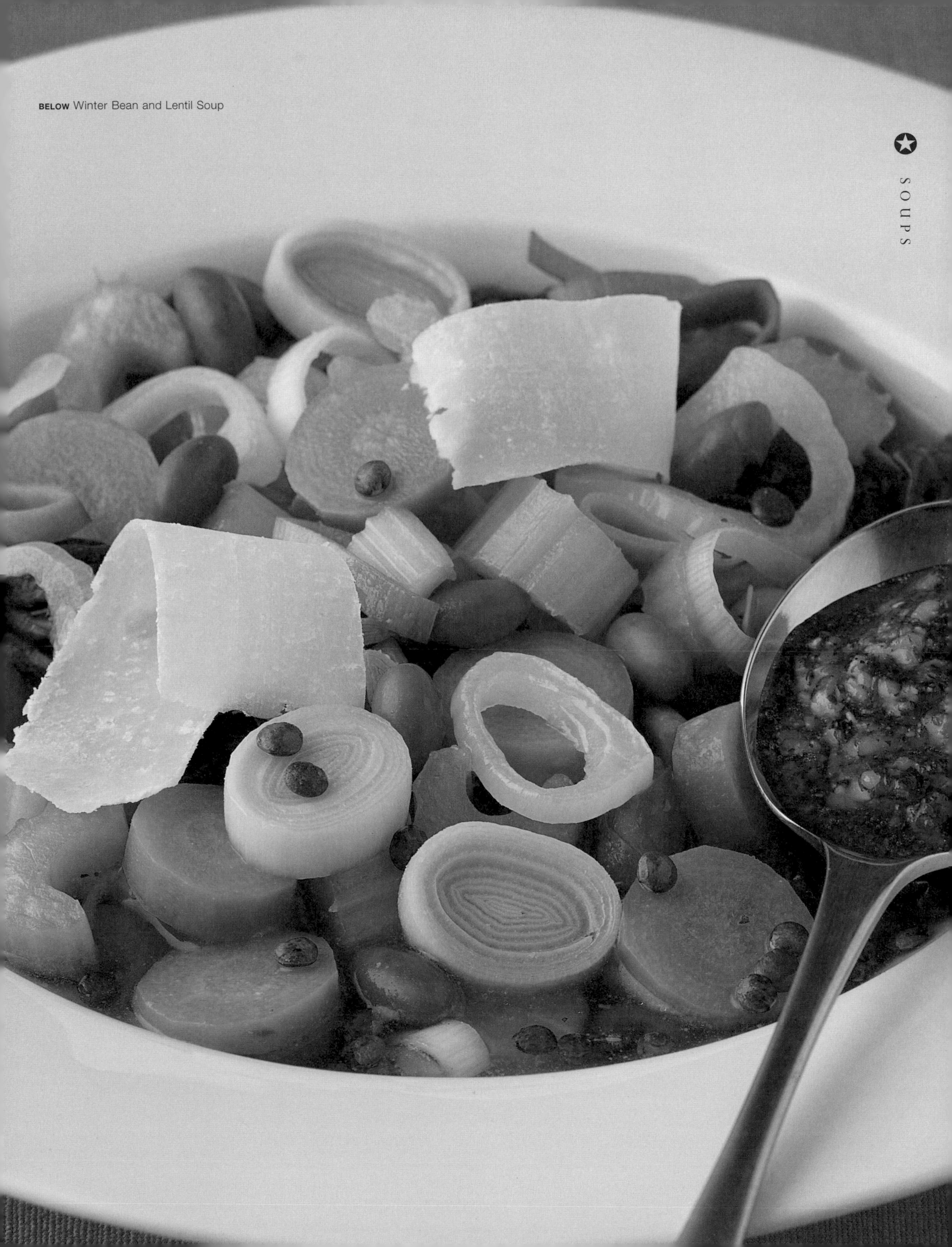

BASIC CHICKEN STOCK

✪

You can make two sorts of chicken stock: a light stock made from raw carcasses and a brown stock made from a cooked carcass. It is more usual to prepare the latter because we often have a carcass left over from a roast chicken, while it is very unusual to have a whole fresh carcass.

Makes about 4 cups
Preparation time: 10 minutes
Cooking time: 1½–2 hours

INGREDIENTS

1 carcass from a roast chicken
6¼ cups water
1 onion, peeled and sliced
1 carrot, peeled and sliced
1 celery stalk, sliced
1 tsp dried thyme
1 bay leaf
3 sprigs fresh parsley
salt and pepper

You will need a large, lidded pan (about 15 cups), a cook's knife, a cutting board, a measuring cup, a wooden spatula, a slotted spoon, a large bowl, and a strainer

METHOD

1 Break up the carcass and place it in a large pan. Add the water, vegetables, and herbs. Season well and bring to a boil over medium heat. Skim the surface if any scum forms.

2 Cover the pan, lower the heat and simmer for 1½–2 hours.

3 Remove from the heat, let cool a little, and strain into a large bowl. Discard all the meat, vegetables, and herbs.

4 Cool thoroughly, then remove all traces of fat from the top of the stock. If required, you can then reboil for up to 30 minutes to reduce the stock and give a more intense flavor. Cover the cool stock with plastic wrap, and chill in the refrigerator for up to 1–2 days before use.

*Suitable for freezing. Chill thoroughly, pour into a rigid, lidded container, and freeze for up to 3 months. To use, thaw at room temperature and use as instructed.

BASIC VEGETABLE STOCK

Makes 4 cups
Preparation time: 10 minutes
Cooking time: 1 hour, plus reduction time

INGREDIENTS

1 tbsp olive oil
1 onion, peeled and coarsely chopped
1 carrot, peeled and sliced
2 celery stalks, sliced
1 leek, trimmed and sliced
4 cups shredded lettuce, or 2½ cups shredded cabbage
5 cups water
1 bouquet garni (see page 50)
salt and pepper

You will need a large, lidded pan (about 15 cups), a cook's knife, a cutting board, a wooden spatula, a measuring cup, a slotted spoon, a large bowl, and a strainer

METHOD

1 Heat the oil in a large pan over medium heat and add the prepared vegetables. Stir well and cook for 3–4 minutes until the vegetables become slightly golden. This will give the stock a good color.

2 Pour in the water, add the bouquet garni, and season well. Bring to a boil, half-cover the pan, and simmer for 30 minutes to 1 hour. The stock should reduce slightly.

3 Remove from the heat, let cool a little, and strain into a bowl. Discard all the vegetables and bouquet garni and use the stock as required. If not used immediately, cover with plastic wrap and keep in the refrigerator for 1–2 days only. Alternatively, reduce the stock by boiling for 30 minutes until reduced by half, then cool completely, and freeze.

• *Any vegetables can be used: cauliflower stalks, beans, broccoli, outside leaves of cabbage, and other vegetable trimmings. Do not use beet because the color will be too strong, and do not use potatoes or other starchy vegetables because they will make the stock cloudy and also may "sour" it.*

* *Suitable for freezing. Cool first, and then pour into a rigid, lidded container. Freeze for up to 3 months. To use, thaw at room temperature and use as instructed.*

GIBLET STOCK

This stock can be made with chicken or turkey giblets and is essential when you need a good gravy to accompany the roasts.

Makes about 2½ cups
Preparation time: 10 minutes
Cooking time: 1½–2 hours

INGREDIENTS

1 packet chicken or turkey giblets
3 cups water
1 onion, left unpeeled, but thickly sliced
1 carrot, peeled and thickly sliced
1 celery stalk, sliced
1 tsp dried thyme
1 bay leaf
3 sprigs fresh parsley
salt and pepper

You will need a large, lidded pan (about 7½ cups), a cook's knife, a cutting board, a measuring cup, a wooden spatula, a slotted spoon, a large bowl, and a strainer

METHOD

1 Place the giblets in the pan. Add the water, vegetables, and herbs. Season well and bring to a boil over medium heat. Skim the surface to remove any scum.

2 Cover the pan, lower the heat, and simmer for 1–1½ hours.

3 Remove from the heat, let cool a little, then strain into a large bowl. Discard all the giblets, vegetables, and herbs.

4 Cover with plastic wrap, chill thoroughly, and use as required. This stock will keep in the refrigerator for up to 1–2 days before use.

SMOOTH GAZPACHO

This delicious soup is Spanish in origin and is very refreshing served chilled on hot summer days.

Serves 6–8
Preparation time: 20 minutes, plus marinating

INGREDIENTS

10 ripe tomatoes
½ cucumber
1 red bell pepper
½ white onion, peeled
½ red onion, peeled
2 garlic cloves, peeled
2 slices white bread (crusts removed)
1 cup tomato juice
1 tbsp balsamic vinegar
2 tbsp wine vinegar
10 fresh basil leaves, torn in half
1 tbsp chopped fresh cilantro
pinch of ground cumin
pinch of cayenne pepper
1 cup olive oil
salt and pepper

To garnish
1 tbsp finely chopped tomato
1 tbsp finely chopped cucumber
fresh sprigs of cilantro or chervil

You will need a cook's knife, a cutting board, a glass bowl, a measuring cup, a blender, a strainer, and 6–8 serving bowls

METHOD

1 Dice the tomatoes, cucumber, red bell pepper, white onion, red onion, garlic, and white bread.

2 Place all the diced ingredients in a glass bowl. Add the tomato juice, vinegars, herbs, and spices. Pour in 5 tablespoons of the olive oil, cover with plastic wrap, and marinate for a few hours, or overnight if possible.

3 After the mixture has marinated, transfer it to a blender, and process to a smooth purée.

4 Pass the mixture through a strainer. Process again, then gradually add the remaining olive oil until the mixture is smooth. Season to taste, then cover with plastic wrap, and chill well for 2–3 hours or overnight. Pour the soup into chilled bowls and spoon a little tomato and cucumber on top before serving. Top with sprigs of fresh cilantro or chervil.

CARROT AND ORANGE SOUP

Serves 4–6
Preparation time: 15 minutes
Cooking time: 30–35 minutes

INGREDIENTS

6 tbsp butter

2 onions, peeled and finely chopped

2 lb/900 g carrots, peeled and chopped

3¾ cups vegetable stock

1 bay leaf

juice and grated rind of 3 oranges

salt and pepper

⅔ cup crème fraîche, to serve

2 tbsp snipped fresh chives, to garnish

You will need a large, lidded pan (about 10 cups),
a cook's knife, a cutting board, a wooden spatula, a measuring
cup, a blender, and 4–6 serving bowls

METHOD

1 Melt the butter in a large pan over medium heat. Add the
chopped vegetables and sauté gently for 3–4 minutes until
soft but not brown. Pour in the stock, add the bay leaf and
grated orange rind, and simmer, with the lid on the pan, for
about 20 minutes or until the vegetables are cooked.

2 Remove from the heat and process the soup in a blender
until smooth. Return to the clean pan and stir in the orange
juice. Add salt and pepper to taste.

3 Reheat the stock, then serve in warm bowls with a swirl of
crème fraîche and garnished with chives.

** Suitable for freezing. Prepare up to the end of step 2, let cool, and pour
into a rigid, lidded container. Freeze for up to 3 months. To use, thaw at
room temperature, then continue from step 3 above.*

CHICKEN AND CHILE SOUP

Serves 4
Preparation time: 15 minutes
Cooking time: 30–35 minutes

INGREDIENTS

2 tbsp butter
1 tbsp olive oil
2 medium red chiles, seeded and finely chopped
2 slices lean bacon, diced
1 onion, peeled and finely chopped
1 garlic clove, peeled and crushed
2 skinless boneless chicken breast portions, thinly sliced
1 tsp chopped fresh thyme
1 medium potato, peeled and diced
1⅓ cups corn, frozen or canned
5 cups chicken stock
salt and pepper
⅔ cup heavy cream
1 tbsp chopped fresh cilantro, to garnish

You will need a large, lidded pan (about 10 cups),
a cook's knife, a cutting board, a potato peeler,
a measuring cup, and 4 serving bowls

METHOD

1 Heat the butter and oil in a large pan. Cook the chiles, bacon, onion, and garlic over medium heat for 4–5 minutes until soft. Add the chicken and cook until just colored.

2 Add the thyme, potato, corn, and stock and simmer, covered, for about 20 minutes.

3 Season to taste, then pour into warm serving bowls, and top with a swirl of cream and a sprinkling of cilantro.

CURRIED APPLE SOUP

This soup can be served hot, but is also delicious served cold in the summer.

Serves 8
Preparation time: 15 minutes
Cooking time: 30 minutes

INGREDIENTS

4 tbsp butter
2 onions, peeled and finely chopped
2 tbsp curry powder
7½ cups chicken stock
8 eating apples, cored and chopped (peeled if desired)
¾ cup dried apricots, chopped
⅔ cup light cream
salt and pepper

To garnish
3 tbsp toasted, sliced almonds
1 tbsp chopped fresh parsley
1 tbsp chopped fresh mint

You will need a large, lidded pan (about 15 cups), a cook's knife, a cutting board, a wooden spatula, a measuring cup, a blender, and 8 serving bowls

METHOD

1 Melt the butter in a large pan over medium heat. Add the onions and sauté gently for 3–4 minutes until soft but not brown. Stir in the curry powder and cook for 1r minute more.

2 Stir in the stock and bring to a boil.

3 Add the apples and apricots, return to a boil, then lower the heat, and simmer, covered, for 20 minutes.

4 Remove from the heat and process the soup in a blender until smooth.

5 Return it to the clean pan and reheat. Add the cream, taste, and season if necessary.

6 Serve in warm bowls, garnished with the toasted almonds and chopped herbs.

* Suitable for freezing. Prepare the soup up to the end of step 4, let cool, then pour into a rigid, lidded container. Freeze for up to 3 months. To use, thaw at room temperature, then continue from step 5 above.

SPICY PARSNIP SOUP

Serves 4
Preparation time: 15 minutes
Cooking time: 20–25 minutes

INGREDIENTS

4 tbsp butter

1 medium onion, peeled and chopped

1 medium potato, peeled and chopped

1 lb 2 oz/500 g parsnips, peeled and chopped

½ tsp curry powder

½ tsp ground cumin

½ tsp ground coriander

½ tsp ground cardamom

6¾ cups chicken stock or vegetable stock made with bouillon powder

salt and pepper

⅔ cup heavy cream, optional

You will need a large, lidded pan (about 12½ cups), a cook's knife, a cutting board, a wooden spatula, a measuring cup, a blender, and 4 serving bowls

METHOD

1 Melt the butter in the pan over medium heat and cook the onion and potato for 3–4 minutes until softened. Add the parsnips and mix well. Stir in the ground spices and continue to cook for 1 minute more.

2 Pour in the stock and bring to a boil. Lower the heat, cover the pan, and simmer for 20–25 minutes until the parsnips are soft.

3 Remove from the heat and process the mixture in a blender until smooth. Taste and season with salt and pepper.

4 Serve hot, with a swirl of cream (if using).

Suitable for freezing. Prepare to the end of step 3, then chill thoroughly, and pour into a rigid, lidded container. Freeze for up to 3 months. To use, thaw at room temperature, reheat, and serve as above.

SMOKED HADDOCK CHOWDER

3

RECIPES

Serves 4 as an appetizer, or 3 as a main course

Preparation time: 10 minutes
Cooking time: 25–30 minutes

INGREDIENTS

2 tbsp butter
2 oz/55 g lardons or lean bacon, sliced
1 onion, peeled and finely chopped
12 oz/350 g undyed smoked haddock, skinned
8 oz/225 g small, waxy potatoes
1¼ cups milk
scant 2 cups fish or vegetable stock
4 tbsp light cream
salt and pepper
2 tbsp chopped fresh parsley, to garnish

You will need a large, lidded pan (about 12½ cups),
a cook's knife, a cutting board, a small skillet,
a measuring cup, a wooden spatula, and 4 serving bowls

METHOD

1 Melt the butter in the skillet over medium heat and cook the lardons for 3–4 minutes until they start to brown. Add the onion and continue to cook for 2–3 minutes until soft.

2 Cut the haddock into 1 inch/2.5 cm cubes, place in a bowl, and cover with plastic wrap until ready to use.

3 Cut the potatoes into ½ inch/1 cm cubes and place in a large pan.

4 Pour in the milk and stock and bring to a boil over medium heat. Reduce to a gentle simmer and cook for 10–15 minutes until the potatoes are just starting to cook. Add the haddock, lardons, and onion and simmer for a further 5 minutes. Remove from the heat, stir in the cream, season to taste, and serve in warm bowls garnished with parsley.

SQUASH AND ALMOND SOUP

Serves 4–6
Preparation time: 10–15 minutes
Cooking time: 50–55 minutes

INGREDIENTS

2 lb/900 g butternut squash, or any type of pumpkin
1 tbsp olive oil
1 onion, peeled and finely chopped
1 cup ground almonds
3¾ cups vegetable stock
juice and grated rind of 1 orange
salt and pepper
⅔ cup freshly grated Parmesan cheese
2 tbsp toasted, sliced almonds, to garnish

You will need a large lidded pan (about 12½ cups), a cook's knife, a cutting board, a roasting pan, a measuring cup, a blender, and 4–6 serving bowls

METHOD

1 Preheat the oven to 400°F/200°C. Cut the squash into slices and remove the seeds. Place the slices in a lightly oiled roasting pan and roast in the preheated oven for 30–40 minutes until tender and just starting to brown.

2 Heat the remaining oil in a large pan over medium heat and cook the onion gently for 2–3 minutes until softened. Add the almonds and stir well.

3 Remove the squash from the oven. Remove and discard the rind, then add the cooked pulp to the pan.

4 Pour in the stock, bring to a boil, then simmer over gentle heat for 10–15 minutes until the onions are soft.

5 Remove from the heat and process the soup in a blender until smooth. Return it to the clean pan, then reheat, and add the orange juice and rind. Taste and season if necessary.

6 Remove from the heat, stir in the Parmesan, and serve immediately in warm bowls garnished with the sliced almonds.

Suitable for freezing. Prepare the soup to the end of step 5, then chill thoroughly, and pour into a rigid, lidded container. Freeze for up to 3 months. To use, thaw at room temperature, reheat and continue from step 6 above.

WINTER BEAN AND LENTIL SOUP

Serves 4
Preparation time: 15 minutes
Cooking time: 25–30 minutes

INGREDIENTS

2 tbsp olive oil

1 onion, peeled and finely sliced

12 oz/350 g carrots, peeled and sliced

3 celery stalks, sliced

2 garlic cloves, peeled and chopped

½ cup Puy lentils, rinsed

5 cups vegetable stock

1 bay leaf

2 medium leeks, trimmed and sliced

3¼ cups shredded cabbage or scant 2 cups shredded spinach

14 oz/400 g canned borlotti beans, drained

salt and pepper

To garnish
4 tbsp pesto sauce

scant ⅔ cup freshly shaved Parmesan cheese

You will need a large, lidded pan (about 15 cups), a cook's knife, a cutting board, a wooden spatula, a measuring cup, and 4 serving bowls

METHOD

1 Heat the oil in a large pan over medium heat. Add the onion, carrots, celery, and garlic and sauté gently for 3–4 minutes until soft but not brown.

2 Add the lentils and cook for 2 minutes more.

3 Pour in the stock, add the bay leaf, and bring to a boil. Simmer, covered, for 15 minutes or until the vegetables are almost tender.

4 Add the leeks, season well, and continue to cook for 5 minutes.

5 Finally, add the shredded cabbage or spinach together with the beans and cook for 2–3 minutes more.

6 Remove from the heat. Check the seasoning and serve in warm bowls with a swirl of pesto and the shaved cheese.

E G G S

Eggs are one of the most versatile and nutritious foods, whether used whole or in their separate—whites and yolks—components. They should be a stock item: you will need large eggs for main recipes and smaller ones for cooking processes like coating and glazing. You can store them in the refrigerator, but always bring them to room temperature before use.

Make sure you buy your eggs from a reliable supplier and use them as fresh as possible. You can choose between intensively farmed, free-range, and organic eggs—a matter of preference and price. Shell color is irrelevant.

We will be concentrating here on hens' eggs. There are others: quail eggs are increasingly popular, duck eggs are widely available, and even ostrich eggs are appearing now.

Choosing and buying eggs
The freshest eggs are the best but it is often impossible to ascertain when the eggs were laid unless you have a local supplier or a friend who keeps hens. In supermarkets we must rely on the date stamped. This is the "best before" date and is set at three weeks after the eggs were laid, so look for ones with the date furthest ahead. Always buy from a reliable supplier or from a supermarket where there is a fast turnover.

You can buy eggs in four sizes: extra large, large, medium, and small. Extra large eggs are 2¼ oz/60 g or over, large are 1¾ oz/50 g or over, medium and small are anything below 1¾ oz/50 g. The eggs used in the recipes in this book are all extra large but when they are served alone (for example a boiled egg) a very large size would be preferable. Smaller eggs can be bought for glazing and binding and they are also useful for small children for their boiled eggs and soldiers (toasted fingers of bread).

Check the freshness of an egg by floating it in water: an egg that lies on its side at the bottom of a bowl is fresh, one that stands vertically with the rounded end up is less fresh, and one that floats completely is stale and should not be used.

Storage
There is great debate as to whether you should keep your eggs in the refrigerator or at room temperature. Eggs kept in the refrigerator last longer than those kept at room temperature.

However, eggs are best cooked from room temperature so you will need to get them out of the refrigerator 2–3 hours before they are needed. If you regularly cook for a large number of people, you could keep your eggs in a cool place and not in the refrigerator because you will have a quick turnover, but if you use eggs only now and then. they are best kept in the refrigerator. Store them with the pointed ends downward. If you can, it is a good idea to store them in the boxes in which they were bought, rather than in the egg racks in the door of the refrigerator, because this helps to prevent them picking up smells. Separated egg whites can be kept in a lidded container in the refrigerator for up to one week. Egg yolks and beaten whole eggs can be stored in the refrigerator for two days.

Eggs can also be frozen. Separated egg whites will freeze for up to three months if lightly forked and stored in a lidded container. Egg yolks will also freeze satisfactorily, but they should be beaten with a little salt or sugar to prevent them becoming too gelatinous. Label the containers clearly with what they contain and the date they were frozen. Whole eggs may be frozen, lightly beaten and also mixed with a little salt.

Salmonella
Salmonella bacteria in eggs can, in some rare cases, cause food poisoning. However, thorough cooking will usually prevent this. Undercooked or raw eggs can be the main source of the problem and so recipes that contain raw or lightly cooked eggs should be avoided by vulnerable groups. People in vulnerable groups include the elderly, pregnant and breast-feeding women, young children, sick people, and convalescents. This means that foods such as mousses, cold soufflés, mayonnaise, egg custards, home-made ice-creams, and royal frosting should be avoided. Luckily some supermarkets are now stocking pasteurized egg so that these dishes can be made without any danger to health.

SEPARATING EGGS

For some recipes it is necessary to separate the white from the yolk of an egg.

1 There are some gadgets available that help to achieve this, but if you have not got a gadget, you can use the shell method described here. You will need a bowl. Crack the egg shell in half on the edge of the bowl.

2 Pass the yolk into one of the shell halves, letting some of the white to drop into the bowl.

3 Pass the yolk into the other shell half, at the same time letting more of the egg white to drop into the bowl. Take care not to break the yolk on the sharp edges of the egg shells.

4 Repeat passing the yolk between the egg shells until all the white is in the bowl. Remember that any egg white needed for a meringue should have no trace of yolk in it or it will not whisk properly.

N ote: the fresher the egg, the easier it is to separate because the white is more gelatinous and the yolk firmer. It also helps to chill the egg first before separating.

WHISKING EGG WHITES

Absolutely fresh eggs are not ideal for whisking: those that are 3–5 days old are best. Make sure everything is scrupulously clean and that there is not a trace of grease anywhere on the equipment. Place the separated egg whites in a large bowl and whisk, using a balloon whisk, a hand-held electric mixer, or a large, free-standing electric mixer. Depending on whether you are going to incorporate the whites with other ingredients as in a soufflé or make a meringue, you must whisk them to the correct consistency. If they are to be mixed, the consistency should be "soft peaks," that is, the peaks should be firm enough to hold their shape but are still soft and will flop over. "Firm peaks" are achieved when the mixture is beaten so that it is dry and when the whisk is lifted from the bowl the peaks are firm and stand rigid. Once the whites are whisked, the other ingredients should be folded in very carefully so that the air is retained. Use a plastic spatula or a metal tablespoon for folding in because they cut through the mixture more easily.

COOKING EGGS

It is always advisable to have eggs at room temperature before starting to cook them. They are very sensitive to heat and start to cook (coagulate) at 140°F/60°C. This makes eggs useful in cookery as a binding agent, for thickening sauces, in egg custards, and as a food in their own right. However, it is very easy to overcook eggs and end up with some indigestible mass, so gentle and swift cooking is essential.

Baking

A delicious way of serving eggs is to bake them. This is a good way of serving a large number of people without too much trouble. You will need individual ramekins or heatproof teacups. Generously butter the dishes and break one egg into each dish, season well, and spoon a tablespoon of light cream into each dish. Place the dishes in a small roasting pan with enough hot water to come halfway up the sides of the dishes. Bake at 375°F/190°C for 15 minutes for a soft egg and 18–20 minutes for a firmer egg. Other ingredients like fried mushrooms and bacon pieces can be added. This makes a good breakfast dish or a simple appetizer.

Boiling

You will need a pan large enough to hold the eggs you need to boil but not so large that the eggs move around too freely and crack. The water (which should be deep enough to cover the eggs) should be at a gentle simmer. Lower the eggs into the water using a long-handled, metal tablespoon, and simmer for 3–4 minutes for soft-cooked (runny yolk and soft set white), 5–6 minutes for a medium-cooked egg (creamy yolk and firm set white), and 10 minutes for a hard-cooked egg (both yolk and white are firm). If you are serving hard-cooked eggs cold, always run them under cold water immediately after boiling to prevent black discoloration (iron sulfide), which results from the reaction of hydrogen sulfide in the white with iron in the yolk, during cooking.

Poaching

For poaching you really need the freshest of eggs—do not attempt to cook by this method if this cannot be guaranteed because the eggs will break up in the water. You will need a small, shallow pan (a small skillet is ideal), particularly if you are cooking more than one egg (do not attempt to poach too many in one go). The water needs to be deep enough to just cover the eggs. You can add 1–2 teaspoons of vinegar at this stage if you like; it does help to coagulate the egg white but I don't like the flavor, which always permeates the egg. Break the egg into a cup. If you are more experienced, you could break it directly into the water, but sometimes the egg refuses to break well and I think a cup is an insurance policy. Bring the water to a gentle simmer and carefully pour in the egg—the white should immediately cover the yolk; if not, a gentle help with a slotted spoon works. Let the egg cook gently for 2–3 minutes until the white is just set and the yolk still soft, or 4–5 minutes if you like your eggs firmer. You can also baste the top of the egg with the hot water to make sure that the egg is completely cooked. Use a slotted spoon to remove it from the water and drain quickly on a paper towel. Serve the eggs immediately.

Frying

A fried egg is most delicious when accompanied by bacon for a filling traditional breakfast. If you have cooked some bacon, you have the ideal fat in which to cook your egg, but if you just want a fried egg you should heat a tablespoon of oil in a skillet (a nonstick skillet is best for eggs). Set the skillet over medium heat because you need quite a high temperature for frying. Break the egg into a cup and slide the egg into the hot skillet. Fry the egg for a few seconds until the white sets, then tip the skillet to one side so that the fat accumulates at the edge and you can baste the egg using a tablespoon, making sure the yolk and white are completely cooked on the top but the yolk is still soft in the center. Use a metal or wooden spatula to remove the egg from the pan. If you like, you can rest it for a few seconds on a paper towel in order to absorb any excess oil before serving.

Scrambling

Scrambled eggs need very gentle cooking or you might end up with very rubbery results. Allow 2 eggs per person and break them into a bowl. Beat well and season with salt and pepper (you can add a dash of milk if you like). Melt 1 tablespoon of butter in a small, nonstick pan over low heat until foaming. Pour in the beaten eggs and stir well using a wooden spoon. The egg will start to set on the base of the pan but just continue to stir, removing the cooked egg from the base of the pan and mixing it well with the runny mixture. When the mixture is starting to be creamy all through, remove from the heat—it will continue to cook in the hot pan. You can, if you like, add a small pat of butter or a tablespoon of cream at the end for an added treat. Serve immediately. Do not try to cook too many eggs at one time: you will have a better result if you cook each portion individually.

Making an omelet

A basic omelet is still one of the quickest meals you can cook without resorting to prepared convenience foods. You really need an omelet pan, which is just a small skillet kept purely for making omelets (about 7 inches/18 cm). It should have curved sides and a heavy base, made from aluminum, steel, or cast iron—it can also be nonstick.

Begin by breaking two eggs into a bowl and beating gently, just enough to break up the eggs. Season well. Heat the pan over medium heat, add 2 tablespoons of butter, and melt until foaming. Pour in the eggs and stir quickly with a wooden spatula or the back of a fork to spread them evenly over the pan. As the egg begins to cook, draw the egg slightly from all around the outside toward the center of the pan, letting the liquid egg run toward the outside. This takes only a few moments. Stop as soon as the egg is almost set but still a little liquid. Remove from the heat and fold half the omelet over the other half. Serve immediately on a warm plate. If you want to add a filling, prepare it ahead and add it to the omelet just before folding.

Here are a number of recipes for using eggs and cooking with them. They follow traditional lines but some of the dishes have foreign influences.

TOP LEFT Quail eggs
TOP RIGHT Free-range hens' eggs
MIDDLE LEFT Kahki Campbell's small white eggs
MIDDLE RIGHT Coll duck eggs
BOTTOM LEFT Aylesbury large white eggs
BOTTOM RIGHT Goose eggs

ZUCCHINI AND MUSHROOM FRITTATA

A frittata is the Italian equivalent of a French omelet. It is nearer to the Spanish tortilla because it is thick and firmly cooked. The frittata is also good served cold for a picnic or a brown bag lunch.

Serves 2
Preparation time: 10 minutes
Cooking time: 15 minutes

INGREDIENTS

1 tbsp butter

1 tbsp olive oil

1⅛ cups sliced zucchini

1⅝ cups sliced crimini mushrooms

1 garlic clove, peeled and finely chopped

4 eggs

6 tbsp milk

3 tbsp chopped fresh parsley

salt and pepper

You will need a 9 inch/23 cm nonstick skillet (with a heatproof handle if possible, but not essential), a wooden spatula, a bowl, a balloon whisk, a cook's knife, and a cutting board

METHOD

1 Melt the butter with the oil in a skillet over low heat.

2 Raise the heat to medium and cook the zucchini for about 5 minutes, turning occasionally, until golden brown.

3 Add the mushrooms and cook for 2–3 minutes more until they are soft. Stir in the garlic.

4 Break the eggs into a bowl and beat well using a balloon whisk. Pour in the milk and continue to mix well, then season with salt and pepper.

5 Lower the heat under the pan and pour the egg mixture over the vegetables and sprinkle in the parsley. Stir gently and then leave to cook for about 5–6 minutes or until the mixture is almost set and the base is cooked.

6 To complete the cooking, place the pan under a hot broiler for 2 minutes until the top is set (if the handle is not heatproof, or you have not got a broiler, turn the frittata onto a plate, slip it back into the pan, and cook it on the other side over low heat for 2 minutes). Serve while still warm, cut into wedges.

WINE SUGGESTION

This frittata is delicious with an Italian white Chardonnay or a red Chianti.

TAGLIATELLE CARBONARA

This is a traditional Italian pasta dish. It can be made with any sort of pasta but to be authentic it should always contain bacon pieces and eggs.

Serves 2
Preparation time: 10 minutes
Cooking time: 15 minutes

INGREDIENTS

6 oz/175 g tagliatelle
1 tbsp olive oil
4 bacon strips, thinly sliced
1 garlic clove, peeled and finely chopped
3 eggs
salt and pepper

To garnish
⅔ cup freshly grated Parmesan cheese
1 tbsp chopped fresh parsley

You will need a large pan (about 15 cups), a skillet, a cook's knife, a cutting board, a bowl, a colander, and 2 serving plates

WINE SUGGESTION
Try an oaky New Zealand or Pays d'Oc Chardonnay with this dish.

METHOD

1 Cook the pasta over medium heat in a large pan of salted boiling water, according to the instructions on the packet.

2 Heat the oil in a skillet and fry the bacon over high heat for 3–4 minutes until crispy. Add the chopped garlic and mix well.

3 Break the eggs into a bowl and beat well. Add seasoning, but remember that the bacon is salty.

4 When the pasta is cooked, drain it in a colander.

5 Scrape the bacon, garlic, and fat from the skillet into the pan and then return to the heat. Add the pasta and stir well.

6 Pour in the eggs and very quickly stir into the pasta so that the eggs start to set. Remove from the heat and serve immediately on hot plates, sprinkled with the Parmesan. Garnish with the parsley.

ONION TART

You can use this recipe to make six small, individual tarts instead of one large tart.

Serves 6–8
Preparation time: 45 minutes, plus chilling
Cooking time: 30 minutes

INGREDIENTS

2 cups all-purpose flour, or half whole-wheat flour and half all-purpose flour
½ tsp salt
½ cup butter
4 tbsp vegetable shortening
1 egg yolk
cold water, to mix
1½ lb/675 g onions, peeled and thinly sliced
1 tbsp olive oil
salt and pepper
freshly grated nutmeg
3 egg yolks, beaten well
1 cup heavy cream

You will need a 10 inch/25 cm quiche pan or rectangular ovenproof dish, a cookie sheet, a cook's knife, a bowl, and a cutting board

METHOD

1 Sift the flour and salt into a bowl and gently rub in half of the butter and all the shortening until the mixture resembles bread crumbs. Stir in the egg yolk and sprinkle in enough cold water to form a soft dough. Wrap in plastic wrap and let rest in the refrigerator for 1–2 hours.

2 Roll out the dough to form a round or rectangle, depending on the shape of your dish; it should be large enough to line it. Carefully line the dish without stretching the dough, trim around the edges and let rest in the refrigerator again for 1 hour.

3 Melt the remaining butter with the oil in a large, heavy pan over medium heat and add the onions. Stir until they are well coated and cook, covered, for about 30 minutes until they are soft and lightly golden. Season well and add a good grating of nutmeg. Let cool a little.

4 Preheat the oven to 400°F/200°C. Stir the egg yolks and cream into the onion mixture. Pour the filling into the prepared pie shell and bake in the center of the preheated oven, on a heated cookie sheet, for 30 minutes.

5 Remove from the oven and serve hot with salad greens either as an appetizer or a light lunch.

WINE SUGGESTION

Try serving a medium French red like Beaujolais or a Pays D'Oc Syrah with a touch of oak.

SALAD NIÇOISE

Serves 2
Preparation time: 20 minutes

INGREDIENTS

2 Boston, Bibb, or baby romaine lettuces
2 hard-cooked eggs (see page 73–74)
8 baby plum tomatoes
7 oz/200 g canned tuna, drained
⅓ cup green beans, blanched for 2 minutes
4 anchovy fillets, sliced
12 black olives, pitted
French bread, to serve

Dressing
4 tbsp extra-virgin olive oil
1 tbsp tarragon vinegar
1 garlic clove, peeled and crushed
salt and pepper
¼ tsp French mustard
2 tbsp chopped fresh tarragon, parsley, and chives

You will need a screw-top jar, a cook's knife, a cutting board, a can opener, and 2 large salad bowls

METHOD

1 First make the dressing by placing all the ingredients in a jar and shaking well.

2 Cut the lettuces into fourths and arrange in two large bowls. Shell the eggs, cut into fourths, and place on top of the lettuce.

3 Slice the tomatoes, flake the tuna, and add to the bowls along with the green beans.

4 Sprinkle the anchovy fillets and olives over the top.

5 Pour on the dressing and serve immediately with chunks of French bread.

WINE SUGGESTION

Serve a cold Rosé from Provence or a light Sauvignon with this salad.

MAYONNAISE

Many people are nervous about making mayonnaise, but if you are careful and not in too much of a rush, the result will be wonderful. One tip: ensure that the egg yolks and the oil are at the same temperature.

Makes 1¼ cups
Preparation time: 10–15 minutes

INGREDIENTS

2 egg yolks
1 tsp Dijon mustard
½ tsp salt
1¼ cups light olive oil, or half olive oil and half peanut oil
2 tsp white wine vinegar
pepper
dash lemon juice, optional

You will need a mixing bowl, an electric hand-mixer or a balloon whisk, and a measuring cup

METHOD

1 Place the egg yolks, mustard, and salt in a mixing bowl and whisk until thoroughly mixed.

2 Pour the oil into a measuring cup and then slowly add it drop by drop to the mixture while continuing to whisk. It is easier to do with an electric mixer in one hand and the cup in the other. Whisk constantly until the mixture begins to thicken, then you can gradually add the oil in slightly larger quantities but still go slowly. Add the vinegar to thin the mayonnaise and then continue until all the oil is used up.

3 Taste the mayonnaise and add a little pepper and some more salt if needed. If the mayonnaise is too thick, you can thin it with a little boiling water, and if it is not sharp enough, add a little lemon juice.

4 Store the mayonnaise in a screw-top jar in the refrigerator for up to one week and use as needed.

Note: if your mayonnaise curdles, start again with one newly whisked egg yolk and add the curdled mayonnaise as if it were the oil, and it will be fine.

CHEESE SOUFFLÉ

Serves 3–4
Preparation time: 20 minutes
Cooking time: 25–30 minutes

INGREDIENTS

1 tbsp butter, melted
1 tbsp finely grated Parmesan cheese
2 tbsp butter
¼ cup all-purpose flour
1¼ cups milk
1 cup finely grated Cheddar cheese
1 tsp grainy mustard
a good grating of nutmeg
4 extra large eggs, separated
salt and pepper

You will need a 7½ cup soufflé dish or 3–4 ramekins, a medium pan, a wooden spoon, an electric hand-held mixer or a balloon whisk, a plastic spatula, and a cookie sheet

METHOD

1 Preheat the oven to 400°F/200°C. Grease the base and sides of the soufflé dish with the melted butter. Then sprinkle the dish with the Parmesan, turning the dish in your hands so that all the surface is covered with the cheese.

2 Melt the remaining 2 tablespoons of butter in a pan (preferably nonstick) over medium heat. Add the flour, mix well using a wooden spoon, and cook for 1 minute, stirring constantly. Remove from the heat and gradually stir in the milk until you have a smooth consistency.

3 Return the pan to low heat and continue to stir while the sauce comes to a boil and thickens. Simmer gently, stirring constantly, for about 3 minutes until the sauce is creamy and smooth.

4 Remove from the heat and stir in the cheese, mustard, and nutmeg. Taste, then season well. Set aside to cool a little.

5 Whisk the egg whites until soft peaks have formed but are not too dry.

6 Beat the egg yolks into the sauce mixture and then carefully stir in a little of the beaten egg white to slacken the mixture. Then carefully fold in the remaining egg whites.

7 Turn into the prepared dish or ramekins. Place on a cookie sheet and cook in the preheated oven for 25–30 minutes until well risen and golden brown. Serve immediately, perhaps with light salad greens and crusty bread.

WINE SUGGESTION
Serve this with a light white Sauvignon—perhaps Pouilly-Fumé from the Loire.

3

CRÊPES

You can serve these crêpes with lemon and sugar or with warmed honey or jelly. They can also be served with ice cream and chocolate sauce or with stewed fruit. For savory dishes, use them like cannelloni and stuff them with meat, cheese, or vegetable fillings.

Makes 10
Preparation time: 5 minutes
Cooking time: 15–20 minutes

INGREDIENTS

generous ¾ cup all-purpose flour
pinch of salt
1 egg, beaten
1¼ cups milk
10 tsp butter or oil

You will need a 7 inch/18 cm nonstick skillet, a wooden or metal spatula, a mixing bowl, a balloon whisk and a measuring cup

1 Place the flour and salt in a mixing bowl. Make a well in the center, add the egg and half of the milk. Using a whisk, beat the egg and milk together and gradually incorporate the flour. Continue beating until the mixture is smooth and there are no lumps. Gradually beat in the remaining milk. Pour the batter mixture into a pitcher.

2 Heat the skillet over medium heat and add 1 teaspoon of the butter or oil, depending on what you are going to eat with the crêpes. If you are cooking traditional Mardi Gras crêpes to serve with sugar and lemon, then butter is best, but if you are doing something else, for example filling them with broiled vegetables, the oil would be a better choice.

3 Pour in enough batter to just cover the base, then swirl the batter around the skillet while tilting it so that you have a thin, even layer. Cook for about half a minute, then lift up the edge of the crêpe and see if it is brown. Loosen the crêpe around the edges and flip it over with a spatula. Alternatively, have a go at tossing it by shaking the pan quickly with a deft flick of the wrist and catching the crêpe carefully.

4 Cook on the other side for 1 minute until golden brown. Turn out onto a warm plate. Cover with kitchen foil and keep warm. Use all the remaining butter and oil, a teaspoon at a time, until all the crêpes have been cooked. Layer them with baking parchment so that you have a separated stack at the end.

Suitable for freezing. Freeze the crêpes interleaved with plastic wrap or baking parchment, sealed in a plastic bag. To use, thaw at room temperature, then reheat, wrapped in foil in a warm oven.

ZABAGLIONE

This is a delicious Italian dessert. It is made by beating egg yolks with sugar and Marsala wine until thick.

Serves 4
Preparation time: 5 minutes
Cooking time: 10–15 minutes

INGREDIENTS

4 egg yolks
2 tbsp superfine sugar
½ cup Marsala wine
8 ladyfingers, to serve

You will need a large pan, a large, heatproof mixing bowl (make sure it fits snugly on top of the pan), a hand-held electric mixer or a balloon whisk, a measuring cup, and 4 glasses for serving

METHOD

1 Whisk the egg yolks and sugar together in a large, heatproof mixing bowl until light and creamy.

2 Place the bowl over a pan of hot water over low heat and continue to whisk until the mixture begins to thicken. Gradually add the Marsala, and continue whisking until the mixture is very thick and frothy and increased in volume. Take care not to overcook it on the base of the bowl.

3 Remove from the stovetop and lift the bowl off the pan. Pour into individual serving dishes and serve immediately with ladyfingers.

BLACK CURRANT MOUSSE

Serves 4–6
Preparation time: 30 minutes, plus 2–3 hours chilling

INGREDIENTS

3½ cups fresh black currants, or frozen and thawed

generous 1 cup superfine sugar

3 eggs, separated

1 tbsp gelatin

3 tbsp cold water

⅔ cup heavy cream, lightly whipped

1 tbsp confectioners' sugar

4–6 small mint leaves, to decorate

⅔ cup light cream, to serve

You will need a medium pan (about 7½ cups), a wooden spatula, a strainer, a large mixing bowl, a hand-held electric mixer, a small pan, a heatproof bowl (to fit snugly over the small pan), a small bowl, a metal spatula, and a 4 cup glass serving dish or 4–6 individual serving dishes

METHOD

1 First prepare the black currant purée. Put the black currants and half the superfine sugar in a medium pan and cook over low heat for 2–3 minutes until the sugar is dissolved and the berries have formed a rich syrup. Let cool, then pour into a strainer over a bowl and press the fruit through to form a purée. You should get about 1¼ cups.

2 In a separate bowl, whisk the egg yolks and remaining superfine sugar with an electric mixer until thick and light.

3 Soak the gelatin in the 3 tablespoons of water in a heatproof bowl for 1–2 minutes. Place the bowl in a small pan with enough hot water to come halfway up the bowl, and heat gently for 2–3 minutes to dissolve the gelatin. When it is warm and clear, stir it into the fruit purée. Fold the fruit purée evenly into the egg mixture and then fold in the cream.

4 Whisk the egg whites until stiff but not too dry and then fold gently into the mixture. Pile the mixture into a serving dish and smooth over the top with a spatula. Cover with plastic wrap and chill for 2–3 hours in the refrigerator until firm.

5 To serve, shake the confectioners' sugar through a strainer over the surface of the mousse and decorate with the mint leaves. Serve with a little cream poured over the top.

CHOCOLATE AND RASPBERRY PAVLOVA

A pavlova is a meringue cake, but it is not dry like meringue. It has a marshmallow center, which is made of cornstarch, vanilla extract, and wine vinegar. It makes a delicious, melt-in-your-mouth dessert.

Serves 8–10
Preparation time: 1 hour 20 minutes
Cooking time: 1 hour

INGREDIENTS

4 egg whites
generous 1 cup superfine sugar
1 tsp cornstarch
1 tsp white wine vinegar
1 tsp vanilla extract

To serve
1¼ cups heavy cream
1 tbsp superfine sugar
2 tbsp framboise liqueur
1 cup fresh raspberries
2 oz/55 g bittersweet chocolate, shaved

You will need a large mixing bowl, a hand-held electric mixer, a plastic spatula, a cookie sheet with a sheet of baking parchment that has a 10 inch/25 cm circle drawn on the underside, and a large serving dish

METHOD

1 Preheat the oven to 300°F/150°C. In a large mixing bowl, whisk the egg whites until stiff and gradually whisk in generous ½ cup of the sugar. In a separate bowl, mix the remaining sugar with the cornstarch and then whisk it into the egg white mixture; it should be very shiny and firm.

2 Quickly fold the vinegar and vanilla extract into the egg white mixture.

3 Pile the meringue onto the baking parchment on the cookie sheet and spread evenly to the edge of the circle; swirl it around on top to make an attractive shape. Bake in the center of the preheated oven for 1 hour.

4 Remove from the oven, cool slightly, then peel off the parchment. Place the pavlova on a large serving plate. It will shrink and crack, but do not worry about this. It will keep in an airtight container for up to 2 days.

5 One hour before serving, whip together the cream, sugar, and liqueur until thick and floppy. Pile on top of the pavlova and decorate with fruit and shaved chocolate. Chill before serving.

DAIRY PRODUCTS

Traditional farmhouses remain the main source of this range of rich and natural ingredients. Do not be put off by the fat content. Most dairy products come in a range of fat levels, and cheese is also rich in protein and minerals. The basic raw material is milk, mainly from cows, but nowadays also from goats, sheep, and even buffalo. It is available in full-fat or reduced-fat forms, as well as powdered and canned.

Cream is the higher fat form, and is generally used to thicken and enrich soups and savory dishes, or to enhance desserts. Yogurt has similar uses, but is generally lower in fat and has healthy properties attributed to it.

Butter, sweet and salted, contains about 82 percent fat. It has a huge range of uses in cooking, and is added to sauces, cakes, pastries, and cookies.

Cheese is very versatile and can be served simply as part of a cheeseboard or in sandwiches. The range of cheeses now available opens up many new recipe possibilities—soft cheeses that melt and blue cheeses with very powerful flavors.

MILK

Milk is our most basic food. We all start life drinking milk of some sort: cow's milk is the most complete of all foods, containing nearly all the nutrients important to humans. There is now a wide variety of milk available, and the largest growth area is the organic market.

Pasteurized milk

Most milk is now pasteurized to kill bacteria and enzymes, although some 'raw milk is available in some places, often straight from the farm.

Whole milk

This is milk just as it comes direct from the cow, with nothing removed or added. It contains 4 percent fat and is the ideal milk for young children, who need concentrated sources of energy. Above the age of 5 years, children can be given skim milk if their diet and weight so dictate. Whole milk is used in all these recipes, particularly in desserts, white sauces, batters, and soups.

Skim and low-fat milk

Skim milk contains only 0.1 percent fat and low-fat milk must by law have between 1.5 and 1.8 percent fat. The calcium content of these milks is the same as whole milk, but there is a reduction in vitamins A and D.

Homogenized milk

This milk has had the fat globules mechanically broken up so that the cream is evenly distributed throughout the milk. This means there is no cream layer at the top of the milk, so no arguments at breakfast! It is good for making sauces.

Longlife/UHT milk

This milk has been subjected to "ultra-high temperature" of 275°F/135°C for 1–2 seconds. The milk is then cooled rapidly and packed in special containers, and will keep for several months. Once opened, the milk should be treated as fresh. It is a very useful standby in the kitchen for sauces and other recipes, but not so nice in coffee or on cereals.

Evaporated milk

This milk has been treated to remove about 60 percent of its water. It is then sterilized in cans, which gives it its distinctive flavor. It has 9 percent fat and is used in many recipes, either as it is or diluted, and used instead of whole milk.

Condensed milk

This very thick, sweet milk is used in desserts, particularly Banoffee pie. It contains 40–50 percent sugar. It is a favourite with hikers and mountaineers because it can be used as a sweetener in hot beverages. For sweet tooth fanatics, it is also delicious spread on bread.

Buttermilk

Buttermilk is traditionally made from the whey from butter-making, but is now made from skim milk that has been soured with lactic acid. It tastes rather like plain, low-fat yogurt. Buttermilk is used for baking soda bread and biscuits. If you cannot find it, you can make your own by adding 1 tablespoon of lemon juice to 1 cup of whole milk.

Dry milk

This is a fine granule milk made when all the water is removed by evaporation. It is usually low in fat. It is used in recipes by reconstituting it with water. It has a poor flavor, but is useful as an emergency item in the pantry.

Goat's milk

Goat's milk is now widely available. It is useful for people with a lactose intolerance because it is more easily digested by humans than the more difficult to digest cow's milk. The flavor is much stronger than cow's milk, which is why it is so popular with cheese-makers.

Soy milk

This is very popular because more people are now avoiding dairy foods. It is easily available and can be used as ordinary milk, for adding to drinks, and in recipes. It is also quite good on cereals, but you might need a little time to adjust to the flavor, as it is slightly bitter. Some soy milk has added sugar, so check the label.

Storage

Keep milk in the refrigerator, always covered to avoid contamination by odors from other foods. Make sure you always use a clean pitcher when serving: do not refill it once the milk has been used. You can freeze homogenized milk in cartons for an emergency.

CREAM

Cream is made from the concentrated fatty part of milk. It is delicious and adds flavor, texture, and richness to food. Unfortunately, because of its high fat content, cream has a poor reputation but, like all things, it can be enjoyed occasionally as a treat. There are low-fat varieties available, but a half-quantity of the real thing seems a better option.

Half-fat cream

This has the lowest fat content of 12 percent, rather like the traditional top of the milk. It can be used on fruit, in coffee and hot chocolate, and in sauces.

Light cream

This is a pouring cream to be used over desserts. It is not thick enough to whip because it has a fat content of only 18 percent. Use it in sauces, and garnish soups with a little before serving. It is rather rich for ordinary cereals, but delicious on hot porridge. Extra-thick light cream is available for spooning on top of pies and other desserts. It has the same fat content, but has been thickened by homogenization.

Whipping cream

This cream contains 34 percent fat, allowing it to be whipped to a good consistency. Always use a clean bowl and a hand-held electric mixer or a balloon whisk. The cream should double in bulk and produce a light, airy consistency for piling on desserts, or for piping if desired.

Heavy cream

This has a minimum fat content of 48 percent and is exceedingly rich. Use it on special occasions to decorate cakes and desserts. It is good added to sauces because it does not curdle when heated. Take care when whisking it though, because it is so rich it is easy to overbeat and produce a separated butter mixture. Always whisk it cold from the refrigerator. It is used in decadent desserts like crème brûlée and syllabubs. Extra-thick heavy cream is prepared in the same way as the light variety and produces a thick, spoonable cream, with the same fat content, ready for serving.

Clotted cream

This is the richest cream available; it has a 55–60 percent fat content. Clotted cream is traditionally made in Devon and Cornwall in England: it is very thick and can be cut with a knife. Serve it with biscuits and jam for a cream tea. It can also be served with apple pie or fruit tarts for a really luxurious dessert.

Sour cream

This is a rich, thick cream, thickened by bacterial action, which gives it a richer appearance than its fat content of 18 percent would suggest. It is used to make sauces, salad dressings, and dips. It is also good in soups and in traditional Russian, Polish, and Mexican food, such as borscht, stroganoff, and tortillas. It has a slightly acidic flavor.

Crème fraîche

This is like sour cream, but richer. It has a fat content of between 30 and 50 percent, depending on the brand. Check the labels before buying it. Crème fraîche was originally made in France; it has a velvety texture and can be added to hot food without risk of curdling. The low-fat and half-fat varieties seem very acceptable.

Storage

Keep cream in the refrigerator because it deteriorates quickly. Buy it in small quantities and use before the date on the container. Always keep it well covered to prevent contamination by other flavors in the refrigerator. Crème fraîche has a longer life and will keep for up to 2 weeks, so it is a useful commodity to have at hand.

YOGURT

Yogurt is made by fermenting milk with bacteria, which thickens it and also gives it its unique flavor. It has similar uses to cream, but is generally lower in fat and has healthy properties attributed to it. Use it for breakfast, on cereal or with fruit. You can thicken soups and sauces with it or use it in a marinade.

There are many varieties available: plain strained yogurt is probably the thickest and is useful in recipes such as ice cream or yogurt ambrosia (see page 101). Low-fat varieties are particularly useful for serving with fruit and desserts. Beware of some of the fruit-flavored varieties: they have a high proportion of sugar and are often artificially thickened with modified starches. They also contain artificial colorings, which can trigger allergic reactions in sensitive people, so check labels before purchasing. Organic varieties are now widely available and are becoming very popular.

Storage
Buy yogurt little and often and store it in the refrigerator. Cover any open containers with plastic wrap and use by the date on the pack.

BUTTER

Butter is made from cream, which is churned until it separates into butter and buttermilk. Salted and sweet varieties are available. Butter contains not less than 80 percent milk fat, and 1–2 percent of salt in the salted varieties. Many people prefer the tang of salt on their bread, others prefer the bland flavor of sweet butter so that they can taste the bread. For desserts and cakes, sweet butter is often preferred. Choose salted or sweet according to your taste. Cost is a factor, as is the country of origin; try a new one from time to time. There are new "spreadable" butters, which will stay soft in the refrigerator and spread directly without bringing them to room temperature. These are convenient, but are a blend of butter with other oils. Always read the label on the packet before buying. Small, half-sized packets are useful for people who do not eat much butter.

Storage
Keep butter in the refrigerator, and keep it well wrapped to avoid tainting it with other flavors. Check the label for the "use by" date. Butter freezes well and can be stored in the freezer for up to 5–6 months.

There are thousands of cheeses throughout the world. Here we will concentrate on those that are readily available and which we use regularly both for eating raw and for cooking.

Cheese is formed when milk is separated into curds and whey. The curds are cut and drained and then can be pressed and left to mature, as in our familiar hard cheeses. Soft, fresh cheeses are produced by beating the curds to a smooth paste and then adding seasonings.

BRITISH CHEESE

Cheese-making in Britain has been a long-standing tradition. Many British cheeses are known world-wide and are often served in Britain as a "plowman's lunch," in sandwiches, broiled on toast, and in sauces for vegetables and pasta. They are also served as a cheeseboard at the end of a meal instead of, before, or after a dessert.

Cheddar

This is the best-known British cheese and has been imitated many times. The original Cheddar comes from Cheddar in Somerset and is at its best when prepared on the farm from unpasteurized milk. It has a yellow color and a very creamy texture with a nutty flavor. The flavor varies in strength, which makes it an excellent all-purpose cheese. It is wonderful on a cheeseboard served with some good crusty bread and some mustard or chutney. Mild Cheddar is good for grating and sprinkling over au gratin dishes or for incorporating into a sauce.

Stilton

This is known as the king of cheeses. It has a very strong, tangy flavor, which comes from its distinctive blue-green mold. This mold gives the cheese its attractive veining. The best Stiltons are very expensive but have a wonderful flavor. In Britain, this cheese is traditionally eaten at Christmas with walnuts and a glass of port. It is also very good in sauces, soufflés, and in soups, where its strong flavor enhances blander ingredients.

Lancashire

This is a pale-colored cheese with a crumbly texture. It has a mild, sharp flavor. Lancashire cheese is good on a cheeseboard served with celery and pickle. It is also good in cooking because it crumbles and melts well.

Double Gloucester

This cheese resembles Cheddar, but has a rich orange color. It has a mellow flavor and a smooth, firm texture. Eat it on its own or in sandwiches. Double Gloucester can also be used in cooking wherever Cheddar is required.

Wensleydale

Another white, crumbly cheese with a milk flavor. This cheese comes from Yorkshire, where it is served to accompany apple pie. It is good for cooking too.

FRENCH CHEESE

Brie

A large, round, mild, soft cheese, which is one of the world's greatest favorites. It is perfect for ending a meal with a few grapes or as part of a summer's lunch. Try to buy it cut from the whole cheese and eat it within 1–2 days before it dries out. Unpasteurized brie made on the farm is the best.

Camembert

Another famous French cheese, from Normandy. It is stronger and made in smaller rounds, which can be bought whole or halved. Allow it to ripen (it should be soft inside) before eating it with a crisp baguette.

Roquefort

A famous sheep's-milk cheese with green veining. Roquefort is a very salty cheese with a very pungent flavor. It is France's king of cheeses.

ITALIAN CHEESE

Many delicious Italian cheeses are now widely available, from hard cheeses such as Parmesan and romano, to soft cheeses such as mascarpone.

Parmesan

This hard cheese is widely used both for eating and for cooking. It has a good, strong, sweet flavor. Parmigiano Reggiano is the original and still the best you can buy. Buy a large piece and keep it handy for slicing off a piece to have with some fruit at the end of a meal, or grate some ready to serve with pasta or to sprinkle on baked au gratin dishes. Shaved Parmesan, prepared with a vegetable peeler, is a popular way to serve it sprinkled over salad greens. Never buy ready-grated powder in little plastic bags—it has an inferior taste and consistency.

Mozzarella

This is a soft, white, slightly rubbery cheese, which is best when made from buffalo milk. It often comes in small, white plastic bags to keep it moist. You can also buy it from cheese shops, where it is often kept in large bowls. Mozzarella is traditionally used on pizzas, but it is equally delicious in a tomato salad with fresh basil leaves.

Cheddar

Blue Stilton

Lancashire

Wensleydale

Brie

Camembert

Roquefort

Gorgonzola

A soft, blue-veined cheese with a strong flavor. Use it to end a meal or to serve with fruit and salad greens as an appetizer.

Dolcelatte

This cheese is similar to Gorgonzola, but is made in a factory. It is slightly blander, has a creamy, moist texture, and keeps well. Torte de dolcelatte is layered with cream cheese and tastes heavenly.

Romano

This is a cheese made from sheep's milk. It is a hard, grainy cheese and can be used in the same way as Parmesan.

Mascarpone

A very rich cream cheese, which is whisked to give it a creamy texture. Mascarpone forms the basis of the dessert Tiramisù. It can also be used in baked pasta dishes.

Ricotta

This is a rich version of cottage cheese. It has quite a grainy texture and can be found on delicatessen counters in its traditional pyramid shape. It is also available in small cartons in supermarkets. Use it in sweet and savory dishes.

SWISS CHEESE

Gruyère

Often known simply as Swiss cheese, this hard, pressed cheese has an oily texture. It has holes throughout and a good flavor and can be used for cooking and as a dessert cheese.

Emmenthal

This is similar to Gruyère but with larger holes. Its nutty flavor goes well with fruit as a dessert, and it can also be used for cooking. Emmenthal and Gruyère are both good melting cheeses and form the foundation of the heated cheese dish known as a "fondue."

GREEK CHEESE

Feta

A soft, white cheese, which is very salty. It has a hard, crumbly texture and quite an acidic flavor. It is best served with olives and tomatoes, as in a Greek salad.

Halloumi

This is a sheep's milk cheese. It is firm and has a salty flavor, and can be sliced and broiled before serving with salad.

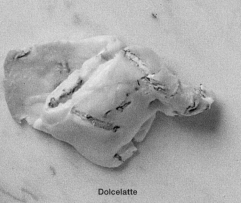

Parmesan

Dolcelatte

Ricotta

Mascarpone

Mozzarella

Gorgonzola

FRESH, SOFT CHEESES

More and more soft cheeses are arriving in our stores. They are gaining popularity and can be used in a variety of ways.

Cream cheese

This is made from light or heavy cream. It is a very creamy cheese and is often used in desserts and cheesecakes. It has a fairly high fat content.

Cottage cheese

This is made from skim milk. It has a low fat content and a lumpy texture. It is rather bland and needs to be mixed with flavorings to make it palatable. However, many people find it acceptable and eat it as part of a weight loss program.

Farmer's cheese

A smooth cheese, which is blended with salt. It has a slightly acidic flavor and is lower in fat content than cream cheese. Use it for spreading on bread or crackers or in recipes requiring a cream cheese.

Fromage frais

This cheese originally came from France. It is made from skim milk but can be mixed with cream to give a range of richness from almost fat-free to a high fat content. You can use fromage frais in the same way as cream or add it to dips and salad dressings.

Storage

A refrigerator is really too cold to store cheese. An ideal temperature is 50°F/10°C, but not many homes have a suitable pantry or a cold room so the refrigerator is the only place. Make sure the cheese is loosely wrapped in waxed paper or a plastic bag, not the wrapper it was bought in because this is too tight and will make the cheese sweat. Remove any cheese at least 2 hours before serving in order for it to come to room temperature. Hard cheeses can be grated ready for use and stored in the refrigerator for up to one week. Grated cheese also freezes well, but is only suitable for cooking, not for salads. Fresh cream cheeses should be bought when needed and used before the "best before" date on the carton.

Emmenthal

Cottage cheese

Cream cheese

Gruyère

Curd cheese

CHEESE AND POTATO GRATIN

Serves 4
Preparation time: 20–30 minutes
Cooking time: 30–35 minutes

INGREDIENTS

1 tbsp butter
1 tbsp olive oil
1 onion, peeled and chopped
1 garlic clove, peeled and finely chopped
¾ cup chopped cured ham
2 eggs
1¼ cups milk
¾ cup grated Swiss cheese
2 tbsp freshly grated Parmesan cheese
whole nutmeg, for grating
1 lb/450 g potatoes, peeled
1 tbsp chopped fresh parsley
salt and pepper

You will need an oval gratin dish (about 5 cup capacity), a cookie sheet, a skillet, a wooden spatula, a large bowl, a balloon whisk, a measuring cup, and a grater or food processor

WINE SUGGESTION

Try a Californian wine—an oaky white Chardonnay, or a soft red Pinot Noir.

METHOD

1 Use a little butter to grease the gratin dish. Melt the remaining butter with the oil in a skillet over low heat. Add the onion and garlic and soften for about 10 minutes. Add the ham and keep it warm on the stovetop.

2 Preheat the oven to 375°F/190°C. In a separate bowl, beat the eggs, then add the milk. Stir in three-fourths of the cheese and season. Grate about a fourth of the nutmeg into the mixture.

3 Grate the potatoes using a grater or a food processor if you have one. Squeeze them between your hands to extract as much water as possible. Add them to the egg mixture along with the ham and onion and the parsley and mix well.

4 Pour into the prepared dish, sprinkle the remaining cheese on top, place on a cookie sheet, and bake at the top of the preheated oven for about 30 minutes until golden brown.

5 Serve warm for lunch or supper with a tomato salad.

BAKED CHEESE SAVORY

Serves 4
Preparation time: 15 minutes
Cooking time: 20–30 minutes

INGREDIENTS

6 thick slices day-old white bread
4 tbsp butter, softened
1 tbsp olive oil
3 extra large eggs
1¼ cups milk
⅔ cup plain strained yogurt
1 garlic clove, peeled and left whole
1½ cups grated Cheddar or Double Gloucester cheese
4–8 scallions, thinly sliced
1 tbsp chopped fresh parsley or mint
2 tbsp grated Parmesan cheese
salt and pepper

You will need a bread knife, a cook's knife, a cutting board, a bowl, a pastry brush, a large cookie sheet, a measuring cup, a grater, and a 10 x 8 inch25 x 20 cm deep ovenproof dish

METHOD

1 Preheat the oven to 325°F/160°C. Spread the bread slices with butter on one side only. Brush a large cookie sheet with a little of the olive oil and lay out the bread on it. Bake in the preheated oven for 5–10 minutes until the bread is nearly dry and slightly brown. Remove the bread from the oven but leave the oven switched on.

2 In a separate bowl, beat the eggs and add the milk and yogurt. Season generously with salt and pepper.

3 Use the remaining oil to brush the ovenproof dish. Cut the crisp bread into thick fingers and rub them with the garlic clove. Lay half the pieces in the dish and sprinkle with the cheese, scallions to taste, and chopped parsley or mint.

4 Cover with the remaining bread and pour in the egg mixture. Let the dish stand for about 15 minutes to absorb the liquid.

5 Sprinkle over the Parmesan and bake in the preheated oven for 20–30 minutes until almost set and golden brown. Serve warm for lunch or supper with salad greens.

WINE SUGGESTION

Try a sturdy Australian red Cabernet Sauvignon or an oaky Australian Chardonnay from the same area.

HOT GOAT CHEESE SALAD

This salad makes a good lunch or light supper dish.

Serves 2
Preparation time: 5 minutes
Cooking time: 25 minutes

INGREDIENTS

8 oz/225 g cherry vine tomatoes

4 garlic cloves, unpeeled

1 tbsp olive oil

7 oz/200 g soft rind goat cheese, such as Pyramid

2 oz/55 g wild arugula, about 1 bunch

2 tbsp balsamic vinegar

salt and pepper

a few fresh basil leaves, to garnish

You will need a small roasting pan, a sharp knife, a cutting board, a heatproof dish, and 2 serving plates

METHOD

1 Preheat the oven to 350ºF/180°C. Put the tomatoes and garlic in a small roasting pan. Sprinkle them with the oil and season well. Cook at the top of the preheated oven for 20 minutes.

2 Remove the top and bottom rinds from the goat's cheese and cut in half horizontally. If you are using two smaller cheeses, cut them both in half horizontally.

3 Place the cheese pieces on a heatproof dish and cook under a hot broiler for 3–4 minutes until they begin to melt and turn golden.

4 Arrange the arugula on two plates. Remove the tomatoes and garlic from the oven. Use a slotted spoon to remove them, and reserve the roasting juices. Arrange the tomatoes and garlic around the plates and put the cheese in the center.

5 Add the balsamic vinegar to the juices in the roasting pan and mix well to make a dressing. Drizzle the dressing over the cheese and salad and serve garnished with the basil leaves.

WINE SUGGESTION

A fruity and unoaked white New Zealand Sauvignon, or a South African Chenin

PENNE WITH MUSHROOMS AND DOLCELATTE

*This is a delicious pasta dish, which uses penne (tube pasta)
and rich Italian blue dolcelatte cheese.*

Serves 4
Preparation time: 5 minutes
Cooking time: 15 minutes

INGREDIENTS

3½ cups penne (tube pasta)
1 tbsp olive oil
3⅝ cups sliced crimini mushrooms
8 oz/225 g dolcelatte cheese, crumbled
scant 1 cup half-fat crème fraîche
5½ oz/150 g arugula leaves or spinach
salt and pepper
2 oz/55 g Parmesan cheese, freshly shaved, to garnish

You will need a large pan (about 15 cups), a colander,
a skillet, a wooden spatula, a cook's knife, a cutting board, and
4 serving bowls

WINE SUGGESTION

Try a fresh red Châteauneuf-
du-Pâpe or a simpler Côtes
de Ventoux with this cheese-
flavoured pasta dish.

METHOD

1 Cook the pasta over medium heat in a large pan
of salted boiling water, according to the instructions on
the packet.

2 Heat the oil in a skillet over low heat and gently sauté the
mushrooms for 3–4 minutes until they start to soften.

3 Stir in the dolcelatte and let it melt, then add the crème
fraîche.

4 Add the arugula or spinach and heat for 1–2 minutes until
just wilted. Taste, and add salt and pepper.

5 Drain the cooked pasta in a colander and serve in hot
bowls with the sauce poured over the top. Serve
immediately garnished with the Parmesan shavings.

PANNA COTTA

This is a delicious, creamy, rich Italian dessert, which is lightly set with gelatin.

Serves 6
Preparation time: 15 minutes, plus chilling

INGREDIENTS

1 tbsp vegetable oil
1 vanilla bean
2½ cups heavy cream
4 tbsp superfine sugar
2 tsp powdered gelatin
3 tbsp cold water

To decorate
6 sprigs fresh mint
about 18 strawberries, sliced

You will need a small pan (preferably nonstick), a small, heatproof bowl that fits snugly over the pan, a sharp knife, a wooden spoon, six ½ cup dariole molds or ramekins, a pastry brush, and 6 small serving plates

METHOD

1 Use the oil to grease the molds well. Split the vanilla bean with a sharp knife and scrape out all the seeds. Put the bean and the seeds in a pan with the cream and sugar and stir well over low heat. Carefully bring to simmering point and simmer gently for 2–3 minutes. Remove from the heat and let cool a little.

2 Soak the gelatin in 3 tablespoons of cold water in a small, heatproof bowl. Place the bowl over a pan of hot water and heat gently until the gelatin is dissolved and clear.

3 Remove the vanilla bean from the cream and stir in the gelatin. Pour the mixture into the prepared molds, cover with plastic wrap, and chill for at least 3 hours, or overnight, until set.

4 To serve, dip the molds up to the rim (do not immerse completely) in hot water for 2 seconds and then turn out onto serving plates. Serve decorated with the mint sprigs and fresh berries.

YOGURT AMBROSIA

*This sweet, creamy dessert is very simple to make, but it
tastes absolutely heavenly.*

Serves 6
Preparation time: 10 minutes, plus chilling overnight

INGREDIENTS

1¼ **cups heavy cream**
1¼ **cups plain strained yogurt**
6 **tbsp dark molasses sugar**

You will need a large bowl, a balloon whisk, and a large,
shallow serving bowl (about 8 inches/20 cm in diameter) or
6 small ramekins

METHOD

1 In a large bowl, use a balloon whisk to beat the cream until
thick. Add the yogurt and mix together well. Pour into the
serving dish or ramekins.

2 Sprinkle the sugar over the surface of the mixture in quite a
thick layer. Cover with plastic wrap and chill in the
refrigerator overnight. The sugar will dissolve, leaving a luscious
toffee layer.

APRICOT BREAD AND BUTTER PUDDING

Serves 4
Preparation time: 10 minutes, plus
15 minutes standing
Cooking time: 30–40 minutes

INGREDIENTS

6 tbsp sweet butter, softened
6 slices thick, white bread
2 tbsp apricot jelly
½ cup ready-to-eat dried apricots, chopped
3 extra large eggs
⅔ cup heavy cream
1¼ cups milk
scant ½ cup superfine sugar
grated rind of 1 orange
1 tbsp raw brown sugar
½ cup light cream, to serve

You will need a 10 x 8 inch/25 x 20 cm ovenproof dish,
a cookie sheet, a bread knife, a cutting board, a measuring cup,
a bowl, and a balloon whisk

1 Use a little of the butter to grease the ovenproof dish and butter the slices of bread. Butter three slices on one side only and three on both sides.

2 Spoon the apricot jelly onto the three slices of bread that have been buttered on one side only. Put a slice of double buttered bread on top of each one to make three sandwiches.

3 Cut the sandwiches into fourths and arrange them, overlapping, in the dish. Sprinkle the chopped dried apricots over the bread.

4 Whisk the eggs well and stir in the heavy cream, milk, sugar, and orange rind. Pour the mixture over the pudding and let stand for 15 minutes to allow the bread to soak up some of the egg mixture. Sprinkle over the raw brown sugar.

5 Preheat the oven to 350°F/180°C. Place the pudding on the cookie sheet. Bake at the top of the preheated oven for 30–40 minutes until just set and golden brown.

6 Remove the pudding from the oven and serve immediately with light cream.

FISH AND SHELLFISH

Thank heavens eating fish is regaining popularity. The days of only eating it as a penance on Fridays are long past, and recipes are no longer limited to just steaming or deep-fat frying. We do not have to worry about filleting or gutting fish anymore either: fish stores and supermarkets have taken the pain out of preparation.

Nowadays we recognize the health benefits of fish. They are a good source of protein and are rich in healthy oils. television programs and foreign travel have also made them popular.

The range of fish now available is much wider too. Times have changed since oysters were a cheap staple and salmon was expensive. Now we have white flat fish, such as flounder, or round fish, such as cod. There are healthy oily fish, such as herrings, mackerel, and tuna, and pink freshwater fish, such as salmon and trout. We can also buy smoked fish, a delicious range of shellfish, and more exotic types of fish, such as shark, red snapper, and monkfish. Now is the time to experiment with this abundance of healthy flavors and textures.

Buying fish

There is no need to worry about buying and cooking fish nowadays. Fish stores and the fish counters in our supermarkets are very reliable and have a good turnover of fish, so we are able to buy it really fresh. Preparation need not be a problem either. We do not expect to butcher our own meat, and likewise we should not have to worry about gutting our own fish. Experts at the task do a better job than we can, so it is best to let them do it. The supermarket counter staff are well trained and will do any job asked of them.

Always buy fish that is in season to get the best flavor and value. Cod and haddock are always on sale, but they may have been frozen and come from Australia. The best cod and haddock come from fishing grounds in the colder waters around the northeast coast and from the North Atlantic, and have the finest flavor and the best texture. The season is from May/June to February. Due to air freight, it is possible to get most fish fresh all the year round, but it is still good to wait for our own season before buying shellfish, especially oysters and mussels.

Storage

Always buy your fish at the end of your shopping trip so that you can take it home immediately. Ask the fish store to wrap it in some ice to make sure it stays cool on the journey. In hot weather I keep a cool box in the trunk of my car to carry home any fresh fish and frozen foods. When you get it home, remove the fish from its wrapping and wipe it over with some paper towels. Then place it in a dish, cover with plastic wrap, and place in the refrigerator before using the same day.

Smoked fish is often bought vacuum-packed: store it in the refrigerator and use by the date shown on the pack. Fresh smoked fish should be well wrapped and chilled for as short a time as possible to avoid contamination with other foods.

Frozen fish is very good and can be stored in the freezer for up to 6 months without deterioration. It is a good idea to buy small fillets or steaks and freeze them individually so that you can have a quick meal at any time. Frozen fish should be thawed in the refrigerator; this helps to retain the flavor and texture. Thaw the fish for at least 8 hours or overnight. Small fillets can be cooked from frozen, but they might need a little longer cooking time.

WHITE FISH

These are divided into round and flat fish. The most familiar round fish is cod and its relatives are haddock, hake, whiting, and coley. They can all be bought as fillets, steaks, or cutlets. Flat fish include sole, flounder, and halibut.

Cod

This can be as large as 14 lb/6.5 kg. It has a firm, flaky flesh, which is soft and white when cooked. It can be baked, broiled, poached, pan-fried, or deep-fried in batter or bread crumbs.

FILLETING A FISH

There is no need to fillet your own fish nowadays—your local fish store can do it for you. If you prefer to fillet your own, however, here is an example.

1 Wash the fish under cold running water, then place it on a clean counter. Remove any scales first.

2 Using a pair of kitchen scissors, cut off the tough fins: this Dover sole has a few small ones on top on either side, whereas salmon and sharks only have one fin.

3 To take the fillet off, slide the knife across the top of the bone, from the neck end right down to the tail.

4 Turn the fish over and, once again, take the fillet off by sliding the knife across the top of the bone, from the neck end right down to the tail. The head and tail will come off automatically.

D epending on its size, a flat fish can yield two or four fillets. Always make sure you trim and scale the fish before you start filleting.

Haddock

This is usually smaller than cod and has a finer texture. It can be used in the same way as cod.

Hake

This is a thinner version of the cod family, so the steaks tend to be smaller. You can bake or steam it; it is also useful in soups and stews.

Whiting

This is a succulent fish and can be fried or baked.

Coley

This has gray-looking flesh and is rather unappealing when raw; also, it does not have a good flavor. However, it is useful in fish cakes, fish pies, and well-flavored recipes such as curry.

Sole

There are two varieties of sole: Dover and lemon. Dover sole has the better flavour. It comes in different weights, from 8 oz/225 g to 2 lb/900 g. The smaller ones are ideal for cooking whole, either by pan-frying or broiling. The larger ones are filleted and can be broiled, fried, baked, or poached. Since the flavor is so fine, a little seasoning and a squeeze of lemon are all that is required. Lemon sole has not got the flavor of its Dover sole relation, but it is good when the fillets are used in recipes with stuffings or other flavorings. Lemon sole can also be made into goujons (small pieces of white fish, usually crumbed and fried).

Flounder

This is very similar to sole but it does not have the fine flavor. If you are buying fillets, buy the white underside ones because the skin is very tender and can be eaten, whereas the greenish brown skin of the upperside needs removing. Flounder can be baked, poached, broiled, or pan-fried, and made into goujons. A sauce accompaniment, such as tartare, is often served with flounder to pep up the flavor.

Dab

Also known as dab sole or sand dab, this is an inexpensive, but very tasty flat fish. It can range in size from quite small to about 1½ lb/650 g and is sandy brown on one side and white on the other. Small dabs are best dipped in flour and pan-fried whole, while larger specimens can be filleted and then broiled, baked, steamed, or poached.

Halibut

This is the largest flat fish and can measure up to 6½ feet/ 2 meters long and 3¼ feet/1 meter wide. It is expensive but has a good flavor and texture. It can be used in the same way as turbot. It can also be cut into cubes and made into kabobs.

FROM TOP Brown trout, Dover sole, herring, mackerel, and red snapper

OILY FISH

These fish are rich in omega-3 fatty acids, which are believed to help reduce cholesterol in our blood and prevent heart disease. They are a healthy food and have a delicious flavor owing to their fat content. Oily fish must be absolutely fresh.

Herring family

This consists of herrings, sprats, sardines, and whitebait. They all have a similar texture and unfortunately lots of small bones. They are best broiled or pan-fried (or grilled) so that the skin crisps and the flesh stays moist. Ask your fish store to remove all the innards and as many bones as possible. Whitebait are the very young fish of the family, so they can be tiny herrings or small sprats or sardines. They should be washed thoroughly, then tossed in seasoned flour, and deep-fried whole. Drain well and serve immediately.

Mackerel

Mackerel have a wonderful silver-gray skin, with shadows of blue and green. They are delicious but must be eaten on the day they are caught, so eat them while you are on vacation or use a reliable supplier. They have a good flavor and are at their best when simply broiled. They can be oven-baked with a piquant stuffing. Traditionally, they are served with gooseberry sauce.

Tuna

Tuna is now widely available and very popular. Its solid steaks are cooked simply by broiling or pan-frying. Tuna is a "meaty" fish, so it is acceptable to people who normally avoid fish. It has a good flavor but do not overcook it or it will dry out. Cook for 2–3 minutes on each side, depending on thickness. For the best flavor, it should be a little underdone in the center.

Salmon

This is probably the most popular fish. Farming methods keep it cheap and it is available all year round. If you can ever get wild salmon (in season from February to October), then do so because it is quite different. Salmon can be cooked whole, in fillets, in steaks, and in cutlets, and by many methods including poaching, broiling, pan-frying, steaming, and "en papillote" (baked inside a parcel of baking parchment). It is very versatile and can be served with butter, in sauces, or in more complex recipes, from soups and appetizers to main courses. Do not overcook the salmon or the result will be dry.

Trout

The wild brown trout is hardly ever seen now, but the farmed rainbow trout is easily available. An average whole trout makes a perfect meal for one person—poach, broil, pan-fry, or bake it in the oven. Make sure the fish store guts the fish and removes the head for you first.

SMOKED FISH

Smoking imparts a wonderful flavor, and with some fish the process of hot-smoking actually cooks the fish too so that we can eat it cold, for example as smoked salmon, trout, or mackerel. Other fish, such as haddock and cod, are cold-smoked to avoid cooking the fish. These then need to be cooked before they can be eaten. Sometimes these fish have been dyed to give them a stronger yellow color. However, there is now a return to undyed, naturally smoked fish. All these fish are usually available in the shops.

Smoked salmon

This is a traditional delicacy, usually served cold with some brown bread and butter. A sprinkling of freshly milled pepper and some lemon wedges are usually offered, but you should try really good smoked salmon as it is to appreciate the delicate flavor. Buy a whole side if possible, and cut it as you need it. Presliced smoked salmon tends to dry out, so eat it soon after purchase.

Smoked trout

Delicately flavored smoked trout is available whole (minus the head). Serve it simply with lemon wedges and some horseradish sauce mixed with a little crème fraîche.

Smoked mackerel

This is rather rich and oily, and needs a sharp sauce to accompany it. A dill and mustard sauce, or horseradish sauce mixed with a little crème fraîche, would be good. Smoked mackerel can also be used to make a quick smoked fish pâté with lots of lemon juice and grated lemon zest and a little butter.

Smoked haddock

This is the best-known smoked fish. It is delicious simply poached and then served with a poached egg on top. It is also good with buttered spinach or lentils. It forms the basis of kedgeree (a breakfast dish consisting of rice, lentils, onions, smoked fish, hard-cooked eggs, and a rich cream sauce).

Smoked cod

This is similar to smoked haddock, but quite often is thicker with chunkier flakes. It makes a fine fish pie and can be used in fish cakes.

Smoked herring

These are smoked fish, which can be reheated by quickly broiling or poaching them. A traditional method is to put the herring in a tall pitcher, fill the pitcher with boiling water, and leave them for 5 minutes. They are usually served for breakfast but they also make a good supper dish.

NEWER VARIETIES OF FISH

We have more varieties of fish available than ever before and some are gaining in popularity. The following are the most popular of the newer types of fish.

Monkfish

Just the tail of this fish is used. It has a very fine texture and a reasonably sweet flavor. It is very firm and can be cooked on skewers; it is also good broiled. Monkfish has no bones, which is a great attraction. The fish store will remove the skin and divide the tail into two fillets for you, ready for cooking.

Red snapper

This fish is easily recognized on the fish counter. It is a vivid red and is wonderful broiled or cooked on a barbecue. It can also be pan-fried. It has a firm texture with a mild flavor.

Other newcomers are sea bass, bream, mahi-mahi, red gurnard, shark, and swordfish. All are worth trying.

SHELLFISH

We are very lucky that there is such a wide variety of shellfish available, both fresh and frozen, in the stores today. Extra care should be taken with shellfish because they can cause food poisoning. Always order direct from your supplier to make sure you get what you require, then use them on the day of purchase. If you are collecting them, get them home as quickly as possible, and keep them in the refrigerator.

Shrimp

These can be bought frozen, raw or cooked, and in different sizes. Ordinary shrimp are sold cooked, either shelled or unshelled. The shelled variety are available frozen. It is a good idea to have a packet of shelled, cooked shrimp in the freezer because a handful can be added to rice dishes or other fish dishes to add interest. They are also useful as a garnish. Large freshwater shrimp are the next in size and they are usually sold uncooked and headless. Some jumbo shrimp are warm-water shrimp and can be bought cooked or uncooked, with or without heads. They are round and fat and have a good flavor. Whole shrimp, with their shells on, are useful for a garnish and to eat simply as an appetizer with a bowl of mayonnaise.

Scallops

These are now becoming very popular. They are expensive, but their delicate flavor and texture make them a worthwhile special purchase. They need the lightest of cooking and are best pan-fried for 1–2 minutes on each side.

Mussels

These are still relatively cheap and they have a great flavor. Buy them only when in season (October to March) and eat on the day of purchase. Before using, make sure all the shells are closed; if not, discard them along with any broken shells. Scrub to remove any deposits and pull away the "beards." Wash them well in two or three changes of water, then leave in clean, cold water until you are ready to cook them. After cooking, check the shells again, and if any have not opened, discard them.

Oysters

Oysters are usually eaten raw. They are farmed in carefully monitored water conditions. They can also be cooked in many ways, by steaming or broiling or adding to fish soups and stews. Serve them well chilled with a little lemon or vinegar on the side. Some finely chopped shallots can also be added.

You need a special oyster knife to open them. Hold the oyster in a cloth to protect the hand. The flatter shell should be on top. Put the blade of the knife in between the shells at the narrowest point. Work the knife backward and forward to break the hinge. Twist the knife and remove the top shell.

Squid

Squid looks more like a little octopus, but it is a mollusk, like mussels and oysters. You can buy it already prepared, and even cut into rings. However, it is best to buy it whole and cut it to size yourself, to preserve the tentacles and give a less uniform appearance. Squid has a good flavor but a bad reputation for being rubbery—that is because people overcook it. It should be sautéed quickly for only 2–3 minutes and served immediately.

Crab

Crab is usually cooked before buying, but it is difficult to remove the meat from the shell and claws. If you practice, you will be able to master it eventually. The easiest way to eat it is to buy it ready prepared. Sometimes you can even buy the white meat separated from the brown, but usually you have a mixture. Crab has a very delicate flavor and is often served simply, on its own with some brown bread and butter. If it is to be mixed with other foods, they need to be subtle so the flavor is not overpowered. Pasta, savory tarts, and salads are good with crab. Crab cakes are also in fashion at the moment.

Lobster

This is a real extravagance, but it is the ultimate of all shellfish. The flavor is unsurpassable and the experience one to be remembered. You can find prepared lobsters in stores. but they are not so good as those you will find by the sea where they are caught. If you want to buy a lobster, go to a good fish store and order a live one to be cooked specially for you—this way it will be at its best.

HERB CRUSTED COD

Serves 4
Preparation time: 10 minutes
Cooking time: 15–20 minutes

INGREDIENTS

4 thick pieces of skinless cod, about 6 oz/175 g each
2 tbsp olive oil
2 cups fresh bread crumbs (white or whole-wheat)
1 garlic clove, peeled and chopped
2 tbsp chopped fresh parsley
grated rind of 1 lemon
salt and pepper
cooked whole green beans, to serve

You will need a shallow, ovenproof dish (lightly brushed with a little of the oil), a mixing bowl, a blender, a cook's knife, a cutting board, and a grater or lemon zester

METHOD

1 Preheat the oven to 375°F/190°C. Arrange the cod pieces in the dish, brush with oil, and season well.

2 In a separate bowl, combine the bread crumbs, garlic, parsley, and lemon rind and season well.

3 Pile the bread crumb mixture carefully on top of the fish pieces and press down well.

4 Place the dish in the center of the preheated oven and bake for 15–20 minutes until the fish is cooked and the crust is crisp and golden brown. Serve on a bed of freshly cooked green beans.

WINE SUGGESTION

A white Rioja or an Australian white Semillon will go well with this herbed fish dish.

TARTARE SAUCE

Tartare sauce is based on mayonnaise (see page 80), but for this recipe you can use a good branded mayonnaise instead. It is traditionally served with fish.

Makes 1 cup
Preparation time: 20 minutes

INGREDIENTS

1 cup mayonnaise
1 tbsp chopped capers
1 tbsp chopped cornichons
1 tbsp chopped fresh parsley
1 tsp chopped chives
1 tbsp lemon juice
salt and pepper

You will need a bowl and a plastic spatula

METHOD

1 Place the mayonnaise in the bowl and fold in the other ingredients. Check the seasoning and adjust if necessary.

2 Cover the bowl with plastic wrap and chill in the refrigerator for at least 30 minutes. This sauce will keep in a screw-top jar in the refrigerator for up to one week.

BAKED TROUT

Trout makes an ideal quick supper. It can be broiled or pan-fried in just 10 minutes. For more than two people, oven baking is best and it also avoids frying odors. Serve one trout per person.

Serves 4
Preparation time: 20 minutes
Cooking time: 12–15 minutes

INGREDIENTS

2 shallots, peeled and finely chopped

2 tbsp butter, melted

1 garlic clove, peeled and finely chopped

1 tbsp finely chopped fresh ginger root

1 stalk lemongrass, crushed and finely chopped

2 oz/55 g baby spinach

pinch crushed dried chile, optional

4 fresh trout, about 12 oz/350 g each, cleaned and fins removed

1 tbsp light soy sauce

salt and pepper

To serve
2 scallions, finely chopped

1 tbsp butter, melted

½ cup white wine

2 tbsp fish sauce

½ tbsp chopped fresh cilantro

½ tbsp chopped fresh basil

1 lime, cut into fourths, to garnish

You will need a shallow, ovenproof cookie sheet covered with foil, a cook's knife, a cutting board, a medium pan, a wooden spatula, a small pan, and 4 serving plates

WINE SUGGESTION
This dish suits the juicy flavors of a New Zealand Semillon or Semillon Chardonnay blend.

METHOD

1 Put the shallots and the 2 tablespoons of melted butter in a medium pan and soften over medium heat for 2–3 minutes. Add the garlic, ginger, and lemongrass. Cook for 2 minutes more, then add the spinach. Cook it for 2–3 minutes, then add the chile (if using). Season well. Remove from the heat and let cool. Drain if necessary.

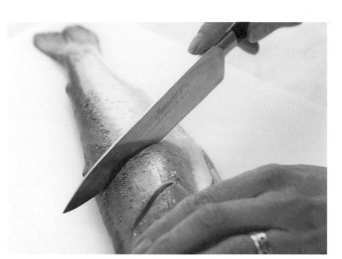

2 Preheat the oven to 425ºF/220ºC. Wipe the trout carefully with paper towels and, using a sharp knife, slash the skin of each fish diagonally on both sides about five times—this lets the fish to cook quickly. Season well inside and out, and rub with the soy sauce.

3 Fill the trout with the spinach stuffing, then reshape them as neatly as you can.

4 Lift the trout carefully onto the prepared cookie sheet. Cook at the top of the preheated oven for 12–15 minutes until the skin is crispy and golden.

5 In a small pan, soften the scallions in the melted butter over low heat for 1–2 minutes, then add the wine and the fish sauce. Season to taste. Raise the heat and cook rapidly for 1 minute to produce a slightly thickened sauce. Add the herbs and stir well.

6 Serve the trout on warmed serving plates with the sauce poured over them. Serve immediately, garnished with the lime fourths.

FISH CAKES

This recipe makes 4 large fish cakes. You can make 8 smaller cakes if you prefer, but they are more awkward.

Serves 4
Preparation time: 30 minutes
Cooking time: 10 minutes

INGREDIENTS

1 lb/450 g potatoes, peeled

1 lb/450 g mixed fish fillets, such as cod, haddock, and salmon, skinned

2 tbsp chopped fresh parsley or tarragon

grated rind of 1 lemon

1 tbsp all-purpose flour

1 egg, beaten

2 cups white or whole-wheat bread crumbs, made from one-day-old bread

4 tbsp vegetable oil, for frying

salt and pepper

You will need a large pan, a vegetable peeler, a cook's knife, a cutting board, a colander, a potato masher, a skillet, a mixing bowl, a cookie sheet, and a metal spatula

METHOD

1 Cut the potatoes into chunks and cook in a large pan of boiling, salted water for 15 minutes. Drain well and mash with a potato masher until smooth.

2 Place the fish in a skillet and just cover with water. Bring to a boil over medium heat, then cover, and simmer gently for 5 minutes until just cooked. Remove from the heat and transfer the fish to a plate, draining it well. When cool enough to handle, flake the fish and make sure that there are no bones.

3 Mix the potatoes with the fish, herbs, and lemon rind in a bowl. Season well and shape into four round, flat cakes.

4 Dust the cakes with flour, dip them into the beaten egg, then coat thoroughly in the bread crumbs. Place on a cookie sheet and chill for at least 30 minutes.

5 Heat the oil in the skillet and cook the cakes over medium heat for 5 minutes on each side. Use a metal spatula to turn them carefully.

*Suitable for freezing. Complete to the end of step 4 and open freeze on a cookie sheet. When frozen, remove the cookie sheet and wrap the fish cakes in freezer bags. Seal well. Store in the freezer for up to 3 months. To use, thaw in the refrigerator overnight and then continue to cook from step 5 above.

FRIED SQUID AND ZUCCHINI

Serves 2
Preparation time: 15 minutes
Cooking time: 8–10 minutes

INGREDIENTS

2 tbsp olive oil
3 zucchini, trimmed and cut into ½ inch/1 cm cubes
14 oz/400 g prepared squid, cut into rings
4 plum tomatoes, seeded and chopped
1 red chile, seeded and very finely chopped
1 garlic clove, peeled and finely chopped
2 tbsp white wine
salt and pepper
2 tbsp chopped fresh cilantro, to garnish

You will need a cook's knife, a cutting board, a heavy skillet, a wooden spatula, a slotted spoon and a heated serving dish

WINE SUGGESTION

A New World Sauvignon has the guts to match the spicy flavoring of this recipe.

METHOD

1 Heat the oil in the skillet over high heat and cook the zucchini quickly for 3–4 minutes until they are dark golden brown. Remove the zucchini from the skillet using a slotted spoon and place in a hot dish to keep warm.

2 Add the squid to the skillet and cook over high heat for 2 minutes.

3 Reduce the heat, add the tomatoes, chile, and garlic and continue to cook for 1 minute more. Pour in the white wine and let the mixture bubble for a few seconds.

4 Remove from the heat and pour on top of the zucchini. Sprinkle with the cilantro and serve immediately with lots of warm crusty bread.

GOUJONS OF SOLE

Serves 2
Preparation time: 20 minutes
Cooking time: 5–6 minutes

INGREDIENTS

2 lemon sole fillets, about 6 oz/175 g each, skinned

2 tbsp all-purpose flour

1 egg, beaten

2 cups white or whole-wheat bread crumbs, made from one-day-old bread

1 tbsp finely chopped fresh parsley

1 garlic clove, peeled and crushed (optional)

1 cup vegetable oil, for frying

salt and pepper

1 lemon, halved, to serve

You will need a cook's knife, a cutting board, a bowl, a shallow dish, a plastic bag, a skillet, and a slotted spoon

METHOD

1 Cut the fillets across diagonally into thin strips, about ½ inch/1 cm wide.

2 Season the flour well and put onto a plate. Roll the strips of fish in the flour until well covered.

3 Place the beaten egg in a shallow dish and then dip the fish into it.

4 Mix the bread crumbs with the parsley and garlic, if using, and season well. Put the mixture into a plastic bag, add the goujons, and toss to coat thoroughly. Chill in the refrigerator for at least 30 minutes.

5 Heat the oil in a skillet and fry half the goujons over medium heat for 2–3 minutes, turning them with a slotted spoon. Remove from the skillet and drain on paper towels. Keep warm. Repeat using the remaining fish.

6 Serve immediately with a half lemon per portion to squeeze over the goujons.

Suitable for freezing. Complete to the end of step 5, let cool, then cover with plastic wrap, and chill quickly. Open freeze on a cookie sheet, then store in the freezer in a lidded, rigid container. To use, reheat from frozen: place on a cookie sheet in an oven preheated to 400°F/200°C until hot, cooked through, and crispy.

MEDITERRANEAN FISH CASSEROLE

Serves 6
Preparation time: 25 minutes
Cooking time: 30 minutes

INGREDIENTS

2 tbsp olive oil

1 red onion, peeled and sliced

2 garlic cloves, peeled and chopped

2 red bell peppers

14 oz/400 g canned chopped tomatoes

1 tsp chopped fresh oregano or marjoram

a few saffron threads soaked in 1 tbsp warm water for 2 minutes

1 lb/450 g white fish (cod, haddock, or hake), skinned and boned

1 lb/450 g prepared squid, cut into rings

1¼ cups fish or vegetable stock

1 cup cooked shelled shrimp

salt and pepper

chunky bread, to serve

To garnish
6 cooked whole shrimp in their shells
2 tbsp chopped fresh parsley

You will need a 9 cup lidded casserole dish, a skillet, a wooden spatula, a cook's knife and a cutting board, a measuring cup, and 6 bowls

METHOD

1 Heat the oil in a skillet and cook the onion and garlic over medium heat for 2–3 minutes until beginning to soften.

2 Seed and thinly slice the bell peppers and add to the skillet. Continue to cook over low heat for 5 minutes more. Add the tomatoes with the herbs and saffron and stir well.

3 Preheat the oven to 400°F/200°C. Cut the white fish into 1¼ inch/3 cm pieces and place with the squid in the casserole dish. Pour in the cooked vegetable mixture and the stock, stir well, and season to taste.

4 Cover and cook in the center of the preheated oven for about 30 minutes until the fish is tender and cooked. Add the shrimp at the last minute and just heat through.

5 Serve in hot bowls garnished with the whole shrimp and the parsley. Provide lots of chunky bread to mop up the casserole juices.

WINE SUGGESTION
Try a light white Pinot Grigio, or a Tokay d'Alsace for more bite.

POACHED SALMON

A whole salmon can often be bought in supermarkets and it makes a good centerpiece for a buffet or large party. It can be served hot or cold.

KETTLE METHOD

A fish kettle is necessary for larger fish. If you haven't got one in your household, you can usually hire one from your local supermarket or fish store.

Serves 12
Preparation time: 10 minutes
Cooking time: 20 minutes, plus cooling (if serving cold), or 45 minutes (if serving hot)

INGREDIENTS

1 whole salmon (head on), about 6 lb/2.7 kg to 8 lb/3.6 kg prepared weight
3 tbsp salt
3 bay leaves
10 peppercorns
1 onion, peeled and sliced
1 lemon, sliced

You will need a large fish kettle (with a two-handled rack), a cook's knife, a cutting board, and a pair of scissors

METHOD

1 Wipe the salmon thoroughly inside and out with paper towels, then use the back of a cook's knife to remove any scales that might still be on the skin. Remove the fins with a pair of scissors and trim the tail. Some people prefer to cut off the head but it is traditionally served with it on.

2 Place the salmon on the two-handled rack and place in the kettle. Fill the kettle with enough cold water to cover the salmon adequately. Sprinkle in the salt, bay leaves, and peppercorns and add the onion and lemon slices.

3 Place on the stovetop, over two low burners, and bring just to a boil very slowly.

4 Put on the lid and simmer very gently. To serve cold, simmer for 2 minutes only, remove from the heat, and let cool in the cooking liquid for about 2 hours with the lid on. To serve hot, simmer for 6–8 minutes and let stand in the hot water for 15 minutes before removing.

WINE SUGGESTION
Ideally you should choose a French white Sauvignon, preferably Sancerre.

OVEN METHOD

This method is suitable for fish under 5 lb/2.25 kg in weight.

Serves 8
Preparation time: 10 minutes
Cooking time: 40 minutes, plus cooling (if serving cold), or 1 hour (if serving hot)

INGREDIENTS

4 lb/1.8 kg fresh whole salmon, prepared weight
2 tbsp butter, melted
1 lemon, sliced
a few sprigs fresh parsley
½ cup white wine or water
salt and pepper

You will need a sharp knife, a cutting board, a pair of scissors, a large roasting pan, a measuring cup, a pastry brush, and kitchen foil

METHOD

1 Preheat the oven to 350°F/180°C. Wipe the salmon thoroughly inside and out, removing any scales that might still be on the skin. Remove the fins with a pair of scissors and trim the tail.

2 Line the roasting pan with a double layer of foil and brush with the melted butter. Season the salmon with salt and pepper both inside and out.

3 Lay the salmon in the foil and place the lemon and parsley in the body cavity. Pour in the wine or water and gather up the foil to make a fairly loose packet.

4 Bake in the preheated oven for about 30–40 minutes. When cooked, test with the point of a knife; if the fish is cooked thoroughly, the flesh should flake. To serve hot, leave for 15 minutes before removing from the foil. To serve cold, leave for 1–2 hours until lukewarm.

PACIFIC PIE

Serves 6
Preparation time: 30 minutes
Cooking time: 45 minutes

INGREDIENTS

1½ lb/675 g small potatoes, unpeeled
1 tbsp olive oil
9 oz/250 g small leeks, trimmed and finely sliced
1⅔ cups small mushrooms, sliced
1 lb/450 g white fish fillets, such as cod or haddock, skinned
2½ cups milk
4 tbsp butter
1½ cups cooked shelled shrimp and/or mussels, optional
1 tbsp chopped fresh parsley or tarragon
3 tbsp all-purpose flour
1¾ cups grated Cheddar cheese
salt and pepper

You will need a cook's knife, a cutting board, a medium pan, a skillet, a wooden spatula, a colander, a 7½ cup ovenproof dish, and a cookie sheet

METHOD

1 Slice the potatoes into thick slices. Cook in a large pan of boiling, salted water for 5 minutes, then drain well.

2 Put the oil and the leeks in a skillet and cook gently over low heat for 2–3 minutes until soft. Add the mushrooms and cook for about 2 minutes.

3 Place the fish in the rinsed pan and just cover with a little milk. Over gentle heat, bring to a simmer and poach for 5 minutes until tender. Drain and reserve the poaching milk.

4 Use a little of the butter to grease the ovenproof dish. Flake the fish and place in the dish with the leeks, mushrooms, and shrimp (if using). Sprinkle in the parsley or tarragon.

5 Preheat the oven to 400ºF/200ºC. In the same pan, make a white sauce. Melt the remaining butter in the pan and add the flour. Stir well and cook over low heat for 2–3 minutes. Remove from the heat and gradually stir in the remaining milk, beating well after each addition. When all the milk has been added and the sauce is smooth, return the pan to the heat. Cook over low heat, stirring constantly, until thickened. Cook for 2–3 minutes more, then add scant 1 cup of the cheese. Season to taste.

6 Pour half the sauce over the fish, arrange the potato slices on top, and cover with the remaining sauce.

7 Sprinkle on the remaining cheese and cook on a cookie sheet, in the center of the preheated oven, for 45 minutes until golden brown.

WINE SUGGESTION

A chilled white Viognier would be delicious with this fish pie.

SEARED TUNA

Serves 4
Preparation time: 15 minutes, plus marinating
Cooking time: 6 minutes

INGREDIENTS

four 5 oz/140 g tuna steaks
2 tbsp soy sauce
rind and juice of 1 lime
1 tbsp olive oil

To serve
2 scallions, trimmed and finely chopped
4 plum tomatoes, seeded and chopped
pinch chili flakes
1 tbsp shredded fresh basil leaves
2 tbsp olive oil, plus extra for brushing
1 tbsp balsamic vinegar
4 bagels or soft rolls, to serve (optional)

You will need a griddle pan or heavy skillet, a cook's knife, a cutting board, a small bowl, a shallow, nonmetallic dish, a pastry brush, a metal spatula, and 4 plates

METHOD

1 Put the tuna in a shallow, nonmetallic dish. Add the soy sauce and the lime rind and juice, and let marinate for 1–2 hours, or overnight if possible.

2 Make the salsa by combining the scallions, tomatoes, chili, basil, oil, and vinegar in a small bowl. Season well. Put to one side for 15–30 minutes to let the flavors to mix.

3 Preheat the griddle pan or skillet over high heat for 2–3 minutes until very hot. Brush the fish with oil, then place on the hot pan for 2–3 minutes; do not move it until the time is up, so that it can brown. Then brush the other side of the fish with oil and turn carefully. Cook for 2–3 minutes more without moving it. The tuna should be just pink in the center.

4 Transfer the fish to warm plates and serve with the salsa, in rolls if you like, or with simple salad greens.

WINE SUGGESTION

A full-bodied red, such as a Chilean Merlot or Australian Shiraz, would be perfect with this dish.

MEAT

Meat has had a bad press recently, with its fat content linked to heart disease and the publicity given to various diseases. But do not let that put you off. Meat is rich in protein, vitamins, and minerals and lean cuts are low in calories. Surplus fat can always be trimmed off before cooking or drained off after cooking.

The wide variety of cuts of beef, lamb, and pork that are available can be confusing but are easily divided up. Large, tender cuts are ideal for roasting, and cheaper, tougher cuts are suitable for casseroling.

Smaller and leaner cuts are quicker to cook and have less fat, such as lamb loin or pork tenderloin, or chops and beef steaks. They are delicious broiled in the winter or cooked on the barbecue in the summer. They are also useful thinly sliced and stir-fried quickly with lots of vegetables—a modern healthy alternative to traditional cooking. Do not forget the many uses of lean ground meat—beef, pork, or lamb—to make quick meals with herbs and spices.

Here are the different sorts of meats available and the best ways to cook them. Some of the recipes that follow are traditional, and one or two newer ideas reflect more contemporary eating.

Choosing Meat
Red meats should look fresh and moist, but not too red. If the meat is bright red, it will not have been hung long enough to develop a good flavor. A ruby/burgundy color is better. The fat should be creamy rather than white. Do not worry too much about the amount of fat around a cut because it will keep the meat moist and will naturally protect the flesh during the cooking process. You can remove it after cooking if you feel there is too much for your taste. Flesh that has a marbling of fat will be richer and moister when cooked than that which has no fat. Braising steak with a good marbling is

best because this melts during the long, slow cooking and gives a tender, well-flavored result.

Pork flesh should be smooth and moist, and a pale pink color. There should be a reasonable amount of fat covering it. Organic pork will have a higher percentage of fat than intensively farmed pork and will certainly have a better flavor. The rind should be clean and hairless and cuts should be of an even thickness for even cooking.

Always use a reliable supplier, either your supermarket counter or your local butcher. Farmers' markets can also be a good source of locally produced meat.

For roasting, buy about 6 oz/175 g to 8 oz/225 g per person for a boneless cut and about 12 oz/350 g per person if the meat is on the bone. For casseroling, allow the same amount as a boneless cut and for steaks allow individual appetites to dictate.

Storage
Make sure that you take home fresh meat as soon as possible after buying. Unwrap the meat and place it in a clean dish, cover with plastic wrap or foil, and store in the refrigerator. Use ground and diced meat on the day of purchase; roasts can be stored for up to 3 days and chops for 2 days. If you buy prepacked meat, make sure you read the label and use by the date stated on the pack; do not unwrap these packs because they have been prepared under controlled atmospheric conditions to preserve the meat longer. Always let the meat return to room temperature before cooking.

Beef

Lamb

Pork

Not only has beef suffered from health scares over the last few years, it has also suffered from intensive agricultural methods, poor hanging times, and poor butchery. However, if you want to eat beef as it used to be, with a wonderful flavor and texture, you can buy it organically reared. This will cost more, but it will be worthwhile. And if you buy it in smaller quantities, it will be more economical and you will be satisfying the health lobby not to eat too much red meat.

CUTS FOR ROASTING

Sirloin
This is the tenderest cut from the back of the loin. It can be a large cut on the bone but more usually it is boned and rolled so you can choose the size you need.

Ribs
Rib and standing rib roast are excellent roasting joints, and are best roasted on the bone. They have a good layer of fat, which cooks out during the roasting, producing a well-flavored roast. Ribs can be boned and rolled to give the smaller cut known as a rolled rib roast.

Rump roast
This cut is often sold for roasting, but it is better if pot-roasted or braised.

Round
This is similar to rump roast, from the hind leg. It has a good flavor but can be tough. It can be slow-roasted, but pot-roasting or braising is recommended.

Roasting times and temperatures
Start by roasting at 450°F/230°C for 15 minutes, then cook for :
- 15 minutes per 1 lb/450 g plus 15 minutes at 375°F/190°C for rare
- 20 minutes per 1 lb/450 g plus 20 minutes at 375°F/190°C for medium
- 25 minutes per 1 lb/450 g plus 25 minutes at 375°F/190°C for well done

Let the roasted meat stand for 20 minutes, in a warm place, before carving.

CUTS FOR CASSEROLING
These cuts of meat require long, slow cooking to become really tender.

Chuck steak
This cut comes from the shoulder area of the animal and is quite lean. It is sold either sliced or diced and is frequently labeled "braising steak."

Hind and fore shank
Both of these cuts come from the leg. Fore shank is very gristly and should only be used for stock, but hind shank can be stewed for 6–8 hours to soften the connective tissue. This is rather heavy on fuel, but produces a rich, gelatinous stock that is also used for traditional beef tea.

FRYING AND BROILING
Only the very best tender meat is suitable and requires very little cooking.

Porterhouse steak
This is the finest cut of beef: it is lean and boneless. It comes from below the sirloin and is the most expensive. It can be roasted whole, but it is usually sold in steaks cut into sizes dictated by appetite and price—anything from 4 oz/115 g to 10 oz/280 g. Also cut from the loin, T-bone steak contains some tenderloin or fillet, but club steak does not.

Entrecôte steak
This is the lean and tender eye muscle of the sirloin. It is also boneless, and can be cut into even-sized steaks, about 1¼–1½ inches/3–4 cm thick. It can also be used cut into thin strips for stir-frying.

Round steak
This comes from the hind quarter of the animal. It has a good layer of fat, which melts quite a lot on cooking. It is thought to have the best flavor of all the steaks and can be cut into any size, the usual being from 8 oz/225 g to 12 oz/350 g.

Below: Always use separate utensils for cutting and preparing raw and cooked meats. Wash utensils well after use, and keep raw and cooked meats away from each other.

The sweet flavor of lamb and its tender flesh make it the most delicious of all meats and my favorite. We have home-reared lamb from quite early in the year, about April. In the winter we have lamb imported from New Zealand. There is not really any need to buy organic lamb because most have lived healthy outdoor lives, but it is available if you want to be assured of its provenance.

CUTS FOR ROASTING

Leg
This tender and lean meat is probably the most popular cut for roasting.

Shoulder
This is more economical than leg and, in my opinion, it has the sweeter flavor. It has more fat than leg but that cooks out while roasting and can be poured off after cooking. It is a difficult cut to carve, but you can get your butcher to bone it first and then it is simple.

Rack of lamb
This is a very small roast, cut from the top end of the loin. It has very tender meat and looks like a row of chops. It is easy to carve by cutting down between the bones to serve as individual chops. It is a very useful roast if you are cooking for only two people.

Saddle
Also known as a loin or double loin roast, this is the largest cut, consisting of a whole pair of loins. It is excellent for a large gathering of people.

Roasting times and temperatures
Start by roasting at 450°F/230°C for 20 minutes, then cook for:
• 25 minutes per 450 g/1 lb/450 g at 350°F/180°C for medium
• 30 minutes per 1 lb/450 g at 350°F/180°C for well done
Shoulder will need a little more cooking than leg, about 5 minutes per 1 lb/450 g. Cook a rack for only 10 minutes at the higher temperature. Let stand for 15 minutes, in a warm place, before carving.

CUTS FOR CASSEROLING

Leg
When boned and cut into cubes, leg makes extremely good casseroles. The cut is quite expensive, but the cooking time is shorter and therefore more economical.

Shoulder
This can be boned and cut into cubes and used for casseroles. It has more fat so it needs to be well trimmed before using.

Lamb shanks
Braised lamb shanks are often on the menu at top restaurants. They are convenient because you can allow one per person, but they do take a long time to cook—at least 3 hours. However, they have a lovely flavor and the meat is very tender.

FRYING AND BROILING

Gigot of lamb
These are also known as leg chops. The top end of the leg is sliced into large, round steaks with the bone going through the center. They are delicious marinated in red wine with garlic and rosemary, and can be grilled. Serve one per person (but the size can vary with the thickness of the cut).

Loin and sirloin chops
These are chops cut from the loin. They have a T-shaped bone and are best broiled to reduce the fat content.

English chops
These are smaller chops with a central bone. They can be broiled or pan-fried.

Rib chops
These are very small chops, cut from the ribs, with tender sweet meat and long, thin bones. Serve 2–3 per person.

Shoulder chop
This is a boneless strip of meat, cut from the top of the shoulder. It is good cubed and made into kabobs with onions and bay leaves. It can also be cut up into strips and stir-fried.

Below: Lamb cut into cubes is ideal for casseroling. Make sure that you trim off all the excess fat first.

Pigs are now bred to have less fat than in the past because it was thought that the consumer wanted it that way. Unfortunately, these newer breeds do not have so much flavor as their predecessors and it is quite difficult to get crispy cracklings. Luckily, organic farmers are now producing pork with a higher fat content because, as the pigs live outdoors, they have to build up their own insulation. This is an improvement for the people who want to enjoy well-flavored pork with cracklings.

CUTS FOR ROASTING

Ham roast
The leg is sold whole or divided into fillet end and knuckle. The knuckle is cheaper because it has a larger bone content. Boneless ham roast is also available.

Loin
This is the best choice for roasting. The hind loin, from the back of the animal, is superior to the fore loin from the rib end. These roasts can be cut by the butcher to the size of your choice and you can even buy a whole loin, weighing about 12 lb/5.4 kg. Loin roasts are available on the bone or can be boned and rolled. Loin on the bone gives the best cracklings.

Tenderloin
This can be roasted but, because it is so lean, it is best used for other methods of cooking. If it is roasted, however, it is usually wrapped in bacon or prosciutto to give it some fat or cooked in a roasting bag so that it is self-basting; it is also often stuffed to add moisture to the meat.

Roasting times and temperatures
Start by roasting at 450°F/230°C for 20 minutes, then cook for:
• 25 minutes per 1 lb/450 g at 350°F/180°C for loin
• 35 minutes per 1 lb/450 g at 350°F/180°C for ham roast
Let the roasted meat stand for 15 minutes, in a warm place, before carving.

CUTS FOR CASSEROLING

Arm shoulder
This is may be called the shoulder butt. It can be roasted but it is best cut into cubes for casseroles. It produces a delicious, tender meat when cooked in a long, slow, moist way with plenty of vegetables.

Ham
This can be cut into cubes, and is also ideal for casseroles.

Spare ribs
These are cut from the thick end of the belly. They are cooked in the oven but not roasted as such because they are usually cooked in a spicy sauce, slowly, for 2–2½ hours.

FRYING AND BROILING

Tenderloin
This can be thinly sliced and pan-fried quickly. A sauce is often added before serving. It can also be cut into thin strips for stir-frying, which are usually marinated before cooking. It can also be cubed and made into kabobs.

Loin chops
These are large, lean chops with a good edge of fat. Trim off the rind to prevent the chops from curling when cooked. They are best cooked under a hot broiler or on a barbecue.

Top loin chops
These come from the hind loin. Cook them in the same way as loin chops.

Below: To make crispy cracklings, spread plenty of salt over the rind of the roast, then use a sharp knife to score lines over it before roasting in the oven.

Lamb
and
Mint

Pork
and
Sage

Beef

Vegetarian

CURED AND SMOKED HAM

Smoked ham also comes from the pig: it is the hind leg, which is removed before processing. Cured and smoked ham comes from the same part but is processed by curing it in brine, while it is still part of the carcass.

Cooking
Cured and smoked hams are cooked in a pan of just simmering water for about 20 minutes per 1 lb/450 g. If they are being served cold, let them cool in the water. Alternatively, remove the skin and glaze before finishing off in an oven preheated to 400°F/200°C for 15–20 minutes. Whole hams need only 15 minutes of oven time per 1 lb/450 g.

SAUSAGES

No longer are we restricted to pork or beef sausages. We have specific "sausage stores," which sell about 80 different flavors, including vegetarian, chicken, and game. Sausages are an ideal quick food as long as you buy good-quality ones. Always check the label for meat content and only buy those that contain at least 80 percent meat. Cheap sausages contain all sorts of things we would not choose to eat, so only buy the best. If you buy from your butcher or a specialty store, always use the sausages on the day of purchase. Prepacked sausages will contain preservative and can therefore be stored in the refrigerator for a few days. Check the label before storing. If the sausages are particularly spicy, make sure you keep them well wrapped to avoid the flavors spoiling other foods.

Cook them by broiling, baking, or frying at not too hot a temperature to stop the casings splitting, but make sure they are cooked through. Try experimenting with different flavors.

GROUND MEAT

This is available as beef, lamb, pork, veal, and poultry. Ground meat can be a very useful commodity but it needs to be chosen with care. There are some awful examples of "economy" meats, which should be avoided because they are high in fat and contain unpleasant gristle. The source of the meat can also be questionable. The proportions of meat and fat in ground meat are variable. As a guide, the fat content of ground beef should not exceed 20 percent, lamb 25 percent, and pork 30 percent. "Lean" ground meat should contain less than 7 percent fat. Supermarkets have their own system and the fat content should be clearly labeled on the packaging.

Ground meat can be used to make meatballs, hamburgers, shepherd's pie, cottage pie, spaghetti bolognese, chile con carne, and to stuff vegetables.

BEEF IN GUINNESS

A casserole benefits from being made the day before and then being reheated before serving. If you do this, cool the casserole as quickly as possible and store it in the refrigerator or a cool pantry overnight.

Serves 6
Preparation time: 20–25 minutes
Cooking time: 2½–3 hours

INGREDIENTS

3 tbsp olive oil
2 onions, peeled and thinly sliced
2 garlic cloves, peeled and chopped
2 lb 4 oz/1 kg stewing steak
2 tbsp all-purpose flour
1¼ cups Guinness
bouquet garni (see page 47)
⅔ cup beef stock or vegetable stock, or water
salt and pepper
1 tbsp chopped fresh parsley, to garnish

To serve
mashed potato
a cooked green vegetable, such as cabbage or spinach

You will need a casserole dish (about 7½ cups capacity), a large skillet, a wooden spatula, a slotted spoon, a measuring cup, a cook's knife, and a cutting board

METHOD

1 Preheat the oven to 300°F/150°C. Heat 1 tablespoon of the oil in a large skillet and cook the onions and garlic over medium heat for 4–5 minutes until soft and brown. Remove the onions and garlic from the skillet using a slotted spoon, then place them in the casserole dish.

2 Cut the meat into thick strips. Using the remaining oil, cook the meat over high heat for about 5 minutes, stirring well until it is brown all over. Sprinkle in the flour and stir well to prevent lumps from forming. Season well.

3 Lower the heat to medium, pour in the Guinness, and continue to heat, stirring constantly, until boiling.

4 Remove from the heat and carefully turn the contents of the skillet into the casserole. Add the bouquet garni and the stock. Cover the dish and cook gently in the center of the preheated oven for 2½–3 hours.

5 Remove from the oven, discard the bouquet garni, and check the seasoning. Garnish with parsley and serve immediately with mashed potato and a cooked green vegetable, such as cabbage or spinach.

Suitable for freezing. Follow the recipe to the end of step 6, cool quickly, and turn into a rigid lidded container. Freeze for up to 3 months. To use, thaw overnight in the refrigerator, then reheat either on the stovetop or in the oven at 350°F/180°C for 30–40 minutes before serving.

WINE SUGGESTION

This dish should be served with a classic red Cabernet Sauvignon, perhaps from Australia—try a Barossa or a Coonawarra.

ROAST LOIN OF PORK

The best cuts of pork for roasting are the ham and the loin. The ham is best for larger numbers of people. The loin can be bought in smaller sizes and is the best for cracklings.

Serves 4
Preparation time: 20 minutes
Cooking time: 1 hour 20 minutes

INGREDIENTS

2 lb 4 oz/1 kg piece of pork loin, chined (backbone removed) and the rind scored by the butcher

1 tbsp all-purpose flour

1¼ cups hard cider, apple juice, chicken stock, or vegetable stock

roast potatoes and a selection of cooked vegetables, to serve

Stuffing
1 tbsp melted butter

½ onion, peeled and finely chopped

1 garlic clove, peeled and finely chopped

½ inch/1 cm piece fresh ginger root, peeled and finely chopped

1 pear, cored and chopped

6 fresh sage leaves, chopped

1 cup fresh bread crumbs, white or whole-wheat

salt and pepper

You will need a good, solid roasting pan, a small pan, a wooden spatula, some string, aluminum foil, a skewer, a balloon whisk, a measuring cup, a cook's knife, and a cutting board

METHOD

1 Preheat the oven to 425°F/220°C. Make the stuffing by heating the butter in a small pan and cooking the onion and garlic over medium heat for 3 minutes until soft. Add the ginger and pear, mix well, and cook for 1 minute more.

2 Remove from the heat and stir in the sage and bread crumbs, and season well.

3 Put the stuffing along the middle of the loin, then roll it up, and tie with string; you will need 4–5 pieces to hold the roast in shape. You can cover the stuffing on the ends with small pieces of foil to stop it burning.

4 Season well, and in particular use a lot of salt on the rind to make crisp cracklings. Place the meat in a roasting pan and roast in the center of the preheated oven for 20 minutes.

5 Reduce the oven temperature to 350°F/180°C and cook for an hour until the skin is crispy and the juices run clear when the joint is pierced with a skewer.

6 Remove from the oven, lift out the meat, and place on a hot serving plate. Cover with foil and leave in a warm place.

7 Pour off most of the fat from the roasting pan, leaving the meat juices and sediments behind. Sprinkle in the flour and whisk well. Cook the paste for a couple of minutes, then add the cider, apple juice, or stock, a little at a time, until you have a smooth gravy. Boil for 2–3 minutes until the gravy is the required consistency. Season well and pour into a hot serving pitcher.

8 Cut the string from the roast and remove the cracklings by cutting into the fat. Carve the stuffed pork into slices and serve on hot plates with the cracklings and the gravy. Serve with roast potatoes and cooked vegetables in season.

WINE SUGGESTION

Try an Italian Sangiovese red, such as Chianti, with this dish.

GREEK LAMB CASSEROLE

Serves 6
Preparation time: 25 minutes
Cooking time: 1–1½ hours

INGREDIENTS

3–4 tbsp olive oil

1 small eggplant (about 8 oz/225 g), sliced

2 onions, peeled and chopped

1 garlic clove, peeled and chopped

2 lb/900 g lamb (either leg or shoulder), cubed

1 tsp ground coriander

whole nutmeg, for grating

14 oz/400 g canned chopped tomatoes

2 tbsp tomato paste

1¼ cups vegetable stock (fresh, or made using bouillon powder)

14 oz/400 g canned apricot halves in juice

3 bay leaves

salt and pepper

1 quantity Fruit and Nut Pilaf (see page 190), to serve

To garnish

1 tbsp chopped fresh cilantro

grated rind of 1 orange

You will need a casserole dish (about 7½ cup capacity), a skillet, a wooden spatula, a cook's knife, a canelle knife, a cutting board, a grater, a bowl, a measuring cup, and a large, deep serving dish

METHOD

1 Heat 3 tablespoons of the oil in a large skillet and cook the aubergine over high heat for 3 minutes each side until browned. Remove from the pan and drain on paper towels.

2 Cook the onions and garlic in the skillet (adding another tablespoon of oil if necessary), over medium heat for 3–4 minutes until transparent.

3 Add the meat and continue to cook over high heat until it has a good dark brown color. Stir in the ground coriander and grate in a good fourth of the nutmeg. Season well.

4 Preheat the oven to 350°F/180°C. Pour the tomatoes into the skillet and stir in the tomato paste. Add the stock and the juice from the drained apricots, keeping the fruit for a garnish.

5 Add the bay leaves and bring to a boil. Transfer the lamb mixture and the fried eggplant to a casserole dish. Cover, and cook in the center of the preheated oven for 1–1½ hours until the lamb is cooked (depending on which cut is used—see page 125).

6 Ten minutes before the end of cooking, pour the apricot halves into a dish, cover with foil, and heat in the oven at the same temperature for 10 minutes.

7 Prepare the orange rind by using a canelle knife or a zester so that you have long strips of rind to use as a garnish.

8 Serve the lamb casserole in a deep serving dish. Arrange the warm apricot halves around the lamb, sprinkle with the cilantro, and top with the orange rind.

9 Serve hot with a tasty pilaf.

WINE SUGGESTION

Full-bodied reds are needed here—try a rich Chilean Malbec or a powerful Spanish Rioja.

PORK SCALLOPS WITH APPLES AND CRÈME FRAÎCHE

Serves 4
Preparation time: 25 minutes
Cooking time: 25–30 minutes

INGREDIENTS

1 lb 4 oz/550 g pork tenderloin

2 tbsp olive oil

2 tbsp butter, melted

1 small onion, peeled and finely chopped

1 garlic clove, peeled and finely chopped

2 eating apples, cored and diced into ½ inch/1 cm cubes

1 tbsp soft brown sugar

1 cup hard cider

½ cup apple vinegar

2 tbsp crème fraîche

salt and pepper

1 tbsp chopped fresh parsley, to garnish

mashed potato, to serve

You will need a cook's knife, a cutting board, a large skillet, a rolling pin, a measuring cup, some plastic wrap, and a heated serving dish.

WINE SUGGESTION

Try a traditional hard cider with this apple dish, or a Gewürztraminer.

METHOD

1 Cut the pork into slices ½ inch/1 cm thick. Place each piece between two pieces of plastic wrap or inside a plastic food bag and, using any part of a rolling pin, beat out the meat until it is very thin and twice the size. Season the meat well.

2 Heat half the oil and butter in a skillet and cook the pork scallops on high heat for 2–3 minutes on both sides. You may need to do this in two or three batches. Remove from the skillet and keep warm in a hot serving dish.

3 Heat the remaining oil and butter in the skillet over medium heat and then cook the onion and garlic for about 5 minutes until soft.

4 Add the apples and sugar to the skillet and cook over high heat for about 4–5 minutes until they are caramelized and turning golden brown.

5 Lower the heat, add the hard cider and the vinegar, and then gently simmer for about 5 minutes until the mixture is thick and glossy.

6 Return the pork scallops to the pan and mix well. Taste, and adjust the seasoning if necessary. Stir in the crème fraîche. Serve the pork scallops on warmed plates with the apple and onion sauce spooned over them. Garnish with the parsley and serve some creamy mashed potatoes alongside.

3

GLAZED CURED HAM

There is great debate as to whether the best way to cook a cured ham is to boil it or roast it. A compromise of doing both seems to be the best answer, resulting in a moist and well-flavored meat.

Serves 6
Preparation time: allow time for soaking (see step 1), plus 10 minutes for glazing
Cooking time: 1 hour 20 minutes

INGREDIENTS

3 lb/1.3 kg boneless cured ham
2 tbsp Dijon mustard
scant ½ cup raw brown sugar
½ tsp ground cinnamon
½ tsp ground ginger
18 whole cloves
1 quantity Apricot Sauce (see page 139), to serve

You will need a roasting pan, a large lidded pan, a plate, a cook's knife, and a cutting board

WINE SUGGESTION
Try a French Tavel Rosé or a Riesling from Alsace with this dish.

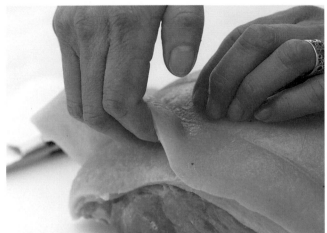

1 Check with your butcher or on the wrapper to see the supplier's instructions regarding soaking the ham. Some cured hams are presoaked and some are not. Place the ham in a large pan, cover with cold water, and slowly bring to a boil over gentle heat. Discard the water and cover with fresh water (this removes all the scum). Bring to a boil again, then cover, and simmer very gently for 1 hour.

2 Remove the cured ham from the pan and drain. Remove the rind from the ham and use a sharp knife to score the fat into a diamond-shaped pattern.

3 Preheat the oven to 400°F/200°C. Spread the mustard over the fat. On a plate, combine the sugar, cinnamon, and ginger, then roll the ham in it, pressing down well so that there is an even coating all over.

4 Stud the diamond shapes with the cloves and then place the ham in a roasting pan. Roast in the center of the preheated oven for 20 minutes until the glaze is a rich golden color. To serve hot, let stand for 20 minutes before carving. Serve with hot apricot sauce. If the ham is to be served cold, it can be cooked the day before and stored, covered with plastic wrap, in the refrigerator before using.

STUFFED SHOULDER OF LAMB

This roast can be difficult to carve, so get your butcher to bone the lamb for you first and you will then have no trouble carving this delicious meat.

Serves 6–8
Preparation time: 20 minutes
Cooking time: 1½ hours

INGREDIENTS

4 lb/1.8 kg shoulder of lamb, boned
salt and pepper

Stuffing
1 tbsp butter, melted
1 onion, peeled and finely chopped
1 garlic clove, peeled and finely chopped
4 oz/115 g ground veal or pork
2 cups fresh bread crumbs, white or whole-wheat
grated rind and juice of 1 lemon
1 tbsp chopped fresh parsley
1 tbsp chopped fresh rosemary
1 tbsp olive oil
1 cup red wine

To serve
small navy beans, cooked with a crushed clove of garlic
and 1 tbsp chopped fresh parsley (see step 6)

You will need a trussing needle and some fine string,
a roasting pan, a small pan, a large bowl, a measuring cup, and
a wooden spatula

METHOD

1 Preheat the oven to 400°F/200°C. Wipe the lamb with paper towels and season well inside and out. To make the stuffing, melt the butter in a small pan and cook the onion and garlic over medium heat for about 3 minutes until soft and transparent. Transfer to a large bowl and combine with the veal, bread crumbs, lemon rind and juice, and herbs.

2 Season the mixture well. Using your hands, carefully put the stuffing into the shoulder.

3 Sew up the pocket to form a good shape (do not worry about the stitches—they will be removed—but try to use only one piece of string).

4 Place the lamb in a roasting pan and rub it with the oil. Season with salt and pepper and roast in the center of the preheated oven for 1½ hours, basting from time to time.

5 Remove the pan from the oven, then lift out the meat, and place on a warm serving plate. Remove all the string, cover the meat with foil, and keep it warm.

6 Pour off the excess fat from the pan and make gravy with the juices. Add the red wine, scrape all the sediment off the base of the pan, and boil vigorously for 2–3 minutes until well reduced. Pour the gravy into a warm pitcher. Serve the lamb thickly sliced with small navy beans, simply heated with a crushed clove of garlic and a tablespoon of chopped parsley.

STIR-FRIED BEEF

This is a substantial dish, but if you like, you can serve some Chinese noodles or rice to accompany the dish.

Serves 4
Preparation time: 35 minutes, including marinating
Cooking time: 15–20 minutes

INGREDIENTS

1 lb/450 g steak (round or entrecôte)

2 tbsp light soy sauce

2 tbsp rice wine or dry sherry

2 tbsp tomato paste

pinch of Chinese five-spice powder

1 garlic clove, peeled and finely chopped

2 small bok choy, shredded

1 red bell pepper, cut into thin batons

2 carrots, cut into thin batons

2 zucchini, cut into thin batons

4 scallions, sliced diagonally

scant 2 cups bean sprouts

2 tbsp vegetable oil

3 tbsp sesame seed oil

2 tbsp toasted sesame seeds

salt and pepper

cooked Chinese noodles or rice, to serve (optional)

You will need a wok or a large, deep skillet, a shallow bowl, aluminum foil, a cook's knife and a cutting board, a serving dish, and 4 plates

METHOD

1 Cut the steak into very thin slices, about 2 inches/5 cm long and ½ inch/1 cm thick.

2 Place the beef in a shallow bowl and combine with the soy sauce, rice wine, tomato paste, and five-spice powder. Let marinate for 30 minutes.

3 While the meat is marinating, prepare the vegetables.

4 Heat the vegetable oil the wok or skillet until it is very hot, swirl it around, and then add the steak. Stir-fry over high heat for about 3 minutes. Use a slotted spoon to remove the steak from the pan, and keep warm in a hot serving dish covered with aluminum foil.

5 Heat 2 tablespoons of sesame oil in the wok or skillet and stir-fry the garlic, bok choy, red bell pepper, carrots, zucchini, and scallions over high heat for about 1 minute—they should still be crisp. Add the bean sprouts last and just heat through. Season the vegetables well and spoon onto 4 serving plates. Arrange the steak on top and pour over any remaining sauce from the pan.

6 Drizzle on the remaining sesame oil and garnish with the toasted sesame seeds.

WINE SUGGESTION

A Barossa Shiraz from Australia or Syrah (it's the same) from the French Pays D'Oc would be good with this stir-fry.

R O A S T   B E E F

Roast beef is the most difficult roast to get right. Unlike the other meats, you need to cook it so that it is still pink in the center, so careful timing is important. The best beef is a rib cooked on the bone, but this must be a good size. For a smaller number of people a sirloin, boned and rolled, is a good alternative.

Serves 8
Preparation time: 5 minutes
Cooking time: 2 hours 35 minutes

INGREDIENTS

6 lb/2.7 kg standing rib roast of beef
2 tsp dry hot mustard
3 tbsp all-purpose flour
2½ cups beef stock, or red wine, or hard cider
2 tsp Worcestershire sauce, optional
salt and pepper

To serve
a selection of accompaniments, such as roast potatoes (see page 173), Yorkshire puddings (see page 138), and cooked carrots and cauliflower

You will need a good, solid roasting pan, a wooden spatula, a measuring cup, some foil, and a carving knife

METHOD

1 Preheat the oven to 450°F/230°C. Season the meat and rub in the mustard and 1 tablespoon of the flour. Place the meat in a roasting pan large enough to hold it comfortably.

2 Roast the meat in the preheated oven for 15 minutes, then reduce the oven temperature to 375°F/190°C and cook for 15 minutes per 1 lb/450 g, plus 15 minutes (1 hour 45 minutes for rare beef), or 20 minutes per 1 lb/450 g plus 20 minutes (2 hours 20 minutes for medium beef).

3 Baste the meat from time to time to ensure a moist result. If the pan becomes too dry, add a few tablespoons of stock or red wine.

4 Remove the pan from the oven, lift out the meat, and place on a hot serving plate. Cover with foil and leave in a warm place.

5 Pour off most of the fat from the roasting pan, leaving behind the meat juices and the sediment. Place the pan on the stovetop over medium heat and scrape all the sediments from the base of the pan. Sprinkle in the remaining flour and quickly mix it into the pan juices. A small whisk can be used for this. When you have a smooth paste, gradually add the remaining stock, wine, or cider, whisking constantly. Adjust the seasoning, and add a little Worcestershire sauce if using. Bring to a boil, and stir until thickened and smooth.

6 When ready to serve, carve the meat into medium slices, and serve on hot plates with the chosen accompaniments.

7 Pour the gravy into a warm pitcher or gravy boat and pass it around separately.

WINE SUGGESTION
The greatest dish deserves the greatest wine—a good red Bordeaux. Why not try a St. Emilion.

YORKSHIRE PUDDINGS

Makes 12
Preparation time: 5 minutes
Cooking time: 25–30 minutes

INGREDIENTS

generous ¾ cup all-purpose flour
1 egg, beaten
1¼ cups milk and water mixed (half milk, half water)
3 tbsp roast beef drippings, goose fat, or olive oil
salt and pepper

You will need a mixing bowl, a hand-held electric mixer or a balloon whisk, a measuring cup, a muffin pan with 12 deep molds, and a ladle

METHOD

1 Preheat the oven to 425°F/220°C. Place the flour and a pinch of salt in a mixing bowl. Make a well in the center, add the egg and half the liquid. Using a whisk, beat the egg and milk together and gradually incorporate the flour. Continue beating until the mixture is smooth and there are no lumps. Gradually beat in the remaining liquid. Season with the pepper.

2 Put a little drippings or oil into each mold of the muffin pan. Heat at the top of the preheated oven for 3–4 minutes until very hot. Remove the hot pan very carefully, use a ladle to pour the batter into each mold, then return the pan to the oven.

3 Bake for 20–25 minutes until the Yorkshire puddings are well puffed up and golden brown.

4 Serve immediately with roast beef (see page 137) or any other meat you like.

APRICOT SAUCE

Serves 6
Preparation time: 5 minutes
Cooking time: 2–3 minutes

INGREDIENTS
14 oz/400 g canned apricot halves in syrup
⅔ cup vegetable stock (made from powder)
½ cup Marsala wine
½ tsp ground ginger
½ tsp ground cinnamon
salt and pepper

You will need a small pan, a wooden spoon, a measuring cup, and a blender

METHOD

1 Put the canned apricots and syrup into a blender and blend until smooth.

2 Pour the pureé into a pan, add the other ingredients, and mix well. Heat the sauce gently over low heat for about 4–5 minutes until warm. Season to taste.

3 Remove from the heat and pour into a serving pitcher. This sauce goes well with cured ham.

QUICK HORSERADISH SAUCE

Horseradish sauce is made using freshly grated horseradish, but this is difficult to find. An alternative can be made by using commercial horseradish sauce and mixing it with crème fraîche.

Serves 6–8
Preparation time: 2 minutes

INGREDIENTS
6 tbsp creamed horseradish sauce
6 tbsp crème fraîche

METHOD

1 In a small serving bowl, mix the horseradish and crème fraîche together. Serve the sauce with roast beef or smoked fish, such as trout or mackerel.

MINT SAUCE

Serves 6–8
Preparation time: 10 minutes, plus 30 minutes standing

INGREDIENTS
small bunch fresh mint leaves
2 tsp superfine sugar
2 tbsp boiling water
2 tbsp white wine vinegar

You will need a cook's knife, a cutting board, and a small bowl

METHOD

1 Make sure the mint is clean and tear the leaves from their stems. If the mint is dirty, wash it gently and dry thoroughly before tearing.

2 Place the leaves on the cutting board and sprinkle with the sugar. Chop the leaves finely (the sugar helps the chopping process) and place in a small bowl. Pour in the boiling water and stir to dissolve the sugar.

3 Add the vinegar and let stand for 30 minutes. This sauce goes particularly well with roast lamb.

POULTRY AND GAME

*P*oultry and game represent one of the healthiest sources of protein. They are mostly low in fat but rich in essential vitamins and minerals. And if your butcher or supermarket has done the preparation for you, poultry and game offer a good variety of reasonably quick and easy-to-prepare dishes, particularly roasts and casseroles.

We think of chicken as the main variety of poultry. It comes fresh or frozen, corn fed, or free range. You can eat all the meat—roasted whole, casseroled in quarters, or broiled breast portions and legs—then make a stock with the carcass. There is also turkey, which is traditional at Thanksgiving. And of course goose and duck—available whole or in breast portions—as well as guinea fowl or quail.

On the game side we have pheasant and partridge, squab, wild duck, and grouse. All can be cooked like chicken. However, since it is impossible to know their age, it is generally best to casserole them. Rabbit and venison are also traditional game dishes.

All of these birds and animals are discussed below, along with how to choose, prepare, and cook them. There is also a selection of recipes using poultry and game, both for everyday use and for special occasions. Traditional accompaniments are also included.

CHICKEN

Chicken is the most popular protein food. It is eaten in great quantities all over the world. Chickens are sold, oven-ready, either fresh or frozen, and can be reared in a variety of ways. Many chickens, for example, are kept in chicken houses and have no chance to run around. Free-range chicken categories are now governed by law :

Free-range chickens
These birds can roam in open air runs for half their average life (56 days). They must be fed at least 70 percent cereal.

Traditional free-range chickens
These are similar to the free-range chickens above but they have more space (only 4,888 birds allowed in each house!). They are from slow-growing breeds and have daytime access to open-air runs. Their average life is 81 days and their diet must be 70 percent cereal.

Free-range total freedom chickens
These chickens have free access to pasture land without any fenced runs.

Organic chickens
These chickens live in less crowded conditions, usually between 100–500 in a group. They have permanent access to pasture land. Their feed is at least 80 percent organic and the use of preventive antibiotics is banned.

Corn-fed chickens
These chickens can be reared in the standard or free-range system. The difference is that their feed must contain 50 percent corn, hence the deep corn color of the birds.

Choosing chicken
Always buy from a reputable supplier, such as a good butcher, or buy from the supermarket where you are sure of a quick turnover. Choose fresh birds for roasting, but frozen chickens and cut pieces are useful for casseroles. Fresh birds should look soft, plump, and creamy pink; they should not be scrawny, discolored, or bruised. If you want chicken portions, it is often cheaper to buy a whole chicken and ask the butcher to cut it up for you; that way you also get a variety of meat rather than all legs or breast portions. If you want to do it yourself, see opposite. Buy reputable frozen brands and do not store for too long: check the "use by" date on the packaging. Never buy frozen chicken that has damaged packaging.

Chicken pieces are available in all types and sizes: legs, drumsticks, thighs, and breast portions, whole, part-boned, boned, and skinned. Stir-fry strips and ground chicken are also available, and are economical and quick to cook.

STUFFING A CHICKEN

1 Use your hands or a spoon to place the stuffing in the neck end of the bird. Do not pack the stuffing in too tightly or the bird will not cook all the way through—this could encourage harmful bacteria to develop. Pull the skin over and secure with a poultry pin. Twist the wing tips up and over; tie the wings and legs with string.

CUTTING UP A CHICKEN

1 Put the bird breast-side up on a cutting board. Using a sharp knife, cut one leg away from the bird. Repeat with the other leg, then cut off both wings.

2 Use poultry shears or kitchen scissors to cut the breast in half from tail to neck. Turn the bird over and cut out the backbone. Remove the two breast pieces.

Sizes

Rock Cornish hens are the smallest chickens (4–6 weeks old). They weigh up to 1 lb/450 g and are ideal as a single portion. Larger young chickens (6–10 weeks old) are ideal for cooking on the barbecue, especially when butterflied (cut up the backbone and then flattened out). You can buy them ready prepared in the supermarket.

Roasting chickens are available from 3 lb/1.3 kg up to 6 lb/2.7 kg, and even larger ones are available sometimes. These birds are suitable for roasting and also for casseroling.

Storage

Take the chicken home as soon as possible after buying it. Unwrap and store it, lightly covered with plastic wrap, in the refrigerator. If it has giblets, remove them from the body at once, and use them within 24 hours. Use the chicken within 1–2 days. If you buy a packet of chicken portions and you do not need them all at once, put the remainder in individual freezer bags, seal well, and freeze for up to 3 months. They are very useful for when you just need a meal for one. Frozen chicken should be placed in the freezer at once until you want to use it, then it is best to thaw it the refrigerator overnight. Always make sure the chicken is thoroughly thawed before use. Do not refreeze it once it has been thawed.

COOKING CHICKEN

Roasting times and weights (including stuffing)
- 25 minutes per 1 lb/450 g at 375°F/190°C for a chicken weighing 2 lb/900 g to 3 lb/1.3 kg
- 20 minutes per 1 lb/450 g plus 20 minutes at 375°F/ 190°C for a chicken weighing 3 lb/1.3 kg to 4 lb/1.8 kg
- 20 minutes per 1 lb/450 g at 375°F/190°C for a chicken weighing 4 lb/1.8 kg to 6 lb/2.7 kg

If the bird is getting too brown, cover it with foil toward the end of cooking. Baste well every half an hour and check that it is cooked by piercing the thickest part of the leg with a sharp knife; if it is cooked thoroughly, the juices will run clear. You can also tug the leg to see if it comes away from the body easily. Never eat undercooked chicken—it can cause food poisoning.

Frying and broiling
Chicken legs and breast portions are most suitable for these types of cooking. For broiling, brush the breast portions with oil or melted butter to make sure they stay moist. The legs have enough fat in them not to need this. Season well before cooking. For frying, use a mixture of olive oil and a little butter, to give the chicken color and flavor.

All chicken is suitable for the barbecue. Breast portions are best if left on the bone because they will stay more moist. It is a good idea to marinate chicken pieces before cooking, because this helps the meat to stay moist through a fierce cooking process. It also adds additional flavors to the meat.

TURKEY

Whole turkeys are usually only available fresh in winter, but they are widely available frozen all year round. Turkey is a very healthy meat, and contains less than half the fat of chicken. It can be bought in many sizes, from tiny to massive. The most popular size range is between 6 lb/2.7 kg and 16 lb/7.2 kg. Turkey is extremely good hot or cold, so it makes an ideal meat for over the Thanksgiving period.

Like chickens, most turkeys are reared under intensive conditions, but there are now more free-range and organically reared free-range turkeys available. If you want a well-flavored bird, do consider these alternatives. The traditional breeds, which are more moist, such as the Cambridge bronze turkey, are making a comeback; they are reared specially for their

flavor and are allowed to hang for some time in order to develop it even further.

Choosing turkey
As with chicken, use a reliable supplier and buy according to your needs. If you are buying a frozen turkey, make sure you buy a reliable brand and let it thaw thoroughly before cooking—check on the label for times, but allow at least 10–12 hours in the refrigerator per 2 lb 4 oz/1 kg. At room temperature, allow 4–6 hours for the same weight, but as room temperatures vary, it is impossible to give exact guidance. Personally, I think thawing slowly in a refrigerator seems to be the safest method.

Turkey portions are available throughout the year. Thighs, drumsticks, breast portions, scallops, stir-fry strips, and ground turkey—are all good alternatives to red meat.

Storage
Always store turkey in the refrigerator as soon as possible after buying. There may be a space problem at Thanksgiving if your refrigerator is full to bursting, so collect it as late as possible from your supplier and, if the weather is cold, you can keep it in the trunk of the car overnight. Make sure you remove the giblets before storing in the car and keep the turkey well covered with plastic wrap or foil. Frozen turkeys should always be kept in the freezer until required to thaw. Turkey pieces should be treated like chicken, see above. Allow both types to come to room temperature before cooking.

COOKING TURKEY
It is difficult to give absolute times for roasting a turkey: it will depend on the breed, how it has been reared, how old it is, and the size. Start it off at a high temperature to get the fat running and the skin starting to crisp and color.

Roasting times and temperatures
Start by roasting at 425°F/220°C for 30 minutes, then cover with foil. Then cook for 15 minutes per 1 lb/450 g, plus 15 minutes at 350°F/180°C.

You may need to add 15–30 minutes extra if you are stuffing the body cavity. Baste every half an hour to make sure the bird is moist.

Remove the foil 30 minutes before the end of cooking to allow final browning. Test the bird is cooked by piercing a leg with a knife point: if the juices run clear, the bird is cooked.

Cover lightly with foil and let rest for 30 minutes in a warm place before carving.

Frying and broiling
Use turkey breast strips in stir-fries—turkey can replace chicken in any stir-fry recipe. Ground turkey can be used to make meatballs or turkey burgers.

Quail

Corn-fed chicken

Guinea fowl

Barbary duck

This is a much fattier bird. You need to allow about 1 lb 9 oz/700 g per person when buying a whole duckling or duck. Ducks are readily available in the stores and can be bought all year round. If you want to serve more than four people, it is probably best to buy two smaller ducklings because the meat will be more tender. Duck breast and legs are also available, ready to cook.

Choosing duck

Again, a good supplier is the answer. A fresh duck is preferable but a frozen one will suffice. Make sure it is well thawed and thoroughly dry before cooking. Most of the ducks available are home produced but we are getting more French ducks like Barbary, which are superior when bought as duck breasts.

Storage

You should bring the duck home as soon as possible after purchase and store it in the same way as you would store chicken (see page 141).

COOKING DUCK

Duck is very fatty and requires a high temperature to give it a crisp, golden finish. Cook it on a trivet or wire rack in a roasting pan so that the fat runs off and the base of the duck is crispy. Before cooking, use a skewer to prick the skin of the duck all over. Season well and start by roasting at 425°F/220°C for 15 minutes. Reduce the temperature to 350°F/180°C and cook for 30 minutes per 1 lb/450 g. Pour off excess fat from time to time; keep it in a screw-top jar in the refrigerator for roasting potatoes at a later date. It will keep for one month.

The duck should be really golden and crunchy but, if you feel it is getting too crisp, cover it with foil. Drain well and use kitchen scissors to "carve" the duck into fourths. Alternatively, you can use a knife to carve slices and smaller pieces but, since there is only a small amount of meat, it is a time-consuming task. Serve it with an orange sauce or apricot sauce (see page 139).

Duck breasts are good broiled or grilled, but the legs are rather tough and need precooking (simmering in stock) before roasting. They are also good cooked in casseroles.

Below: Use a carving fork or a skewer to prick the skin of the duck all over before roasting it. This allows the fat to run out. It is best not to stuff duck because it is too fatty. However, you could use a little chopped onion or apple to give it some flavor.

Below: Cooking the duck on a trivet or a wire rack allows the fat to run off and keeps the base of the bird crispy.

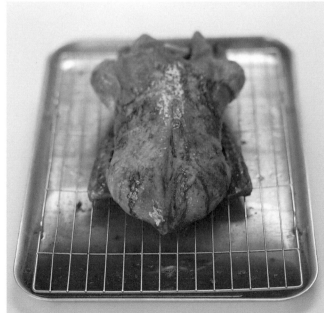

GOOSE

Goose has even more fat than duck, but it has delicious dark meat. You need at least 1½ lb/675 g raw weight per person. Fresh geese are usually only available near to Christmas, although city suppliers will probably be able to get some at other times. They tend to be raised on smaller farms and are often free-range. My own butcher raises his own geese annually. The way to tell a young goose is by its feet—they are soft and yellow; the older birds have drier, firmer feet. Frozen geese are available throughout the year and are a good substitute for fresh because they freeze well. Do make sure you thaw it properly and dry it well before cooking.

COOKING A GOOSE

Like duck, this bird is best cooked on a trivet and benefits from being cooked upside down first so that the base becomes crisp; then turn it over to cook the breast. It is best not to stuff it because so much fat is naturally given off during cooking that the stuffing can become very fatty, but you can place a cut apple and onion inside the cavity instead to give it some flavor. Prick the skin all over and roast the bird at 425°F/220°C for about 30 minutes. Turn the bird over and drain off the fat, which will have collected in the roasting pan. Keep the fat in a screw-top jar for making the best roast potatoes you will ever have. It will keep for one month in the refrigerator. Roast for a further 15 minutes and then turn the oven down to 350°F/180°C and collect the fat again. Store the fat in a screw-top jar in the refrigerator. Continue to roast for 15 minutes per 1 lb/450 g until the bird is really crisp. Cover with foil toward the end of cooking if you feel that the goose is getting too brown. Carve the goose carefully and serve it with some cooked purple sprouting broccoli and red cabbage casserole (see page 168).

GAME

This is the term given to wild animals and birds that are hunted, but nowadays they are often bred specially for the table. Game meat has become very popular because it is less fatty and healthier than meat from other species. Game only used to be available from specialist game dealers, but it is now to be found in most supermarkets, fresh when in season or frozen. Take care, when eating any game, to look for any shot that might still be in the flesh—biting on it can be an unpleasant experience.

Pheasant

These are intensively reared for shooting—the season is from October to February. If you buy from a supermarket, they will not have been hung for long, so they will have a milder flavor than those you might buy from a game dealer. The female is tenderer than the male and tends to be slightly fatter. Pheasant can be roasted but, since the age will be unknown, it is best to casserole it.

Grouse

These birds are in season in from August until December. They are small birds, and weigh about 1lb 10oz/750 g, so one is suitable for one person. The meat is very dark. Roast at 375°F/190°C for 30–35 minutes. It is a good idea to wrap them in bacon to keep them moist. Older birds can be casseroled according to any game or chicken recipes.

Rabbit

These are usually bred for the table but sometimes wild jack rabbit is available, which has a stronger flavor. Farmed rabbit is a bit like chicken. It is best cooked in a casserole because the meat can be very dry. Boned rabbit is available in some supermarkets and would be a good way to try this meat for the first time.

Venison

This is the meat from hunted wild deer, but it is now also available farmed all year round. It is a good, red meat and can be used in many ways like beef. It is a healthier meat, lower in cholesterol, and is becoming very popular. The best meat comes from a male deer under the age of 2 years. It can be bought as a roast (haunch and saddle) and as prepared meat for braising and casseroles (shoulder and neck). Owing to the dry nature of venison, casseroling is the best way to enjoy the meat's flavor and texture. However, if you live somewhere where you have access to freshly hunted venison, a roast saddle would be a great treat.

ROAST CHICKEN

Chicken is an ever-popular favorite. Simply roasted, with lots of thyme and garlic, chicken produces a succulent gastronomic feast for many occasions. You can make a thicker gravy with giblet stock (see page 61), using the method for roast turkey (see pages 152–3).

Serves 6
Preparation time: 15 minutes
Cooking time: 2¼ hours

INGREDIENTS

5 lb/2.25 kg free-range chicken
4 tbsp butter
2 tbsp chopped fresh thyme (lemon thyme if possible)
3 garlic cloves, peeled and crushed
1 lemon, cut into fourths
½ cup white wine
salt and pepper
6 sprigs fresh thyme, to garnish

To serve
1 quantity bread sauce (see page 157)
cooked new potatoes
salad greens

You will need a small roasting pan, a cook's knife, a cutting board, a bowl, a measuring cup, a fork, and a wooden spatula

METHOD

1 Preheat the oven to 425°F/220°C. Make sure the chicken is clean: wipe it inside and out using paper towels and place it in the roasting pan.

2 In a bowl, soften the butter with a fork, mix in the thyme and garlic, and season well.

3 Butter the chicken all over with the herb butter, inside and out, and place the lemon fourths inside the body cavity.

4 Roast in the center of the preheated oven for 20 minutes. Reduce the temperature to 375°F/190°C, add half of the wine, and continue to roast for another 1¼ hours, basting frequently. If the pan dries out too much, add 2–3 tablespoons of wine or water.

5 Test that the chicken is cooked by piercing the thickest part of the leg with a sharp knife or skewer and make sure the juices run clear. Remove from the oven.

6 Lift out the chicken from the roasting pan, place it on a warm serving plate, cover with foil, and let rest for 10 minutes before carving.

7 Place the roasting pan the stovetop, add the remaining wine, and simmer gently over low heat for 2–3 minutes until the pan juices have reduced and are thick and glossy. Taste and adjust the seasoning.

8 Sprinkle over the thyme sprigs, then serve the chicken with the pan juices, along with some bread sauce, new potatoes, and salad greens.

WINE SUGGESTION

A medium red Burgundy, such as Nuits St. Georges, goes well with this chicken.

CHICKEN DAUPHINOISE

Serves 4
Preparation time: 25 minutes
Cooking time: 1–1½ hours

INGREDIENTS

1 lb 8 oz/675 g trimmed leeks
10 oz/280 g small, waxy potatoes
1 tbsp olive oil
1 garlic clove, peeled and chopped
scant 1 cup soft cheese with garlic and herbs
½ cup white wine
¾ cup chicken stock
2 tsp cornstarch
4 skinless, boneless chicken breast portions
2 tbsp butter, melted
salt and pepper
2 tbsp chopped fresh parsley, to garnish

You will need a large, shallow ovenproof dish (about 7½ cup capacity), a skillet, a cook's knife, a measuring cup, a cutting board, and a blender

WINE SUGGESTION

This dish really needs a rich New Zealand Chardonnay, but if a red is preferred, try a cool red Beaujolais.

METHOD

1 Preheat the oven to 350ºF/180°C. Clean and thickly slice the leeks.

2 Slice the potatoes as thinly as possible.

3 Heat the olive oil in a skillet over medium heat and cook the leeks and garlic for 3–4 minutes until beginning to soften. Remove from the heat and put the leeks in the ovenproof dish.

4 Place the cheese, wine, stock, and cornstarch in a blender and process until smooth.

5 Arrange the chicken pieces on top of the leeks, season well, and pour in the sauce.

6 Layer the potatoes on top, season, and brush very thoroughly with the melted butter.

7 Cook in the preheated oven for about 1–1½ hours until the potatoes are well cooked and brown. Serve at once with the parsley sprinkled over.

R O A S T   G O O S E

Goose has become unfashionable in recent times owing to its high fat content and the fact that you get little meat in proportion to the carcass; you need to buy 1½ lb/675 g dressed weight per person. It is best not to stuff it because so much fat is naturally given off during cooking that the stuffing can become very fatty. It is best to place flavorings, such as onions and lemons, inside the body and cook the stuffing separately.

Serves 6
Preparation time: 15 minutes
Cooking time: 2¼–2½ hours

INGREDIENTS

8 lb 8 oz/4 kg goose
1 onion, peeled and coarsely chopped
1 apple, coarsely chopped
1 lemon, cut into fourths
2 sprigs fresh sage
1 tbsp all-purpose flour
1½ cups giblet stock (see page 61)
salt and pepper

To serve
sage and onion stuffing (see page 159)
apple sauce
roast potatoes (see page 173)
red cabbage casserole (see page 168)
cooked vegetable such as purple sprouting broccoli

You will need a large, solid roasting pan with a trivet, a cook's knife, a cutting board, some aluminum foil, and a small whisk or a wooden spatula

METHOD

1 Preheat the oven to 200°C/400°F/200°C. Make sure the goose is clean: wipe it inside and out using paper towels. Remove any excess fat from inside the body cavity. Season well, rubbing the salt into the skin. Place the onion, apple, lemon, and sage inside the body cavity.

2 Place the bird, upside down, on a rack in a roasting pan, and use a skewer to prick the skin all over to let the fat run out during cooking.

3 Roast in the preheated oven for 15 minutes until the skin is starting to crisp, then turn over and roast for 15 minutes more. Pour off the excess fat and retain. Baste, reduce the temperature to 350°F/180°C, and continue to roast for 2 hours more, basting frequently. Carefully pour off the excess fat each time, and keep it for roasting potatoes—it is delicious. If the goose is getting too brown, cover it with foil.

4 Test that the goose is cooked by piercing the thickest part of the leg with a sharp knife or skewer: the juices should run clear if it is cooked thoroughly.

5 Lift out the goose from the roasting place and place on a warm serving plate, cover with foil, and let rest while you complete the meal.

6 Carefully drain the excess fat from the pan, leaving about 2 tablespoons in the pan, and place it over low heat on the stovetop. Sprinkle in the flour and stir well using a small whisk or wooden spatula. Scrape all the crusty bits off the base of the pan and cook for 1 minute. Pour in the giblet stock, a little at a time, whisking constantly until smooth. Simmer over medium heat for 3–4 minutes until the gravy is the correct consistency and has reduced a little. Taste, and adjust the seasoning.

7 Carefully pour the gravy into a warmed serving pitcher and serve with the goose and accompaniments.

> **WINE** SUGGESTION
>
> An Italian red Barolo or merlot will go well with roast goose.

DUCK BREAST SALAD

Serves 4
Preparation time: 10 minutes
Cooking time: 15–20 minutes

INGREDIENTS

4 duck breast fillets, about 6 oz/175 g each

½ inch/1 cm piece fresh ginger root, peeled and finely chopped

2 tbsp soy sauce

2 tbsp honey

2 tbsp lemon juice

4 oz/115 g mixed salad greens, including arugula and watercress or mizuna

4 oz/115 g sugar snap peas, blanched for 1 minute

salt and pepper

You will need a sharp knife, a heavy skillet with a heatproof handle that will go into the oven or an ordinary skillet, a roasting pan and a large serving plate

METHOD

1 Preheat the oven to 450º/230°C. Use a sharp knife to score the skin on the duck breasts diagonally, about ½ inch/1 cm apart. Repeat in the other direction to make a diamond pattern.

2 Heat the dry skillet over high heat and place the duck breasts in it, skin side down, and cook for 4–5 minutes until golden. Turn over the breasts and place the skillet in the oven or transfer the duck to a roasting pan.

3 Cook at the top of the preheated oven for 10–15 minutes, depending how rare you like your duck.

4 Remove the duck from the skillet or pan, cover with foil, and let rest on a warm serving plate in a warm place while you make the sauce.

5 If there is excess fat in the skillet or pan, spoon out all but 2 tablespoons. Place the pan on the stovetop and add the ginger. Stir well and scrape all the sediment from the base. Spoon in the soy sauce, honey, and lemon juice and mix well. Bubble for a minute until thick, then season to taste.

6 Slice the duck thinly and lay on a large serving plate. Arrange the salad greens alongside and pour the sauce over the duck. You can also serve the duck and greens on individual serving plates.

7 Sprinkle over the peas and serve just warm.

WINE SUGGESTION
A Californian Zinfandel or an Australian red blend would go well with this salad.

COQ AU VIN

A delicious chicken casserole, cooked in red wine with pearl onions and mushrooms. Like all casseroles, this benefits from being made the day before. Cool it quickly and then reheat it when needed.

Serves 8
Preparation time: 40 minutes
Cooking time: 1½ hours

INGREDIENTS

2 tbsp all-purpose flour

4 lb/1.8 kg fresh chicken, cut into 8 pieces (ask your butcher to do this or use 8 chicken joints)

2 tbsp olive oil

2 tbsp butter

8 oz/225 g lardons or fatty bacon, cut into strips

1 lb/450 g pearl onions, peeled

3 cups red wine

2 garlic cloves, peeled and crushed

1 bouquet garni (see page 50)

4¾ cups white mushrooms

2 tbsp chopped fresh parsley

salt and pepper

You will need a large, flameproof casserole dish (about 15 cup capacity), a large plastic bag, a cook's knife, a cutting board, a measuring cup, a slotted spoon, and a serving dish

WINE SUGGESTION

A spicy red Burgundy would be good with this dish—try a Côte de Beaume.

METHOD

1 Preheat the oven to 350°F/180°C. Season the flour and put it into a large plastic bag. Add the chicken and shake well to coat it evenly. Heat the oil and butter in the casserole dish. Cook the chicken over high heat for 5–6 minutes until browned. You will need to do this in two batches. Lift it out of the casserole and keep warm. Fry the bacon in the casserole for 3–4 minutes until crisp and well colored. Lift it out and keep it warm.

2 Cook the onions over high heat for 4–5 minutes until they begin to brown. Pour in the wine and stir well to remove any sediment from the base of the casserole dish.

3 Return the bacon and chicken to the casserole dish and add the garlic and bouquet garni. Bring to a boil, cover, then cook in the center of the preheated oven for 1¼ hours.

4 Add the mushrooms and cook for a further 15 minutes. Discard the bouquet garni and use a slotted spoon to lift out the chicken pieces, bacon, onion, and mushrooms. Put them in a serving dish and keep them warm.

5 Return the casserole and its juices to low heat and check for seasoning. Boil rapidly until the sauce is thick and glossy. Pour the sauce over the dish and serve immediately, garnished with the parsley.

Suitable for freezing. Prepare up the end of step 5. Place the chicken in a rigid, lidded container, pour in the sauce, cool, and freeze for up to 3 months. To use, thaw and reheat on the stovetop or in the oven at 350°F/180°C for 40–45 minutes.

CLASSIC ROAST TURKEY

Traditional roast turkey cannot be beaten. It is a seasonal favorite that many people enjoy. There is much discussion as to whether it is good to stuff the bird; here we use a light celery and walnut stuffing for the body, which is not too dense and also keeps the bird moist, and a traditional chestnut stuffing for the neck. Stuffing should not be packed too tightly because it prevents the bird cooking properly. There are also recipes for bread sauce and cranberry sauce (see page 157).

Serves 10

WINE SUGGESTION

Try a Riesling if you prefer white, but a lighter Bordeaux red would be good—Mèdoc for example.

Preparation time: 20 minutes
Cooking time: 3½–4 hours

INGREDIENTS

10 lb/4.5 kg turkey
1 quantity celery and walnut stuffing (see page 158)
1 quantity chestnut stuffing (see page 158)
½ cup butter, softened
10 strips fatty bacon
2 tbsp all-purpose flour
4 cups giblet stock (see page 61)
½ cup red wine
salt and pepper

You will need a large, solid roasting pan, a wooden spatula, a measuring cup, metal skewers, string, some aluminum foil, and a large serving plate

1 Preheat the oven to 425°F/220°C. Make sure the turkey is clean—use paper towels to wipe it inside and out. Season inside and out. Stuff the body cavity with the celery and walnut stuffing and the neck with the chestnut stuffing. Secure the neck skin with metal skewers and the legs with string.

2 Butter the bird all over and squeeze some under the breast skin. Use a little to grease the roasting pan. Place the bird in the pan, season again and cover the breast with the bacon strips. Cover the bird with aluminum foil and roast in the preheated oven for 30 minutes. Reduce the temperature to 350°F/180°C and continue to cook for 2½–3 hours.

3 Baste the turkey with the pan juices every 30 minutes. Forty-five minutes before the end of the cooking time, remove the foil and let the turkey brown, basting from time to time. Remove the bacon when crispy and keep it warm.

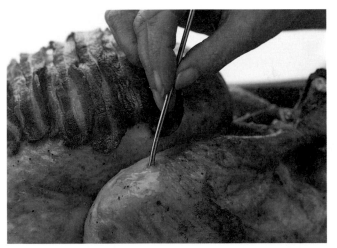

4 Test that the turkey is cooked by piercing the thickest part of the leg with a skewer: the juices should run clear. Also, pull a leg away from the body: it should feel loose. Lift the turkey from the pan, put it on a warm serving plate, cover with foil, and let rest for up to 1 hour.

5 Drain the fat from the pan; place the pan on low heat on the stovetop. Sprinkle in the flour and stir to a smooth paste. Cook for 1 minute. Pour in the stock, a little at a time, whisking constantly until smooth. Add the wine and cook for 3–4 minutes until the gravy is the correct consistency and has reduced a little.

6 Taste, and adjust the seasoning. During the carving of the turkey there will be some meat juices escaping—add these to the pan. Carefully pour the gravy into a warmed serving pitcher and serve.

VENISON CASSEROLE

This casserole benefits from being made the day before to let the flavors develop. Reheat gently before serving, either on the stovetop or in a preheated oven at 350°F/180°C for 35–40 minutes. Make sure you cool the casserole as quickly as possible and store, covered, in the refrigerator or a cool pantry overnight.

Serves 6
Preparation time: 30 minutes
Cooking time: 2½ hours

INGREDIENTS

3 tbsp olive oil
2 lb 4 oz/1 kg casserole venison, cut into 1¼ inch/ 3 cm cubes
2 onions, peeled and thinly sliced
2 garlic cloves, peeled and chopped
1½ cups beef or vegetable stock
2 tbsp all-purpose flour
½ cup port or red wine
2 tbsp red currant jelly
6 juniper berries, crushed
4 cloves, crushed
pinch of cinnamon
small grating of nutmeg
salt and pepper
baked or mashed potatoes, to serve

You will need a casserole dish (about 7½ cup capacity), a cook's knife, a cutting board, a skillet, a measuring cup, a wooden spatula, and a slotted spoon

METHOD

1 Preheat the oven to 350°F/180°C. Heat the oil in a large skillet and cook the cubes of venison over high heat for 2–3 minutes until brown. You may need to cook the meat in two or three batches—do not overcrowd the skillet. Remove the venison from the skillet using a slotted spoon and place in the casserole dish.

2 Add the onion and garlic to the skillet and cook over medium heat for about 3 minutes until a good golden color, then lift out, and add to the meat.

3 Gradually add the stock to the skillet, stir well, and scrape up the sediment, then bring to a boil.

4 Sprinkle the meat in the casserole dish with the flour and turn to coat evenly.

5 Add the hot stock to the casserole and stir well, making sure that the meat is just covered.

6 Add the wine, red currant jelly, and the spices.

7 Season well, cover, and cook gently in the center of the preheated oven for 2–2½ hours.

8 Remove from the oven, check the seasoning, and adjust if necessary. Serve immediately piping hot with baked or mashed potatoes.

* Suitable for freezing. Complete up the end of step 7, then cool, and pour into a rigid, lidded container. Freeze for up to 3 months. To use, thaw at room temperature for 5–6 hours or overnight and reheat gently when needed.

WINE SUGGESTION
Try a full-bodied Bordeaux, such as Pomerol or an Australian Shiraz.

MUSTARD RABBIT

This casserole also benefits from being made the day before to allow the flavors to develop. Make sure you cool the casserole as quickly as possible and store, covered, in the refrigerator or a cool pantry overnight. Reheat gently for 35–40 minutes before serving.

Serves 4
Preparation time: 20 minutes
Cooking time: 1½ hours

INGREDIENTS

2 tbsp all-purpose flour

1 oven-ready rabbit (about 2 lb/900 g), cut into pieces

1 tbsp olive oil

1 tbsp butter

3½ oz/100 g lardons or fatty bacon, cut into strips

4 shallots, peeled and chopped

1 garlic clove, peeled and chopped

⅔ cup dry white wine

1 cup chicken or vegetable stock

3 tbsp wholegrain mustard

1¾ cups white mushrooms, thinly sliced

½ cup heavy cream

salt and pepper

2 tbsp chopped fresh parsley, to garnish

You will need a casserole dish (about 8¾ cups capacity), a cook's knife, a cutting board, a large skillet, a measuring cup, a wooden spatula, a slotted spoon, a large plastic bag, and a large serving dish

METHOD

1 Season the flour well, put it into a large plastic bag, and add the rabbit pieces. Shake well to coat the pieces evenly.

2 Heat the oil and butter in the skillet. Cook the rabbit over high heat for 4–5 minutes until brown. Use a slotted spoon to lift the pieces from the skillet and put in the casserole dish.

3 Preheat the oven to 325°F/160°C. Add the bacon to the skillet and cook over medium heat for 3–4 minutes until crisp and golden, then transfer to the casserole dish.

4 Add the shallots and garlic to the skillet and sauté for 2–3 minutes until soft and brown.

5 Pour in the wine and scrape all the sediment from the base of the skillet. Add the stock and bring to a boil, then simmer for 2 minutes.

6 Stir in the mustard and then pour the contents of the skillet over the rabbit in the casserole dish.

7 Season well, cover, and cook in the center of the preheated oven for 2–2½ hours until the rabbit is tender.

8 Add the mushrooms 15 minutes before the end of the cooking time and stir well. Remove from the oven. Transfer the rabbit, using a slotted spoon, to a warm serving plate.

9 Place the casserole on the stovetop and simmer to the desired consistency. Adjust the seasoning if necessary.

10 Stir in the cream, then pour the sauce over the rabbit in the serving dish. Serve immediately garnished with the chopped parsley.

* Suitable for freezing. Make up to the end of step 8. Cool, then freeze in a rigid, lidded container for up to 3 months. To use, thaw overnight in the refrigerator, then reheat in the oven at 325°F/170°C for 35–40 minutes before adding the cream and garnish.

WINE SUGGESTION
Try a full-bodied Italian red Montalcino with this dish.

PHEASANT AND CHESTNUT CASSEROLE

This casserole benefits from being made the day before. Cool it as quickly as possible, cover, and store in the refrigerator or a cool pantry overnight. Reheat gently on the stovetop or in the oven at 350°F/180°C for 30—35 minutes.

Serves 4
Preparation time: 30 minutes
Cooking time: 1½–2 hours

INGREDIENTS

1 tbsp olive oil
2 tbsp butter
1 large, prepared pheasant, cut into pieces
6 oz/175 g lardons or fatty bacon, cut into strips
8 oz/225 g vacuum-packed chestnuts
2 onions, peeled and thinly sliced
1 garlic clove, peeled and chopped
2 tbsp all-purpose flour
scant 2 cups game or vegetable stock
⅔ cup red wine
rind and juice of 1 orange
2 tbsp red currant jelly
salt and pepper

To garnish
1 whole orange, sliced
small bunch fresh watercress or mizuna

You will need a casserole dish (about 8¾ cup capacity), a cook's knife, a cutting board, a measuring cup, kitchen tongs, a slotted spoon, and a large skillet

METHOD

1 Melt the oil and butter in a large skillet. Add the pheasant pieces and cook over high heat for 4–5 minutes until brown. Use a slotted spoon to remove the pheasant from the skillet and place in the casserole dish.

2 Add the bacon to the skillet and cook over medium heat for 2–3 minutes until crisp and golden, then transfer to the casserole dish.

3 Preheat the oven to 350°F/180°C. Gently cook the chestnuts over low heat for 3–4 minutes until lightly browned, then transfer to the casserole.

4 Add the onions and garlic to the skillet and sauté over medium heat for 2–3 minutes until soft and brown.

5 Stir in the flour and mix well to prevent any lumps. Add the stock, a little at a time, and gradually mix with the onions, scrape up the sediment, and bring to a boil. Pour in the wine.

6 Pour the contents of the skillet over the pheasant in the casserole dish.

7 Add the orange rind and juice and the red currant jelly. Season well, cover, and cook in the center of the preheated oven for 1½–2 hours until the pheasant is tender. Turn the pheasant pieces in the sauce halfway through.

8 Remove from the oven, then check the seasoning, and adjust if necessary.

9 Serve garnished with the slices of orange and a little fresh watercress or mizuna.

* Suitable for freezing. Complete up the end of step 8. Cool, then pour into a rigid, lidded container. Freeze for up to 3 months. To use, thaw at room temperature overnight and reheat gently when needed.

WINE SUGGESTION

Try a powerful red Californian Pinot Noir, or a white Australian Riesling with this casserole.

BREAD SAUCE

This is a traditional accompaniment to turkey, but it is also very useful for serving with cold meats, such as chicken and cured or smoked ham.

Serves 6–8
Preparation time: 10 minutes
Cooking time: 1 hour 20 minutes

INGREDIENTS

1 onion
12 cloves
1 bay leaf
6 black peppercorns
2½ cups milk
2 cups fresh white bread crumbs
2 tbsp butter
whole nutmeg, for grating
2 tbsp heavy cream, optional
salt and pepper

You will need a pan (preferably nonstick), a wooden spoon, a small knife, and a grater

METHOD

1 Make small holes in the onion using the point of a sharp knife or a skewer, and stick the cloves in them.

2 Put the onion, bay leaf, and peppercorns in a pan and pour in the milk. Bring to a boil, then remove from the heat, cover, and leave to steep for 1 hour.

3 To make the sauce, discard the onion and bay leaf, and strain the milk to remove the peppercorns. Return the milk to the cleaned pan and add the bread crumbs.

4 Cook the sauce over very low heat for 4–5 minutes until the bread crumbs have swollen and the sauce is thick.

5 Beat in the butter and season well with the salt and pepper, and a good grating of nutmeg. Stir in the cream just before serving, if using.

CRANBERRY SAUCE

Serves 6–8
Preparation time: 2 minutes
Cooking time: 10 minutes

INGREDIENTS

2 cups fresh cranberries
6 tbsp soft brown sugar
⅔ cup orange juice
½ tsp ground cinnamon
½ tsp grated nutmeg

You will need a pan and a wooden spoon

METHOD

1 Place the cranberries, sugar, orange juice, and spices in a pan and stir well.

2 Cover the pan and bring slowly to a boil over gentle heat.

3 Simmer for 8–10 minutes until the cranberries have burst. Take care because they may splash.

4 Put the sauce in a serving bowl and cover until needed. Serve warm or cold.

CELERY AND WALNUT STUFFING

This is a delicious stuffing for turkey, but it is also good with chicken and duck. If you are using it to stuff a chicken, you will need only half the quantity.

Makes enough for a large turkey about 12 lb/5.5 kg
Preparation time: 15 minutes
Cooking time: 10 minutes, plus extra for the bird

INGREDIENTS

2 onions, peeled and finely chopped
2 tbsp butter
2 cups fresh whole-wheat bread crumbs
4 stalks celery, trimmed and chopped
2 eating apples, cored and roughly chopped
½ cup dried ready-to-eat apricots, chopped
1 cup walnuts, chopped
2 tbsp chopped fresh parsley
salt and pepper

You will need a cook's knife, a cutting board, a small pan, a mixing bowl, and a wooden spatula

METHOD

1 Put the onions and butter in a pan and cook gently over low heat for 2–3 minutes until soft but not colored.

2 In a bowl, combine the bread crumbs, celery, apples, apricots, and walnuts. Add the cooked onions and season to taste.

3 Stir in the parsley and use to stuff a turkey. If you have a small turkey, then you might have some stuffing left over. If you have, cook this in am ovenproof dish in the oven at 350°F/ 180°C for 30–40 minutes. Alternatively, cover with plastic wrap and store in the refrigerator for 3–4 days.

CHESTNUT STUFFING

This recipe makes a classic stuffing for turkey.

Makes enough for a turkey of about 12 lb/5.5 kg
Preparation time: 15 minutes
Cooking time: 10 minutes

INGREDIENTS

4 oz/115 g lardons or fatty bacon, cut into strips
1 onion, peeled and finely chopped
2 tbsp butter
1⅔ cups sliced white mushrooms
scant 1 cup chestnut purée
scant 1 cup fresh whole-wheat bread crumbs
2 tbsp chopped fresh parsley
grated rind of 2 lemons
salt and pepper

You will need a cook's knife, a cutting board, a skillet, a mixing bowl, a wooden spatula, a grater, and a fork

METHOD

1 In the skillet, gently cook the bacon and onion in the butter over low heat for 2–3 minutes until soft and just beginning to color.

2 Add the mushrooms and cook for 1–2 minutes, then remove from the heat.

3 In a mixing bowl, fork over the chestnut purée and break it up. Mix in the bread crumbs, parsley, and lemon rind.

4 Add the contents of the skillet and mix well. Season to taste.

5 Cool before using to stuff the neck end of the turkey.

SAGE AND ONION STUFFING

Sage and onion stuffing is underrated. Sage is a wonderful herb if used carefully and when fresh. It goes really well with fattier meats like duck, goose, and pork, but it can also be used with chicken.

Makes enough for a chicken or small pork roast
Preparation time: 10 minutes
Cooking time: 10 minutes

INGREDIENTS

2 tbsp butter
2 onions, peeled and finely chopped
2 cups fresh white bread crumbs
1 tbsp chopped fresh sage leaves
salt and pepper

You will need a pan, a mixing bowl, a cook's knife, a cutting board, and a wooden spatula

METHOD

1 Melt the butter over low heat in a pan. Add the onions and cook gently over low heat for 2–3 minutes until soft but not colored.

2 In a separate bowl, combine the bread crumbs and sage. Add the cooked onions and season to taste.

3 You can use the mixture to stuff a chicken or a pork roast. If you want to serve this stuffing with goose or duck, place it in an ovenproof dish and bake at 350°F/180°C for 30–45 minutes.

VEGETABLES AND SALADS

*U*nder this heading we have the widest range of food varieties, with different ones available at different times of the year. Buy them fresh when they are in season to get the best quality of flavors and textures.

Root vegetables, such as parsnips, carrots, and rutabaga, are at their best in winter; use them in thick soups or roasts. Potatoes, the best known of the root vegetables, are wonderful roasted, baked, or mashed, or simply boiled when new in the summer.

Brassicas, such as broccoli, cabbage, cauliflowers, and sprouts, are generally best in the winter too. They are usually served with roasts, but can make wonderful dishes on their own. Pods—the various forms of peas and beans—are equally good with meat, fish, game, or in compilation dishes such as risottos.

Greens are even more versatile: spinach is good cooked or raw in salads, as are the range of lettuces and the new range of greens including arugula, bok choy, and mizuna, which now make summer salads so tasty.

There is a range of tomatoes too—for cooking or salads, in sauces and in purées—as well as mushrooms, garlic, bell peppers, and chiles, all of which add flavors to hot and cold dishes. Onions and leeks also add flavor in summer and winter.

Most vegetables used to be boiled before serving, but roasting and broiling brings out the flavors and conserves their nutritional value much better. Remember: eat vegetables raw as much as you can for the healthiest eating of all.

Organic vegetables are making an increasing appearance now and need to be bought to taste the real vegetable flavors. How often you buy them is up to your preference and budget.

ROOTS

Botanically speaking, we should call some of these tubers, but we will stick to roots and include all the vegetables grown below the ground.

Potatoes

Potatoes come in all shapes and sizes. New potatoes mean exactly that and come in different varieties; the most sought after are Jersey Royals. Simply boil them unpeeled with a little mint and serve with butter. Older potatoes can be used in different ways—for boiling, mashing, baking, roasting, and

frying. There are many types of potato, varying from waxy to mealy. Use the small, waxy varieties, such as Pink Fir Apple, for salads and choose mealy ones, such as King Edwards or Maris Piper, for baked and mashed potatoes. A good all-rounder, such as Cara or Desirée, is good for French fries. Buy and use new potatoes as needed, but you can store maincrop potatoes in a cool, dark place for some weeks.

Carrots

Buy baby carrots when in season and maincrop all year round. Eat them raw, whole or grated, boiled, steamed, and roasted.

Parsnips

These are best in winter; buy medium-size roots with a smooth skin. Parboil and then roast them. Parsnips also make a good purée and are good in soups.

Rutabaga and turnips

Large turnips and rutabaga need to be peeled thickly and are best boiled and mashed. Baby turnips are delicious plainly boiled and served with butter; they also roast well.

Celery root

A very knobby looking vegetable with a thick skin. Peel it thickly, boil, and then mash it—it has a delicious celery flavor.

Beet

Buy small to medium-size beet. Peel and grate them raw for salads, or boil, bake, or roast in their skins and serve hot.

Jerusalem artichokes

These are knobby but there are rearing varieties that are easier to peel. They are delicious roasted and are good in soup.

Radish

This is the smallest root vegetable. Use it in salads and as a snack with drinks. Slice larger radishes for use as a garnish.

White sante potato

Maris bard potatoes

Red salad potatoes

Baby new potatoes

Carrots

Parsnips

Radishes

Beet

French onion

Shallots

Scallions

Leek

Red onion

Fresh garlic

BULBS

This category includes all the onions and leeks (see page 161). Buy bulbs that are firm and crisp, and reject any that have discolored skin or that are sprouting. Bulbs can be stored in a dark, airy place.

Onions

Onions are available in yellow, white, and red, in a vast range of sizes. The ordinary yellow onion is the one normally used for cooking—softened before adding to sauces and casseroles, sliced and cooked slowly for onion tart, chopped and used in stuffings, and baked whole. White and red onions are sold for their color and flavor. Red onions have a sweet, mild flavor and are good eaten raw in salads or broiled. White onions have a stronger flavor.

Shallots

These small onions divide into cloves when peeled. They have a very mild flavor and are used in dishes when a gentle onion taste is required. Shallots are also good roasted whole with other vegetables.

Pearl onions

These are the smallest onions and are grown specifically for pickling. They are useful for dishes such as coq au vin, where small, whole onions are required. They are also handy for kabobs, where they can be cooked with pieces of meat or skewered and broiled as part of a vegetable kabob.

Leeks

Buy leeks in small to medium sizes because large ones tend to be tough. Clean them thoroughly before use. Leeks are good simply sliced and boiled as an accompaniment or they can be used in place of onions in some dishes where a milder flavor is required. Leeks can also be served with a cheese sauce as a dish on their own, or wrapped in cured or smoked ham.

Scallions

These young onions are usually eaten raw in salads. They look attractive when sliced and are often used as a garnish. Scallions can also be stir-fried as part of a dish and are a useful addition to soups. Buy them frequently and use within 2–3 days for maximum freshness.

Garlic

Buy whole heads of garlic that are plump and firm. Garlic is an indispensable ingredient in many dishes; use it in any dish that needs its pungent aroma and flavor. Garlic is usually chopped and sautéed as part of a recipe, but it can also be crushed and added to salad dressings and stuffings, or roasted whole with other vegetables.

GREENS

Cabbages

Buy cabbages that feel firm and crisp and heavy in the hand. Avoid any with blemishes or discolorings. For years cabbage had been an unpopular vegetable owing to overcooking. However, it is delicious and also healthy when finely shredded, steamed, boiled, or stir-fried quickly, with a little spice added. Some cabbage can be eaten raw in salads. Red, green, and white varieties are available.

Brussels sprouts

These are available in the winter around Christmas time. Take care not to overcook them or their flavor and texture will be ruined. They are also good shredded in salads or shredded and added to stir-fries.

Cauliflower

Cauliflowers are not really "green," but they fit into this category. Buy really white heads without any blemishes. Divide them into flowerets and steam or boil gently. They can be eaten raw in salads. They are often served with a cheese sauce as a supper dish, and are good mixed with broccoli. They can be used in stir-fries and as part of a vegetable curry to add color and texture, or to make soup.

Broccoli

Purple sprouting broccoli is the original broccoli and is only available for a short period. Steam or boil it gently, and serve it with butter and a grating of nutmeg; it is absolutely delicious. Calabrese (a variety of green sprouting broccoli) is readily available all year round. Buy it when the color is a rich, dark blue-green; avoid any that is turning yellow. Simply divide it into flowerets and then steam, boil, or stir-fry it. It also makes good soup.

Spinach

Spinach is rich in iron and is therefore very nutritious. You should buy it on the day you want to use it, to be sure of maximum freshness. Baby spinach is wonderful raw in salads. Buy fresh leaves without any sign of yellowing. Wash the leaves well in lots of cold running water first, and then quickly stir-fry them or reduce them in a hot pan until just wilted. Season well and serve with butter and nutmeg. Spinach soup is very good.

Napa cabbages

These are available all year round. They are a versatile vegetable because they can be used as a cabbage and as salad greens. Make sure the leaves are fresh and crisp when buying; they will keep for 3–4 days in the refrigerator. Slice finely to serve in salads; steam or stir-fry to serve hot.

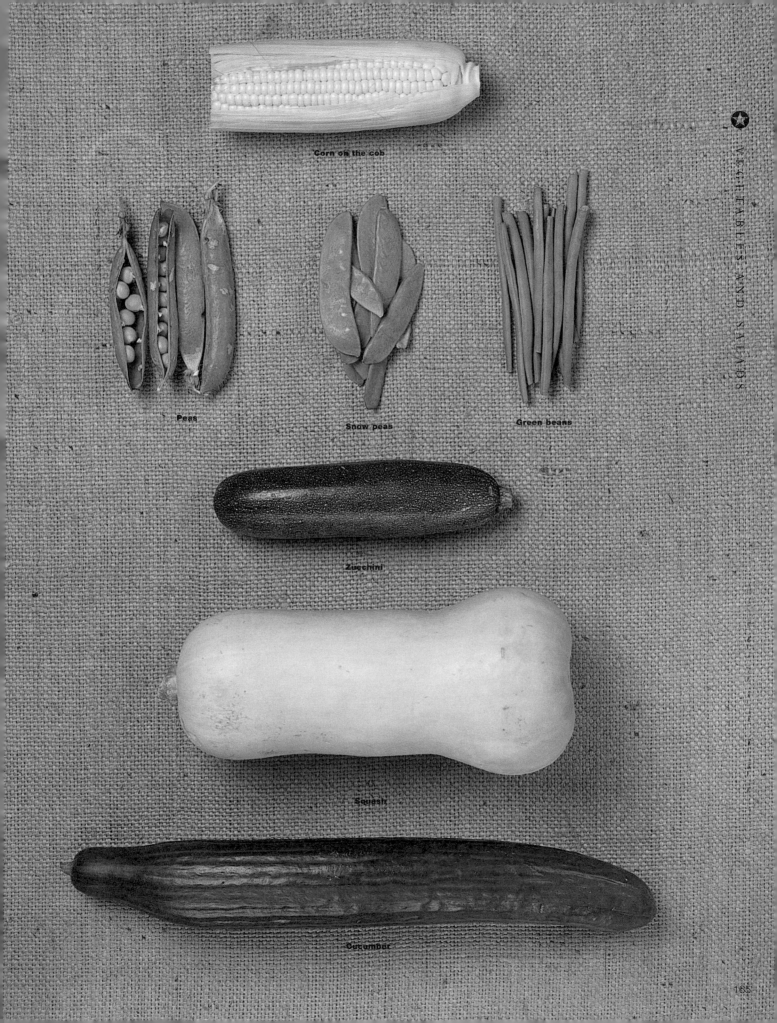

Corn on the cob

Peas

Snow peas

Green beans

Zucchini

Squash

Cucumber

Plum tomato

Cherry vine tomatoes

Salad tomato

Beef tomato

Eggplant

Avocado

Bell peppers

Chiles

Portabello mushroom

Crimini mushrooms

White closed-cup mushrooms

Shiitake mushrooms

VEGETABLE FRUITS

This category covers all the vegetables that are really fruits.

Tomatoes

These are available all year round and come in all shapes and sizes. They are usually eaten raw, but are also delicious when cooked—pan-fried, halved and broiled, baked whole, stuffed and baked, or made into sauces and soups.

Buy tomatoes in season if possible and from a good supplier; they should be of a good, even color and still firm to the touch. Leave soft tomatoes in the store. Eat them soon after buying in order to enjoy their fullest flavor.

Cherry tomatoes

These are the smallest and sweetest tomatoes. Eat them like grapes for a snack, in a salad, or use them as a garnish.

Vine tomatoes

These tomatoes are sold still on the vine. They are more expensive but the flavor is considerably better than others.

Salad tomatoes

These are the most common tomatoes, and they vary in terms of quality. If you are able to buy local produce from a grower or from a farmers' market, they will be wonderful; there is nothing like a home-grown tomato. But so often we are offered tomatoes, which have not been allowed to ripen properly, and their flavor and texture are poor.

Plum tomatoes

These tomatoes can be recognized by their shape. They have a good flavor and, because they have fewer seeds, they are good to use in cooking.

Beef tomatoes

These are the largest tomatoes. Sometimes they have a good flavor, but they can be watery. They are good stuffed and baked.

Eggplant

Buy them in small to medium sizes with a smooth, glossy skin. Slice or dice them before cooking. Eggplant cannot be eaten raw. Their flavor is mild, but they can absorb flavors so they are used in dishes mixed with other strongly flavored ingredients, such as onions and garlic, spices, and chiles.

Avocados

These are probably the most difficult vegetable to buy at the right degree of ripeness. Unripe avocados are inedible and so are overripe ones. You have to buy them a couple of days before you want to eat them and let them ripen on a warm windowsill. A good grocer will always help with your choice.

Never buy any with bruises because they will quickly blacken once cut open. Serve them halved with vinaigrette or sliced in salads (brush with lemon juice to prevent discoloration). They can also be puréed to make a dip.

Bell peppers

These are available in yellow, orange, red, and green. I find the green variety too bitter and do not use it; the red bell pepper is in fact the ripened green one and has a much better flavor. Buy bell peppers that are smooth and firm to the touch. Store them in a plastic bag in the refrigerator for a few days. They can be eaten raw in salads, or stuffed and broiled.

Chiles

These are from the same family as bell peppers, but they are very hot. Usually the smaller the chile, the hotter the flavor. They are available in green or red. Use latex gloves when preparing, because any contact with eyes or delicate skin can give a burning sensation, which will last some time. Remove all seeds before use unless you like a really hot dish.

Mushrooms

Mushrooms are not really vegetables but edible fungi. They are eaten as vegetables, however, and that is why they are included here. There are two types: cultivated and wild. Wild mushrooms have a better flavor. The most commonly available cultivated mushrooms are white or button mushrooms, followed by crimini mushrooms, which are darker in color and slightly larger. Shiitake mushrooms have a silky texture when cooked and have a fine flavor—they are used in Asian recipes. The portabello mushroom is found in the wild—it is larger and has black gills and a good, strong flavor. The flat mushroom is the cultivated equivalent.

Ceps, morels, and chanterelles are other wild mushrooms (although cultivation of some of these is now underway). They are rare to find and very expensive (buy them on vacation in France or Italy if you see them in markets there). These are often available dried, which are still expensive, but keep a small packet in the pantry and add a few to dishes containing cultivated mushrooms and the flavor will be greatly enhanced.

Buy mushrooms fresh: they should be dry on the outside and have a fresh smell. Keep them in a paper bag in the refrigerator and use within 1–2 days of purchase. It is unnecessary to wash them: just wipe them carefully with a soft cloth or a soft brush to remove dirt.

Mushrooms are good cooked whole or sliced in casseroles, pies, soups, pasta and rice dishes, or fried and served on toast for supper. White mushrooms may be sliced and served raw in salads. Large portabello mushrooms may be stuffed and broiled, baked, or cooked on a barbecue. Mushroom sauce can be made to accompany steak. Rehydrate dried mushrooms in a little warm water for 30 minutes before cooking.

RED CABBAGE CASSEROLE

If you are not cooking for a large group of people, it is still worth making this casserole for eight people because it will keep for 2–3 days in the refrigerator and can be served with sausages for a quick supper dish.

Serves 8
Preparation time: 20 minutes
Cooking time: 2½ hours

INGREDIENTS

1 red cabbage, about 1 lb 10 oz/750 g

2 onions, peeled and thinly sliced

1 garlic clove, peeled and chopped

2 small cooking apples, peeled, cored, and sliced

2 tbsp molasses sugar

½ tsp ground cinnamon

whole nutmeg, for grating

2 tbsp red wine vinegar

rind and juice of 1 orange

2 tbsp red currant jelly

salt and pepper

You will need a casserole dish (about 12½ cups), a sharp knife, a cutting board, and a grater

METHOD

1 Preheat the oven to 300°F/150°C. Cut the cabbage into fourths and remove the center stalk. Shred the leaves finely.

2 In the casserole dish, layer the red cabbage, onions, garlic, and apples. Sprinkle with the sugar and cinnamon and grate a fourth of the nutmeg over the top.

3 Pour in the wine, vinegar, and orange juice and sprinkle the orange rind on top.

4 Stir well and season. The dish will be quite full, but the volume of the cabbage will reduce during cooking.

5 Cook in the center of the preheated oven for 1–1½ hours, stirring from time to time. If you prefer, you can cook it more quickly in a flameproof casserole dish on the stovetop over medium heat for 8–10 minutes until the cabbage is just tender. The stove way leaves the cabbage crunchier.

6 Stir in the red currant jelly, and adjust the seasoning if necessary. Serve hot with any meat or game.

BAKED POTATOES

Baked potatoes make a delicious, nutritious snack or meal at any time. To be successful, you need to buy large, mealy potatoes like King Edwards, Cara, or Desirée.

Serves 4
Preparation time: 2 minutes
Cooking time: 1½ hours

INGREDIENTS

4 potatoes, about 7 oz/200 g each
salt and pepper
4 pats of butter, about 2 tsp each, to serve

You will need a pointed knife, a fine skewer, and a potholder

METHOD

1 Preheat the oven to 400°F/200°C. Wash and wipe the potatoes thoroughly. Prick them all over using the point of a knife or a skewer to prevent the skin splitting (you can insert a large metal skewer into each potato to make sure the center is cooked if you like).

2 Bake the potatoes near the top of the preheated oven for 1–1½ hours, until they are soft inside and the skin is crisp. Test by pushing a fine skewer into the center of a potato.

3 Cut a large cross in the top of each potato and, using a clean, thick cloth or potholders, squeeze the potato so that the soft filling starts to push out of the skin. Alternatively, cut each potato in half if you like.

4 Season well and add a pat of butter before serving.

Variations

You can also try some of the following fillings. Each of these makes enough to fill one potato.

Cheese: serve with 25 g/1 oz grated cheese sprinkled on top of the potato.

Chives: crush 1 garlic clove, mix with 1 tablespoon of soured cream and add 2 teaspoons of chopped fresh chives.

Bacon: top the potato with a rasher of crisply fried bacon.

Onion: chop a spring onion and mix it with a tablespoon of crème fraîche.

SPINACH, BACON, AND MUSHROOM SALAD

Serves 4
Preparation time: 5 minutes
Cooking time: 20 minutes

INGREDIENTS

8 oz/225 g baby spinach leaves

8 oz/225 g lardons or fatty bacon, snipped into ½ inch/
1 cm strips

2 garlic cloves, peeled and finely chopped

3¼ cups white mushrooms

2 tbsp olive oil

4 slices thick whole-wheat bread, cut into ½ inch/
1 cm cubes

Dressing
2 tbsp balsamic vinegar

4 tbsp extra-virgin olive oil

1 tsp Dijon mustard

½ tsp sugar

1 tbsp chopped fresh parsley

salt and pepper

4 tbsp freshly grated Parmesan cheese, to garnish

You will need a skillet, a cutting board, a cook's knife,
a bread knife, a small roasting pan, a grater, a wooden spatula,
and 4 salad bowls for serving.

WINE SUGGESTION
Try a cold, white Pouilly
Fuissé with this salad.

METHOD

1 Make sure the spinach leaves are clean and dry and divide them among the serving bowls.

2 Fry the lardons in a dry skillet, with the garlic, over medium heat for 3–4 minutes until they are cooked and crispy. Add the mushrooms and cook for about 2 minutes until just soft. Set aside and keep warm.

3 To make croûtons, heat the olive oil in the skillet and fry the bread cubes over high heat for 4–5 minutes until they are crisp and golden brown. Move them around the skillet quickly to be sure of even coloring.

4 Sprinkle the bacon and mushroom mixture over the spinach and top with the fried croûtons.

5 Combine all the dressing ingredients in a small screw-top jar, season to taste, and shake well. Pour the dressing over the salad and garnish with the Parmesan.

ROASTED WINTER VEGETABLES

Roasted vegetables are very popular, especially since they all cook together and need little attention once prepared. You can use a mixture of whatever is available and vary the mix according to choice. Try to cut all the vegetables to roughly the same size.

Serves 6
Preparation time: 25 minutes
Cooking time: 1 hour

INGREDIENTS

3 red onions
3 medium parsnips
4 baby turnips
3 medium carrots
2⅔ cups peeled, diced butternut squash
21/4 cups peeled diced sweet potato
2 garlic cloves, peeled and chopped
2 tbsp chopped fresh rosemary
1 tbsp chopped fresh thyme
2 tsp chopped fresh sage
3 tbsp olive oil
salt and pepper
2 tbsp chopped fresh mixed herbs, such as parsley, thyme, and rosemary, to garnish

You will need a large roasting pan, a sharp knife, a cutting board, and a wooden spatula.

METHOD

1 Cut the onions into fourths through the root (this will hold them together during the cooking).

2 Peel and cut the parsnips into even-size pieces, about 2 inches/5 cm long.

3 Cut the turnips into fourths.

4 Scrub or peel the carrots as necessary and cut into pieces like the parsnips. Put all the vegetables, including the squash and sweet potato, in one layer in a roasting pan. Sprinkle the garlic and herbs over them.

5 Pour in the oil and season well.

6 Toss all the ingredients together until they are well mixed and coated with the oil (you can leave them to marinate at this stage for 1–2 hours to allow the flavors to be absorbed).

7 Preheat the oven to 425°/220°C. Roast the vegetables at the top of the preheated oven for 45 minutes to 1 hour until they are cooked and nicely browned. Turn the vegetables over halfway through the cooking time.

8 Serve the vegetables with a good handful of fresh mixed herbs sprinkled on top and a final sprinkling of salt and freshly grated pepper.

MASHED POTATO

Serves 4
Preparation time: 10 minutes
Cooking time: 35 minutes

INGREDIENTS

2 lb/900 g mealy potatoes, such as King Edwards, Maris Piper, or Desirée
4 tbsp butter
3 tbsp hot milk
salt and pepper

You will need a large lidded pan, a vegetable peeler, a colander, a small milk pan, and a potato masher

METHOD

1 Peel the potatoes carefully using a vegetable peeler. Place them in cold water while you prepare the others to prevent them from going brown.

2 Cut the potatoes into even-size chunks and cook them in boiling salted water over medium heat, covered, for 20–25 minutes until they are tender. Test that they are cooked by piercing them with the point of a knife, but do make sure you test that they are soft right to the middle to avoid lumps later. Remove the pan from the heat and drain through a colander.

3 Return the potatoes to the hot pan and mash with a potato masher until smooth. Add the butter and continue to mash until it is all mixed in. Then add the milk (it is better hot because the potatoes absorb it more quickly and produce a creamier mash.

4 Taste the mash and season to taste. Serve immediately.

Variations

Herb mash: mix in 3 tablespoons chopped fresh parsley, thyme, or mint.

Mustard mash: mix in 2 tablespoons of wholegrain mustard.

Horseradish mash: mix in 2 tablespoons horseradish sauce.

Pesto mash: stir in 4 tablespoons fresh pesto.

PERFECT ROAST POTATOES

Perfect roast potatoes are what many people try to achieve. Without a crisp potato to accompany the roast, the whole meal can be a disappointment. Make sure you choose the right potatoes: mealy King Edwards, Maris Piper, Romano, or Desirée are the best.

Serves 6
Preparation time: 15 minutes
Cooking time: 1 hour

INGREDIENTS

3 lb/1.3 kg large, mealy potatoes
3 tbsp olive oil
salt and pepper

You will need a lidded pan, a vegetable peeler, a pointed knife, a colander, a heavy roasting pan, and a serving dish

METHOD

1 Preheat the oven to 425°F/220°C. Peel the potatoes carefully using a vegetable peeler. Place them in cold water while you prepare the others to prevent them from going brown.

2 Cut the potatoes into even-size chunks (the size you prefer) and cook in boiling salted water over medium heat, covered, for 5–7 minutes. They should still be firm.

3 While the potatoes are boiling, pour the oil into a roasting pan and place in the hot oven.

4 Remove the potatoes from the heat, drain well, and return them to the pan. Cover with the lid and firmly shake the pan so that the surface of the potatoes is roughened (this helps to give a much crisper texture).

5 Remove the roasting pan from the hot oven carefully and tip the potatoes into the hot oil, basting them carefully to make sure that they are all coated with the oil.

6 Put the pan back into the oven and roast at the top for 45–50 minutes until the potatoes are browned all over and thoroughly crisp. Turn the potatoes once only during the process or the crunchy edges will be destroyed.

7 Transfer the potatoes from the roasting pan carefully into a hot serving dish. Sprinkle with a little more salt and serve immediately. Any potatoes left over are delicious cold.

SPECIAL CAULIFLOWER CHEESE

Serves 4
Preparation time: 15 minutes
Cooking time: 25 minutes

INGREDIENTS

1 cauliflower, about 1 lb 8 oz/675 g prepared weight, trimmed and cut into flowerets

1 tbsp olive oil

1 onion, peeled and thinly sliced

1 garlic clove, peeled and finely chopped

4 oz/115 g fatty bacon, cut into ½ inch/1 cm strips

3 tbsp butter

3 tbsp all-purpose flour

2 cups milk

1 cup finely grated Cheddar cheese

a good grating of nutmeg

1 tbsp grated Parmesan cheese

salt and pepper

To serve
tomato salad or salad greens

crusty bread

You will need a 6¼ cup gratin dish, a cook's knife, a cutting board, a skillet, a measuring cup, a medium pan, a grater, and a wooden spatula

WINE SUGGESTION
A sturdy red Merlot or oaky Australian Chardonnay would go well with this dish.

1 Cook the cauliflower in a pan of boiling salted water for 4–5 minutes; it should still be firm. Drain and place in the hot serving dish, then keep it warm.

2 Heat the olive oil in a skillet over medium heat and cook the onion, garlic, and bacon for 5–6 minutes until the onion is caramelized and golden and the bacon is crisp.

3 Melt the butter in a pan over medium heat. Stir in the flour. Cook for 1 minute, stirring constantly. Remove from the heat and stir in the milk gradually until smooth. Return to low heat and stir until the sauce comes to a boil and thickens. Simmer gently, stirring constantly, for about 3 minutes until the sauce is creamy and smooth. Remove from the heat and stir in the Cheddar cheese and nutmeg. Taste, and season well.

4 Spoon the onion and bacon over the cauliflower and pour on the hot sauce. Top with the Parmesan and place under a hot broiler to brown. Serve immediately with a small tomato salad or salad greens and some crusty bread.

MINTED NEW POTATOES

Potatoes have been staple fare for ages, but began to wane in popularity owing to the growing use of rice and pasta. However, today the potato is back in fashion. It can be served in various ways, as an accompaniment or as a meal in its own right. Make sure you buy the correct variety of potato for the method of cooking. These potatoes can also be served cold, without the butter, as a salad.

Serves 4
Preparation time: 5 minutes
Cooking time: 15–20 minutes

INGREDIENTS

2 lb/900 g new potatoes
sprig fresh mint
1 tbsp butter
salt and pepper
2 tbsp chopped fresh mixed herbs, such as parsley, chives, and mint, to garnish

You will need a lidded pan, a colander, and a small pointed knife

METHOD

1 Wash the potatoes, or just wipe them if they are not dirty. Put the potatoes and the mint in a pan of boiling salted water and cook, covered, for 15–20 minutes until tender. Test with the point of a sharp knife (the timing will vary according to the size of the potatoes).

2 Drain the potatoes well and discard the mint. Return to the pan with the butter. Let the butter melt and mix with the potatoes until they are well covered.

3 Tip the potatoes into a serving dish, season well, particularly with lots of freshly ground pepper, and sprinkle with the herbs. Serve immediately.

Note: new potatoes can also be served "crushed." Simply break them up roughly with a fork in the pan and add more herbs or a few leaves of arugula or spinach until they are wilted.

BROILED SUMMER VEGETABLES

Broiling summer vegetables enhances their flavor and lets you eat them hot, with broiled meats or fish, or cold as a salad with a herb dressing. They are versatile and can be prepared ahead. Cook them under a conventional broiler, on a griddle on the stovetop, or on a barbecue.

Serves 6–8
Preparation time: 25 minutes
Cooking time: 30 minutes–1 hour

INGREDIENTS

2 red bell peppers, seeded and cut into fourths
2 yellow bell peppers, seeded and cut into fourths
2 red onions, peeled and sliced into thick rings
3 zucchini, sliced lengthwise into 3 or 4 pieces
1 eggplant, sliced across into 8 pieces
2 bulbs fennel, trimmed and sliced
3 tbsp olive oil
2 tbsp extra-virgin olive oil
1 lemon, cut in half
salt and pepper

To garnish
2 tbsp chopped fresh mixed herbs, such as parsley, chives, and lemon thyme
2 oz/55 g Parmesan cheese, shaved with a potato peeler

You will need a broiler, griddle, or barbecue, a cook's knife, a cutting board, a pastry brush, some kitchen tongs, a vegetable peeler, and a serving dish

METHOD

1 Brush the vegetables well with the 3 tablespoons of olive oil.

2 Cook under a broiler preheated to high for 4–5 minutes on each side. Alternatively, cook on a griddle over medium heat for 5–7 minutes on each side. The vegetables should have a good brown color. If you are using a barbecue, the vegetables will need to cook for about 4–6 minutes on each side. Cooking times will vary depending on the thickness. Transfer the vegetables to a serving dish. You will need to cook them in different batches until all the vegetables are cooked.

3 Sprinkle with the extra-virgin olive oil and squeeze the lemon halves over the vegetables. Season well and sprinkle with the herbs and cheese.

PEAR AND AVOCADO SALAD

Serves 4
Preparation time: 15–20 minutes

INGREDIENTS

4 small pears, Bartlett or Williams

2 tbsp lemon juice

2 ripe avocados

1 bunch of watercress or mizuna

2 oz/55 g arugula, about 1 bunch

2 tbsp finely chopped walnuts

4 oz/115 g dolcelatte or Roquefort cheese

walnut bread, sliced, to serve

Dressing
3 tbsp balsamic vinegar

2 tbsp extra-virgin olive oil

2 tbsp walnut oil

1 tsp Dijon mustard

½ tsp light soft brown sugar

1 tbsp chopped fresh parsley

salt and pepper

You will need a cutting board, a cook's knife, a pastry brush, a screw-top jar, and 4 serving plates

METHOD

1 Halve the pears, then core, and cut them carefully into thin slices. Brush with lemon juice to prevent discoloration.

2 Cut the avocados in half, remove the pits, and peel them. Carefully cut each half into about five slices. Also brush with lemon juice.

3 Put the watercress or mizuna and arugula on four serving plates and arrange the pears and avocados on top. Sprinkle with the chopped walnuts.

4 For the dressing, combine all the ingredients in a small screw-top jar and shake well.

5 Spoon the dressing over the salad and crumble the cheese over the top.

6 Serve immediately with some sliced walnut bread.

DRESSINGS

BASIC DRESSING

A basic dressing is essential for a good salad. Good olive oil and a fine vinegar or lemon juice should be used. Vary the oil and vinegar according to the salad ingredients and add appropriate herbs at the last minute. Salads should only be dressed immediately before eating or else the greens will go soggy. For the simplest dressing, just sprinkle on some freshly squeezed lemon juice and some olive oil.

Preparation time: 5–10 minutes

INGREDIENTS

2 tbsp lemon juice, or red or white wine vinegar
4–6 tbsp extra-virgin olive oil
1 tsp Dijon mustard
pinch of superfine sugar
1 tbsp chopped fresh parsley
salt and pepper

You will need a screw-top jar or a small bowl and a fork

METHOD

1 Place all the ingredients in a jar, secure the top, and shake well. Alternatively, beat all the ingredients together in a small bowl. Use as much oil as you like. If you have just salad greens to dress, then 4 tablespoons of oil will be sufficient, but if you have heavier ingredients like potatoes, you will need 6 tablespoons of oil.

2 Use the dressing at once. If you want to store it, do not add the herbs—it will then keep for 3–4 days in the refrigerator.

Variations

Asian dressing: replace 1 tablespoon of the oil with sesame oil and add 1–2 teaspoons of soy sauce. Add chopped cilantro instead of the parsley.

Tomato dressing: use balsamic vinegar instead of lemon juice and add 1 tablespoon of chopped sun-dried tomatoes. Replace the parsley with torn basil leaves.

Cheese dressing: add 1 tablespoon of crumbled strong blue cheese, or fork in 1 tablespoon of garlic-flavored soft cheese. A few chopped walnuts, say ¼ cup, would be a nice addition.

Sweet/sour dressing:—add 1 tablespoon of honey and 1 teaspoon finely grated fresh ginger root. Some toasted sesame seeds, about 1 tablespoon, would add a good crunch.

P A S T A ,   N O O D L E S ,   R I C E ,
G R A I N S ,   A N D   P U L S E S

*T*his section covers pasta and noodles (mainly made from wheat), the Asian varieties (made from other grains), other varieties of rice and quickly cooked grains, and pulses. Collectively, they may be called cereals and have a place in the diet on their own or as accompaniments to other foods.

PASTA

There really are hundreds of types of pasta, some made simply from wheat flour and water and some richer ones made with egg. You can make pasta at home but there are so many easily available that I prefer to put the effort into the sauce making. Fresh pasta is now more widely obtainable but the staple is dried pasta, which you can always keep in your pantry. There are two main types of pasta: long and short.

Spaghetti
This is the basic long pasta, and all kitchens should have a packet. Use it for bolognese and carbonara sauces, and as an accompaniment to meat and vegetable dishes.

Macaroni
This is a basic short pasta and is often used for macaroni cheese—a quickly made, economical supper dish.

Lasagne
These are large sheets of pasta, which are used with layers of fillings—such as meat sauce and cheese sauces—and then baked in the oven.

Cannelloni
Large tubes of pasta, which need cooking first before being stuffed with either a meat or vegetable filling.

Fusilli
These are thin spiral shapes, which are particularly good with sauces because they hold the sauces well. They also make good pasta salads.

Farfalle
This is a bow-shaped pasta. It is very attractive in salads and good with meat sauces.

Vermicelli
A very fine pasta—the finest is called "angel's hair." It is best used with fine ingredients, such as shrimp and crab. It is also good with exotic mushrooms.

Tagliatelle
Long, flat noodles, known as ribbon noodles. The ribbons also come in different widths, known as linguine, fettuccine, and pappardelle (this is the widest).

Conchiglie
Shell-shaped pasta, which comes in all sizes from tiny, for soups, to large, which can be stuffed. This is a good, short pasta for use with all sorts of sauces.

Stuffed pasta
Ravioli and tortellini are stuffed pastas with a variety of fillings, including meat, mushrooms, and cheese. They can form the basis of a quick meal and they only need cooking and tossing in melted butter or cream for an easy dish. They are available made from plain or flavored pasta.

Storage
Store dried pasta in a cool, dry place for up to 1–2 years. Egg pastas will not keep so long as the plain varieties, so check labels for storage. Use fresh pasta within 1–2 days of purchase.

LASAGNE

Lasagne is a quick, satisfying, and versatile dish. You can use other ground meat or vegetables in this recipe.

1 Heat 1 tbsp olive oil in a pan. Add 1 chopped onion and 1 chopped garlic clove. Cook over medium heat for 4 minutes. Add 1⅓ cups chopped mushrooms and 3 cups ground beef and cook, stirring, for 4 minutes.

2 Add ⅔ cup red wine, 7 tbsp water, generous 1 cup bottled strained tomatoes, and 1 tsp sugar; cook for 5 minutes. Put 3 sheets of dried "no-cook" lasagne in the base of an ovenproof dish, add half of the sauce, top with 3 sheets, then the remaining sauce, then 3 more sheets.

3 Melt 5 tbsp butter in a pan, stir in ⅓ cup all-purpose flour, and cook for 2 minutes. Remove from the heat, and gradually stir in 2½ cups milk. Bring to a boil, stirring until thickened. Cool slightly.

4 Stir in 1 cup grated Parmesan and 1 beaten egg. Season, then pour onto the lasagne. Sprinkle with 1 cup grated Parmesan, then bake at 375°F/190°C for 30 minutes until golden.

You can replace the beef with the same quantity of chicken or turkey, or make a vegetarian version by replacing the beef with the same quantity of soy substitute. Cook in the same way.

NOODLES

Under this heading we are dealing with Asian noodles, not the Italian variety.

Egg noodles

These are the most common noodles used in Chinese and Thai cooking. They are available in various thicknesses and are very quick to cook (from 1–5 minutes). They can be served with stir-fry dishes or can be a quick meal in themselves mixed with some shellfish and vegetables, and a dash of soy sauce and sesame oil. They can also be stir-fried after cooking.

Rice noodles

These are available as very fine noodles; most of them only need soaking before use, but check the pack for instructions because they vary. Rice noodles can be added to soups and to stir-fries.

Japanese noodles

These are egg noodles like the Chinese noodles, but there are also two specific varieties of Japanese noodles. Soba noodles are made from buckwheat: they have a darker color and are quite thin—they are usually used in soups and broths. Udon noodles are thicker and made from wheat flour—they are used in stir-fries.

Storage

Keep in a cool, dry place and use by the date on the packs.

RICE

Again, there is a large variety available, but a small range opens up a wide area of savory and sweet dishes.

Long-grain rice

This is the easiest to cook and the most easily available. It is very widely grown in America. Long-grain rice is quick to cook and can be the basis of many dishes. It is also cheap. Use it as an accompaniment to meat, fish, and chicken dishes. It is also good in kedgeree. It makes a quick pantry meal—keep some rice into which you can stir some grated cheese, or some tuna and chopped scallion.

Basmati rice

This is long-grain rice from the Punjab region of India. It is the best rice in the world with the best flavor. Use it in the same way as long-grain rice, to accompany delicious food. It is available in white, brown, and as a mixture with "wild rice." Wild rice is not a rice but a grass—it is black and gives a good, nutty flavor.

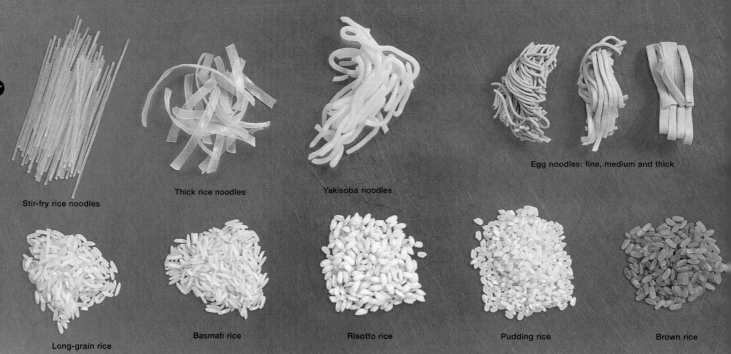

Stir-fry rice noodles

Thick rice noodles

Yakisoba noodles

Egg noodles: fine, medium and thick

Long-grain rice

Basmati rice

Risotto rice

Pudding rice

Brown rice

Risotto rice

This is a short-grain rice, which is specially grown for risotto. Arborio is most widely available, but carnaroli is thought to be superior because it has a creamier texture. Owing to the fashion for Italian food at the moment, risotto is very popular. It is a very soothing dish, both to make and to eat, and can be flavored with different shellfish, meats, and vegetables, along with a few herbs and some grated Parmesan cheese.

Pudding rice

This short-grain rice is suitable for long, slow cooking in milk to make rice pudding. Rice pudding is still a popular dessert with all age groups.

Brown rice

This is available as long-grain or basmati. It is much nuttier than white rice and retains the bran layer and germ of the rice; it therefore has a higher nutritional value. It does take longer to cook, so check the packet for instructions.

Storage

Store in airtight containers in a dry, cool place. Rice will keep for up to three years, so it is a long-term pantry item. If you have enough space and containers, it is a good idea to buy large packs because they are more economical (but only if you are going to use them).

GRAINS

Owing to their availability now in instant form, I suggest you try both of the following grains and keep them as basics in your pantry.

Couscous

This is a fine-grained semolina and is produced from durum flour. It has a mild flavor but a good, nutty texture, which mixes well with other salad ingredients. Now that instant couscous is available, it is really useful in the pantry for a quick meal. Instant couscous just needs a quick soak in hot water or stock for 2–3 minutes and then you can serve it hot with meat, fish, or vegetables. Alternatively, mix it with chopped tomatoes, cucumber, scallions, and lots of herbs for a delicious cold salad. In this case, you will need to soak it in cold water or cooled stock instead.

Polenta

This is another almost instant accompaniment. It is a fine granular cornmeal, which can be made by mixing with boiling stock or water in a pan and cooking for 1–2 minutes. Check packets for instructions because they vary. Polenta can be served hot and soft, like mashed potato with a good pat of butter or some olive oil, or it can be poured into a tray and left to cool. It is then cut into slices and broiled to serve in place of bread.

Storage

Keep in an airtight container in a cool, dry place. Storage times vary, but are often up to 18 months.

BEANS AND LENTILS

These are all known as legumes and are a good, economical source of protein. They are available dried and in cans. Cans cut out the soaking and cooking time and make legumes a useful instant convenience food.

Couscous

Great Northern beans

Garbanzo beans

Small navy beans

Polenta

Red and green lentils

Cannellini beans

Red kidney beans

Great Northern beans

These are probably the most versatile, because they can be used for cassoulet and other casserole dishes, such as Boston Baked Beans. They are white, medium-size beans and are best known canned as baked beans in tomato sauce. The canned varieties are easier to use because they eliminate the need for soaking overnight and cooking for 1–1½ hours.

Garbanzo beans

These are another good, basic food. Garbanzo beans are round and beige and can quickly be made into a mash to serve with fish or meat. They can also be made into hummus with olive oil and garlic. They need to be soaked overnight and then cooked for anything up to 4 hours (depending on their age). I always use the ready-cooked canned variety, but enthusiasts will say that the flavor of the soaked and cooked beans is superior. You will need to make your own choice.

Lentils

These are available in yellow, red, green, gray, and continental brown varieties. Since lentils do not need soaking and do not take much time to cook, I would always use the dried type. However, if you are short of time, then the canned type might suit you better. The red and yellow lentils are actually split, so they are very quick to cook: they become very soft and break down to a creamy purée. These lentils form the basis of Indian dhal, and are also used in stuffings and in vegetarian burgers. The green variety are whole and take a little longer to cook. Serve them in salads, thick soups, and casseroles. Puy lentils are gray/green and are considered to be the finest. They are best served as an accompaniment to meat or fish.

Lima beans

These large, flat, white beans have a lovely buttery flavor. They are good served as an accompaniment with a sprinkling of chopped herbs. They are also good as a purée or roughly forked with a little garlic and chili flavoring. Lima beans can be a useful addition to soups.

Cannellini beans

These beans are popular in Italian cooking, particularly in minestrone. They are also used cold in salads, and hot in some pasta dishes.

Small navy beans

These are delicate, small, green beans, which can be served cold in salads. Traditionally, they are also served hot with lamb.

Red kidney beans

The red kidney bean is the favorite bean of Mexico. It is used in chile con carne, and is also mashed to make refried beans.

Other beans you might like to try include soybeans, pinto beans, borlotti beans, black-eye peas, black beans, and adzuki beans. They all have a different shape and color and can be used to add bulk to a casserole or soup. Use them dried or canned for convenience.

Storage

Buy dried beans and lentils in small quantities from a source that has a quick turnover. The longer you keep these dried legumes, the longer you will need to cook them because they toughen with age. Store in airtight containers in a cool, dry place. Check the packets for storage times.

BAKED CHEESE PASTA

Serves 4

Preparation time: 15 minutes
Cooking time: 35 minutes

INGREDIENTS

3 tbsp olive oil
1 onion, peeled and thinly sliced
2 garlic cloves, peeled and finely chopped
3 zucchini, cut into 2 inch/5 cm batons
2 red bell peppers, seeded and sliced
1 lb 12 oz/800 g canned chopped tomatoes
3 tbsp torn fresh basil leaves
1⅓ cups thinly sliced white mushrooms
3 cups dried fusilli or rigatoni pasta
1½ cups mascarpone cheese
3 tbsp freshly grated Parmesan cheese
salt and pepper
4 sprigs fresh basil, to garnish

You will need a cook's knife, a cutting board, a large pan, a large skillet, a wooden spatula, a 7½ cup ovenproof dish, and a cookie sheet

METHOD

1 Preheat the oven to 400º/200°C. Heat the oil in the skillet and cook the onion and garlic over medium heat for 2–3 minutes until golden. Add the zucchini and bell peppers and continue to cook for 3–4 minutes more.

2 Lower the heat, add the tomatoes and basil, and simmer for 5 minutes until the vegetables are starting to soften. Season well. Stir in the mushrooms and cook for 2 minutes.

3 Meanwhile, cook the pasta in the pan in boiling salted water for 8–10 minutes, or according to the instructions on the packet. When it is "al dente" (tender but still firm to the bite), remove from the heat, and drain well.

4 Pour the drained pasta into the ovenproof dish and pour in the tomato mixture. Stir well.

5 Top with the mascarpone cheese and sprinkle with the grated Parmesan.

6 Bake in the center of the preheated oven on a cookie sheet for 20–25 minutes until bubbling and golden brown. Serve immediately garnished with the basil.

WINE SUGGESTION

Try a rich red Montepulciano d'Abruzzo from Italy with this baked pasta dish.

GARBANZO BEAN SALAD

Dried garbanzo beans need soaking overnight and then up to four hours' cooking. The canned variety are very good as long as you rinse them thoroughly before use.

Serves 4
Preparation time: 15 minutes
Cooking time: 15 minutes

INGREDIENTS

14 oz/400 g canned garbanzo beans
1 red onion, peeled
1 tbsp olive oil
2 garlic cloves, peeled and crushed
1 tsp coriander seeds
1 tsp cumin seeds
1 tsp paprika
4 tomatoes, seeded and roughly chopped
salt and pepper

Dressing
2 tbsp olive oil
juice of 1 lemon
2 tbsp chopped fresh flat-leaf parsley

To serve
4 oz/115 g baby spinach leaves, washed and dried well
½ cup plain strained yogurt
1 tbsp chopped fresh mint

You will need a cook's knife, a cutting board, a skillet, a wooden spatula, a bowl, and 4 serving plates

METHOD

1 Drain and rinse the garbanzo beans thoroughly.

2 Halve the onion vertically and cut each half into small slices, from root to stem.

3 In a skillet, cook the onion in the oil over medium heat for about 8 minutes until soft but not colored. Add the garlic and cook for 2 minutes. Meanwhile, place the coriander and cumin seeds in a mortar and grind with a pestle until fine (or crush with the end of a rolling pin in a bowl). Add these to the skillet with the paprika and continue to cook for 1 minute, stirring constantly. Remove from the heat.

4 Add the garbanzo beans to the skillet and stir well to coat with the spices. Add the tomatoes. Season well.

5 Pour the warm salad into a bowl. Shake the dressing ingredients together in a screw-top jar and pour the dressing over the salad. Serve warm or let stand for 1 hour to let the flavors to develop.

6 Arrange the spinach leaves on the serving plates and top with the garbanzo bean salad.

7 Mix the yogurt with the mint and serve separately.

COUSCOUS SALAD

Serves 6
Preparation time: 10 minutes
Cooking time: 10 minutes

INGREDIENTS

2 cups couscous

2½ cups vegetable stock, made with vegetable bouillon powder

8 oz/225 g cherry tomatoes

8 oz/225 g piece of cucumber

6 scallions

½ cup pine nuts

1 tbsp chopped fresh mint

salt and pepper

1 tbsp chopped fresh mint, to garnish

Dressing
juice and grated rind of 1 lemon

5 tbsp extra-virgin olive oil

You will need a measuring cup, a cook's knife, a cutting board, a mixing bowl, a small skillet, and a serving bowl

METHOD

1 Put the couscous in the mixing bowl and pour in the hot stock. Fork through and soak for 2–3 minutes until all the stock has been absorbed, then let cool.

2 Cut the tomatoes into fourths.

3 Cut the cucumber lengthwise into fourths and remove the seeds, then dice finely.

4 Cut the scallions into ¼ inch/5 mm lengths.

5 Dry-fry the pine nuts over medium heat for 1–2 minutes until they are golden brown. Stir well to avoid burning and remove from the heat once they are ready. Let cool.

6 Place the dressing ingredients in a screw-top jar, season, and shake well.

7 Add all the vegetables to the couscous and stir well. Pour in the dressing and toss together with the pine nuts and mint. Check for seasoning and adjust if necessary.

8 Put the salad into a large serving bowl and sprinkle the mint over the couscous.

LENTILS WITH SAUSAGES

Puy lentils are available in cans, but since they are quite quick to cook and do not need any soaking, I find the dried variety better.

Serves 4
Preparation time: 15 minutes
Cooking time: 35 minutes

INGREDIENTS

generous 1 cup Puy lentils, rinsed

2 tsp vegetable bouillon powder or 1 vegetable bouillon cube

1 carrot, peeled and cut into 4 large chunks

2 shallots, peeled and left whole

4 cloves

2 bay leaves

sprig fresh thyme

1 lb 9 oz/700 g good-quality sausages (about 12)

1 tbsp vegetable oil

2 shallots, peeled and finely chopped

2 garlic cloves, peeled and finely chopped

2 tbsp chopped fresh parsley

salt and pepper

You will need a large pan, a cook's knife, a cutting board, a skillet, a wooden spatula, a slotted spoon, and a serving dish

METHOD

1 Put the lentils in the pan and cover well with water, about 1 inch/2.5 cm above their level. Stir in the bouillon powder or cube and add the carrot. Make two small holes in each of the whole shallots and push in the cloves. Add these to the pan with the bay leaves and thyme.

2 Bring to a boil, reduce the heat, and simmer gently, with the lid half on, for 15–20 minutes. The lentils should be tender but still whole and firm.

3 Meanwhile, in a skillet, cook the sausages in the oil over medium heat for about 15 minutes until they are crusty and brown. Use a slotted spoon to lift them out onto a hot serving dish.

4 Add the chopped shallots and garlic to the skillet and cook quickly over the same heat for 2–3 minutes until soft, stirring the sediment from the base of the skillet.

5 Drain the lentils and remove the vegetables and bay leaves. Tip the lentils into the skillet and mix well. Adjust the seasoning to taste.

6 Stir in the parsley and serve immediately with the sausages.

WINE SUGGESTION

Try a strong red Côtes du Rhône with these sausages.

PEA AND BEAN RISOTTO

Serves 4

Preparation time: 10 minutes

Cooking time: 35 minutes

INGREDIENTS

3 tbsp butter

1 tbsp olive oil

1 onion, peeled and finely chopped

1 garlic clove, peeled and finely chopped

3 cups risotto rice (arborio or carnaroli)

⅔ cup dry white wine

3¾ cups hot vegetable stock

scant 1 cup shelled fava beans (you can use frozen)

1 cup fresh or frozen peas

1⅛ cups freshly grated Parmesan cheese

grated rind of 2 lemons

2 tbsp chopped fresh mint leaves

2 tbsp chopped fresh parsley

salt and pepper

You will need a cook's knife, a cutting board, a large, deep skillet, a pan and ladle, a measuring cup, a wooden spatula, and a grater

WINE SUGGESTION

A cold white Sauvignon matches the flavors of this risotto well.

1 Put 1 tablespoon of the butter and 1 tablespoon oil in the skillet and melt together over low heat. Add the chopped onion and garlic and cook for about 5 minutes until soft but not colored.

2 Stir in the rice and fry for 1 minute. Pour in the wine and keep stirring until the rice has absorbed all the liquid. Keep the vegetable stock simmering in a pan. Add one ladleful of stock to the rice and stir constantly. Wait until the liquid has been absorbed before adding the next ladleful. Gradually use all the stock, stirring constantly. This is a slow process; it will take about 15–20 minutes.

3 After you have added half the stock, add the fava beans and the peas (if using fresh) and cook with the rice. When all the stock is absorbed, the rice should be very creamy in texture. Taste to see if the rice is cooked: it should still be a little chewy, but not hard. Season to taste. If you are using frozen beans and peas, add them now and heat through for 1 minute.

4 Remove the skillet from the heat and stir in the remaining butter and half of the grated Parmesan. Cover the skillet and then let stand for 2–3 minutes for the risotto to become even creamier. Stir in the grated lemon rind and chopped mint and parsley and serve immediately on hot plates. Serve the remaining Parmesan separately.

FRUIT AND NUT PILAF

Serves 6
Preparation time: 10 minutes
Cooking time: 30 minutes

INGREDIENTS

1 tbsp butter

1 tbsp olive oil

1 onion, peeled and finely chopped

1 garlic clove, peeled and finely chopped

1¾ cups long-grain (basmati) rice

pinch ground cinnamon

pinch ground cloves

3 cups chicken or vegetable stock

scant ½ cup raisins

½ cup pistachio nuts

salt and pepper

You will need a cook's knife, a cutting board, a lidded pan, a measuring cup, a wooden spatula, and a serving dish

METHOD

1 Heat the butter and the oil in the pan over low heat. Cook the onion and garlic for about 10 minutes until softened but not colored.

2 Gently stir in the rice and cook for 1 minute more. Stir in the ground spices.

3 Pour in the stock, bring to a boil over medium heat, cover, and simmer gently for 15–20 minutes until the rice is tender and the stock has all been absorbed.

4 Season to taste and stir in the raisins and nuts.

5 Remove from the heat, and serve immediately in a warm serving dish as an accompaniment to any meat, poultry, or fish dish.

SPAGHETTINI WITH CRAB

Serves 2
Preparation time: 10 minutes
Cooking time: 15 minutes

INGREDIENTS

8 oz/225 g dried spaghettini or linguine
1 tbsp butter
1 tbsp olive oil
1¾ cups thinly sliced zucchini
1 garlic clove, peeled and crushed
pinch chili powder or crushed chiles
6 oz/175 g fresh crab meat (or frozen and thawed)
2 tbsp mayonnaise
2 tbsp crème fraîche
salt and pepper
1 tbsp chopped fresh parsley, to garnish

You will need a cook's knife, a cutting board, a large pan, a skillet, a wooden spatula, and 2 serving plates

METHOD

1 Put the linguine in a pan of boiling water and cook for 8–10 minutes, or according to the pack instructions, until "al dente" (tender but still firm to the bite).

2 Meanwhile, heat the butter and oil in a skillet and quickly cook the zucchini over high heat for 2–3 minutes, stirring constantly, until they are quite brown.

3 Add the garlic and chili powder or crushed chiles and stir well.

4 Carefully mix in the crab meat, warm through for about 1 minute, and season well.

5 Drain the pasta, then return it to the hot pan. Stir in the mayonnaise and crème fraîche.

6 Turn the pasta onto two serving plates and pour the crab mixture over it.

7 Serve immediately garnished with parsley.

WINE SUGGESTION

A light Italian Pinot Blanco or a Portuguese Vinho Verde would go well with this crab dish.

WARM CHICKEN NOODLE SALAD

Serves 4

Preparation time: 20 minutes, plus marinating

Cooking time: 25 minutes

INGREDIENTS

12 oz/350 g skinless boneless chicken breast portions

½ tsp ground ginger

½ tsp ground turmeric

½ tsp medium curry powder

½ tsp mustard powder

3 tbsp olive oil

2 zucchini, cut into 2 inch/5 cm batons

1 red bell pepper, seeded and sliced

1 yellow bell pepper, seeded and sliced

1½ cups snow peas, trimmed

1 garlic clove, peeled and finely chopped

¾ inch/2 cm piece fresh ginger root, peeled and finely chopped

3 tbsp honey

2 tbsp lemon juice

6 oz/175 g medium egg noodles

salt and pepper

2 tbsp chopped fresh cilantro, to garnish

You will need a cook's knife, a cutting board, a bowl, a large pan, a skillet, a wooden spatula, a slotted spoon, and a serving dish

METHOD

1 Cut the chicken into thin strips and place in a bowl.

2 Mix in the ground ginger, turmeric, curry powder, and mustard and season well. Cover with plastic wrap and marinate for 1–2 hours.

3 Heat 2 tablespoons of the oil in a skillet and cook the zucchini over high heat for 2–3 minutes until they are well colored. Using a slotted spoon, lift them from the skillet and place in the serving dish. Put the bell peppers in the skillet and cook for 2–3 minutes until slightly softened and just taking on some color. Add the snow peas and cook for 1 minute more. Remove from the heat and add these to the zucchini.

4 Add the remaining oil to the skillet and cook the chicken over high heat until golden brown. Add the garlic and chopped ginger and stir well. Spoon in the honey and lemon juice and let bubble for 2–3 minutes until the chicken is tender. Adjust the seasoning to taste.

5 Cook the noodles for about 3 minutes, or according to the instructions on the packet, and drain well.

6 Mix the noodles with the vegetables in the serving dish and pour in the chicken mixture.

7 Serve immediately, garnished with the chopped cilantro.

WINE SUGGESTION

Try a light, white, unoaked Chardonnay or Pinot Grigio with this salad.

POLENTA

Polenta is the northern Italian equivalent to pasta and can be served soft, like mashed potato, to accompany meat and fish. It can also be served, as here, in a thicker form which is broiled or fried and served with a variety of toppings.

Serves 4
Preparation time: 10 minutes, plus chilling
Cooking time: 10 minutes

INGREDIENTS

4 cups water
1 tsp salt
1¾ cups quick-cook polenta
2 garlic cloves, peeled and crushed
2 oz/55 g sun-dried tomatoes, roughly chopped
½ tsp dried oregano
2 tbsp freshly grated Parmesan cheese
3 tbsp olive oil
salt and pepper

You will need a large pan, a measuring cup, a cook's knife, a cutting board, a skillet or a griddle pan, a wooden spatula, and a small cookie sheet

METHOD

1 Pour the water into a pan, bring to a boil, then add the salt.

2 Pour the polenta, in a steady stream, into the pan, stirring constantly. Lower the heat and simmer for 1 minute (or according to the instructions on the packet).

3 Beat in the garlic, sun-dried tomatoes, oregano, and Parmesan, and season well.

4 Use 2 teaspoons of the oil to grease the cookie sheet, and spoon the polenta mixture onto it. Smooth over the surface and let cool for about 1 hour.

5 Cut into eight slices or wedges and brush with the remaining olive oil.

6 Cook under a broiler preheated to medium, or on a griddle pan over medium heat, for 2–3 minutes each side until golden.

7 Serve two slices per person with any cooked meat or fish, or broiled summer vegetables (see page 177).

FRUIT

W e are exhorted to eat five pieces of fruit and vegetables each day—
what a delight! We are so lucky to have our stores overflowing with
wonderful fruit all year round. Some people think this is sad and that we
should still eat according to season. I certainly believe that when it comes to
summer berries—raspberries and strawberries—we have some of the best.
Home-grown apples are good at the start of the season but toward the end of
their storing time they get rather tired, so it is good to have new season
varieties from Australia and New Zealand.

Some seasonal fruits are around for a short time, like tangerines or
satsumas, and the season for peaches and nectarines passes very swiftly, so we
are limited to eating those in season. Home-grown rhubarb also has a limited
season—it is one of the only fruits that cannot be eaten raw—it needs cooking
and sweetening to make it edible. Here is a selection of the most popular fruits.

TREE FRUITS

These include apples, pears, plums, peaches, nectarines,
apricots, and cherries.

Apples
These are the best-known fruit. There are many varieties,
divided into two types—eating apples and cooking apples.
Eating apples are best bought when they are not too large—
their flavor is best when they are small. Well-known varieties
include Empire, McIntosh, Golden Delicious, Granny Smith,
Red Delicious, and Winesap. The best-known cooking apple is
Bramley's Seedling—a large green apple that is too tart for
eating. When they are cooked, they"fall" and reduce to a soft
pulp, which makes them useful for sauces and other desserts.

Pears
These are a softer fruit than apples, and need careful buying. It
is difficult to buy ripe pears for eating, so it is best to buy
ahead and allow 3–4 days for ripening at home. There are
quite a few varieties available, but some are very hard and are
better for cooking. Conference pears are quite large and
hard—peel and poach them for eating. Comice pears can be
eaten raw or cooked, and the newer types of Red Anjou,

Bartlett, and Williams are smaller, succulent and juicy and can
be eaten for dessert, perhaps with some cheese. They are also
good cooked.

Plums
Plums vary in size and color and are available in dessert and
cooking varieties. Buy plums that have smooth skins and no
blemishes and make sure they are not too soft. The Victoria
plum is a traditional plum and is large and oval in shape. When
it is ripe, it is delicious to eat raw, and it also cooks well.
Damsons are small plums with very dark-blue skins: they are
rather sour and should only be eaten cooked and used for jelly
and preserves.

Peaches and nectarines
Again, it is difficult to buy these fruits when they are ripe—
often they are picked before they are ripe and then only soften
rather than ripen. Make sure you choose the ripest ones
available—they should have a good, pink color, without any
green tinge. If they haven't softened in a couple of days, it
would be best to cook them. A ripe peach or nectarine is a
delight, but a soft "cotton ball" texture is unpleasant. Both

peaches and nectarines come with white and yellow flesh. A peach has a downy skin and the nectarine a smooth skin; if you like, you can also remove the skin by blanching (see page 14). Peaches and nectarines can be eaten raw, whole, cut in half and pitted, mixed in a fruit salad, or cooked by poaching or baking.

Apricots

These are small, orange-colored fruits with downy skins. They are popular in eastern countries, where they are used in both sweet and savory dishes. They have a very short season and it is difficult to find really good ones because they do not travel well. If you find good apricots, eat them as they are—they have a lovely sharp/sweet taste. Otherwise, use them in recipes or simply poach them with a little cinnamon and serve them hot or cold.

Cherries

Some very good cherries are available now, but the season is quite short. Choose even-size cherries with their stalks still attached. The sweet cherries are large and particularly

delicious: just eat them as they are—they will keep in the refrigerator for 2–3 days. Morello cherries are small and very dark and cannot be eaten without cooking. They are often made into jelly, or poached and preserved in brandy.

SOFT FRUITS

This category includes all the fresh currants, strawberries, raspberries, blackberries, cranberries, and gooseberries.

Currants

These are available white, red, and black. We can now buy them easily, albeit for a short season. They are available in small boxes and should look plump and shiny. Black ones are too sour to eat raw, but the red and white varieties can be served in summer puddings or fruit salads, or are good for decorating pavlovas or cheesecakes.

Strawberries

Eat strawberries just as they are with some sugar and cream if you like. Choose small to medium-size strawberries, which are

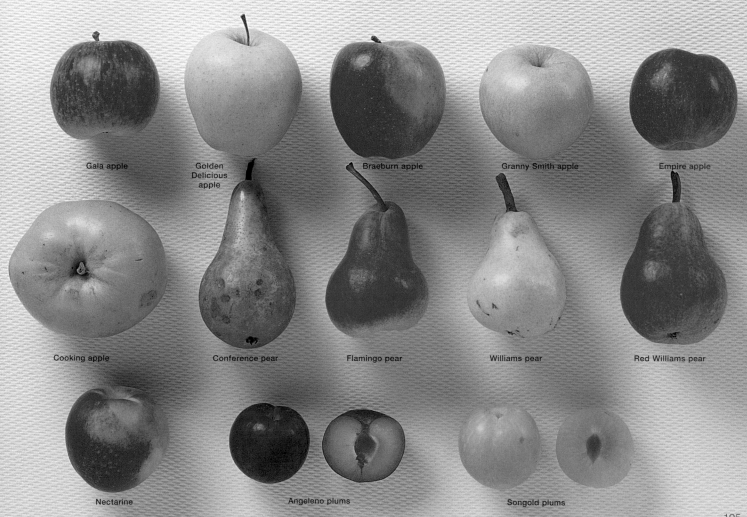

Gala apple
Golden Delicious apple
Braeburn apple
Granny Smith apple
Empire apple

Cooking apple
Conference pear
Flamingo pear
Williams pear
Red Williams pear

Nectarine
Angeleno plums
Songold plums

not too soft. They are not usually cooked, but some people serve them with a dash of black pepper or a splash of balsamic vinegar. Serve them with ice cream or on top of a pavlova, in fruit salads, and in tarts or flans. They also make excellent jelly. Do not attempt to freeze them.

Raspberries

These are the most delicious of all the small fruits. They have a wonderful flavor and look attractive. Again, they are best eaten as they are, simply with sugar and cream. However, they can also form part of a summer pudding, or they can be used to decorate desserts. They are also popular as a modern sauce or "coulis," made by simply rubbing the fruit through a strainer and mixing the purée with a little confectioners' sugar. Unlike strawberries, raspberries freeze very well. They also make delicious jelly.

Blackberries

Cultivated blackberries are available in the shops, but they may also grow wild in hedges. The cultivated ones are larger and sweeter: choose ones that are completely ripe. Blackberries can be served in fruit salads. More usually, and certainly this is the case with the wild ones, they are better

cooked—in crisp desserts, pies, fools, mousses. and summer puddings. They can also be made into jelly.

Gooseberries

Green gooseberries are a traditional favorite, but have gone in and out of fashion over the years. Buy berries that are large and plump, and store them in the refrigerator for 4–5 days. They are not often eaten raw, although some varieties are sweet enough to eat uncooked. Cook them in crisp desserts and pies. You can also make a gooseberry sauce and serve it with oily fish, such as mackerel or trout.

CITRUS FRUITS

Oranges

Oranges are available throughout the year. There are many varieties, mostly sweet, as well as the bitter Seville orange, which is used to make marmalade. Eating oranges should be firm with a clean skin and no blemishes. They will keep for a week at room temperature or longer if stored in the refrigerator. Eat them simply peeled, or segment them and use them in salads. Orange slices can be used for decorating

Currants

Navel orange

Lemon

Strawberries

Mandarin

Lime

Raspberries

Satsuma

Grapefruit

and garnishing all kinds of food. Squeeze out the juice for drinking or to make sherbets, ice cream, mousses, tarts, and desserts. Grate the rind to flavor cakes, pastries, and stuffings (it is best to buy unwaxed fruit or organic if you are using the skin). Temple oranges are in the stores in January to February. The season is short, so buy some as soon as you see them and make some marmalade with them (see page 253).

Lemons

These are also available throughout the year. Buy lemons that are firm with good, yellow skins. Store them in the same way and for the same length of time as oranges. They are very versatile and can be used in many ways. Gin and tonic, for example, would not be the same without a slice of lemon. Many foods benefit from the sharp taste and flavor of lemon. Lemon juice is squeezed over food before serving and lemon rind is added to cakes, stuffings, and fish dishes (use unwaxed ones). Recipes for lemons include lemon tart, lemon curd, lemon sherbet, and ice cream. They can also be used with other citrus fruits to make marmalade.

Limes

These green fruits are like lemons, but smaller, and are used in similar ways. They are now popular in Thai and South American cooking.

Grapefruit

These can be bought all year round. They have different colored flesh, from pale yellow and pink to ruby red. The pinker the fruit, the sweeter the taste. They are usually eaten as a breakfast food, with or without sweetener. The rind is not used because it is too pungent. Grapefruit juice is popular, and the fruit can be segmented and served in some savory salads. It can also be made into mixed fruit marmalades.

Tangerines, satsumas, clementines, and mandarins

All of these are available around Christmas time. They are small, orange-coloured fruits and taste rather like oranges. They vary in sweetness and in the thickness of their skins. Some are easy to peel, which makes them ideal for children, and they are virtually seedless. They are usually eaten uncooked but they can be served in a flavored syrup.

OTHER FRUITS

These fruits do not fall into a particular category.

Rhubarb

This is available in the spring as forced rhubarb, when it is at its tenderest and needs only a little cooking. Buy stalks that are slim and a pale pink color—they should be firm. Baking the rhubarb stalks in the oven will make sure they stay in shape and retain their color. First remove the leaves and the bases of the stems before cutting into 2 inch/5 cm lengths, then sweeten to taste. Rhubarb can also be used for crisp desserts and pies, as well as jelly.

Grapes

Green and red varieties are available, and they can be either seeded or seedless. Grapes can be eaten on their own at any time of day, but they are also a good accompaniment for cheese at the end of a meal. Choose grapes that look dry and firm, and avoid those that are soft and look sticky. Always choose a well-shaped bunch. Grapes can also be used in fruit salads, or as a garnish.

Melons

Melons are best in late summer but they can be bought all year round. There are a variety of colors and flavors available. Honeydew is a largish melon, very sweet with a pale yellow color. Ogen is round with green skin and flesh. Cantaloupe is small and round with a brownish skin and sweet orange flesh. Charentais, a type of cantaloupe, is very small with a strong flavor and deep-orange flesh. Look for melons that have unblemished skins. To test for ripeness, use a finger to press the stalk end of the melon—it should just yield slightly. Do not store melons in the refrigerator—I find they taint all the other foods with their smell. Serve melon cut into segments as an appetizer or light lunch dish. You can also serve it with a little prosciutto. Alternatively, serve it for dessert with some soft fruits. Melon flesh can also be cut into balls and served in a fruit salad.

Bananas

These are starting to become the most popular fruit, and are eaten a lot by sportspeople. Choose yellow bananas for immediate eating or green ones for ripening at home. Do not store them in the refrigerator because they will go black. They are usually peeled and eaten as an instant snack, but they can also be sliced onto breakfast cereal or in fruit salads. Bananas can be baked or broiled and can be used to flavor cakes and ice cream. They are also good with bacon: I was brought up on fried banana with bacon for breakfast.

Kiwi fruit

These are small, dark, rough-skinned fruits, and are bright-green inside. They are a very attractive fruit when sliced and have a very particular flavor. They can be sliced in half and eaten with a teaspoon (like a boiled egg), or peeled and sliced to serve on pavlovas or cheesecakes. The peeled slices can also be added to fruit salads.

APPLE AND BLACKBERRY CRISP

This is one of the simplest desserts—it is easy to make and delicious to eat. Any fruit or combination of fruit can be used to ring the changes.

Serves 6
Preparation time: 20–25 minutes
Cooking time: 25–30 minutes

INGREDIENTS

1 lb/450 g cooking apples
1 lb/450 g blackberries
115 g/4 oz superfine sugar
4 tbsp water
cream, yogurt, or custard, to serve

Crust
1½ cups whole-wheat flour
6 tbsp sweet butter
⅓ cup soft brown sugar
1 tsp apple pie spice

You will need a vegetable peeler, a small, sharp knife, a cutting board, a mixing bowl, a fork, a cookie sheet, and a 7½ cup ovenproof dish (a gratin dish would be good)

METHOD

1 Preheat the oven to 375°F/190°C. Prepare the apples by cutting them into fourths, then peeling, and coring them. Thinly slice them into an ovenproof dish.

2 Add the blackberries and then stir in the sugar. Pour in the water.

3 Make the crisp by placing the flour in a mixing bowl and rubbing in the butter until the mixture resembles bread crumbs. Stir in the sugar and apple pie spice.

4 Spread the crisp evenly over the fruit and use a fork to press down lightly.

5 Put the dish on a cookie sheet and bake in the center of the preheated oven for 25–30 minutes until the crisp is golden brown.

6 Serve warm with cream, yogurt, or custard.

POACHED PEARS IN CASSIS

Serves 4
Preparation time: 15 minutes, plus chilling
Cooking time: 30 minutes–1 hour

INGREDIENTS

4 firm pears
¼ cup superfine sugar
½ cup Cassis
½ cup crème fraîche, to serve

You will need a wide-based, lidded pan, a wooden spoon, a sharp knife, a cutting board, a measuring cup, a vegetable peeler, a slotted spoon, and a serving dish

METHOD

1 Peel the pears carefully, then cut them in half, and remove the cores. Place them in the pan and just cover them with water, then add the sugar.

2 Slowly bring to a boil over gentle heat, making sure the sugar dissolves.

3 Reduce the heat, cover, and simmer for 15–45 minutes until the pears are tender. The cooking time will depend on the ripeness of the fruit.

4 Remove from the heat and use a slotted spoon to lift out the pears. Transfer to a serving dish.

5 Return the pan to the heat and simmer for about 4–6 minutes until the syrup has thickened.

6 Stir in the Cassis, and then pour it over the pears.

7 Cover the dish with plastic wrap and chill well for up to 2–4 hours before serving. Serve with crème fraîche.

APPLE AND GINGER MERINGUE

This spicy baked dessert is full of flavor and is equally good served hot or cold.

Serves 6
Preparation time: 25 minutes
Cooking time: 20–25 minutes

INGREDIENTS

4 oz/115 g ladyfingers
2 tbsp brandy (optional)
2 lb/900 g cooking apples
2 tbsp sweet butter
½ tsp cinnamon
4 tbsp soft brown sugar
3 pieces preserved ginger in syrup, finely diced
3 egg whites
scant 1 cup superfine sugar
cream, to serve

You will need a 10 inch/25 cm round ovenproof serving dish, a pan, a sharp knife, a wooden spoon, a hand whisk, a mixing bowl, and a flexible spatula

1 Preheat the oven to 350°F/180°C. Place the ladyfingers in an ovenproof serving dish and sprinkle the brandy over them (if using). Peel, core, and thinly slice the apples.

2 Melt the butter in a pan over gentle heat and add the apples, cinnamon, and sugar. Cover and cook over medium heat for 6–8 minutes until the apples are cooked and soft. Stir in the chopped ginger, remove from the heat, and let cool a little. Spoon the mixture over the ladyfingers.

3 Whisk the egg whites in a mixing bowl until thick and glossy, and then carefully whisk in the sugar gradually, a tablespoon at a time. Continue until all the sugar is added.

4 Immediately spoon the meringue over the apple mixture and swirl into soft peaks. Make sure the meringue goes right up to the edge of the dish to cover the apple completely.

5 Bake in the center of the preheated oven for 10–15 minutes until the meringue is pale golden brown.

6 Remove the meringue from the oven and serve hot or cold with a little cream.

BAKED STICKY BANANAS

Serves 2
Preparation time: 5 minutes
Cooking time: 12–14 minutes

INGREDIENTS

4 ripe bananas
4 tbsp sweet butter
juice of ½ lemon
3 tbsp soft, light brown sugar
½ tsp crushed cardamom seeds
¼ cup sliced almonds
3 tbsp chilled crème fraîche, to serve

You will need a small, sharp knife, a lemon squeezer, a cutting board, and an ovenproof dish (a gratin dish is good), which is large enough to hold the bananas

METHOD

1 Preheat the oven to 400°F/200°C. Peel the bananas and then cut them diagonally into 1 cm/½ inch slices.

2 Use 1 tablespoon of the butter to grease an ovenproof dish.

3 Place the bananas in the prepared dish and sprinkle with the lemon juice. Add the sugar and the cardamom seeds.

4 Bake in the center of the preheated oven for 6–7 minutes until the sugar has melted.

5 Remove the dish from the oven and baste the fruit with the juices from the dish. Dot on the remaining butter and sprinkle over the almonds.

6 Return to the oven and bake for a further 6–7 minutes at the same temperature until the bananas are cooked and the almonds are browned.

7 Serve immediately with the crème fraîche.

BAKED STUFFED PEACHES

Serves 4
Preparation time: 15 minutes
Cooking time: 20–25 minutes

INGREDIENTS

4 ripe peaches
4 tbsp sweet butter
2 tbsp soft brown sugar
1 cup crushed amaretti or macaroons
2 tbsp Amaretto liqueur
½ cup light cream, to serve

You will need a small, sharp knife, a cutting board, a bowl, a wooden spoon, and an ovenproof dish (an au gratin dish is good), which is large enough to hold the peaches

METHOD

1 Preheat the oven to 350°F/180°C. Prepare the peaches by cutting them in half and removing the pits (if you want to peel them, just dip them into boiling water for 10–15 seconds and then plunge them into cold water).

2 Use 1 tablespoon of the butter to grease an ovenproof dish.

3 In a bowl, combine the remaining butter and sugar until creamy, then add the amaretti or macaroons, and mix well.

4 Place the peach halves in the greased ovenproof dish, cut sides up, and stuff them with the cookie filling.

5 Bake them in the center of the preheated oven for 20–25 minutes until the peaches are soft.

6 Pour the liqueur over them and serve hot with some light cream.

CARAMELIZED ORANGES

Serves 4
Preparation time: 20–30 minutes, plus chilling
Cooking time: 5–7 minutes

INGREDIENTS

4 large oranges
generous ½ cup superfine sugar
1 cup water

You will need a citrus zester or grater, a small, sharp knife, a cutting board, a heavy pan, a measuring cup, a wooden spoon, a bowl, 4 toothpicks, and 4 serving dishes

METHOD

1 Using a citrus zester, carefully remove the rind in strips from two of the oranges, then set aside.

2 Use a sharp knife to peel the remaining oranges. To peel and segment an orange, cut the top and bottom off the orange and place it on a board, then cut down onto the board, removing the peel and all the pith. Slice the oranges horizontally into 5 thick slices and then secure them through the center with a toothpick to re-form. Place them in individual serving dishes.

3 In a pan, heat the sugar over medium heat for 1–2 minutes until melted. Continue to heat for 2–3 minutes more until it turns a good caramel color.

4 Remove the pan from the heat and, holding it at arm's length, slowly and carefully pour in the water. It will bubble and spit. Use a potholder or a cloth to hold the cup of water.

5 Stir well to dissolve any lumps. If there are still lumps, you might need to heat it again very gently. Let cool thoroughly for 15–20 minutes before pouring the syrup over the oranges.

6 Cover with plastic wrap and chill in the refrigerator for up to 24 hours until needed.

7 Just before serving, sprinkle on the prepared orange peel.

ASIAN GREEN FRUIT SALAD

Serves 6
Preparation time: 20 minutes, plus chilling
Cooking time: 5 minutes

INGREDIENTS

6 oz/175 g lychees
8 oz/225 g green, seedless grapes
1 small melon (Honeydew or Ogen)
2 kiwi fruit, peeled and thinly sliced
2 green apples, cored and sliced
juice of 1 lemon
1 pear, cored and sliced
sprigs fresh mint, to decorate

Syrup
generous ½ cup granulated sugar
1¼ cups water
2 tsp China tea leaves

You will need a pan, a wooden spoon, a sharp knife, a cutting board, a measuring cup, a vegetable peeler, and a melon baller

METHOD

1 For the syrup, put the sugar and water into a pan and bring slowly to a boil over low heat. Stir to make sure the sugar is dissolved. Pour the syrup over the tea leaves in a bowl and let cool.

2 To prepare the fruit, peel the lychees and remove the pits. Wash the grapes and cut in half if large. Cut the melon in half and scoop out the seeds. Using a melon baller, make small spheres of fruit. (If you have not got a baller, cut the fruit into even-size chunks.)

3 Use a vegetable peeler to peel the kiwi fruit, then slice thinly with a sharp knife.

4 Carefully cut the apples into halves and then fourths, and remove the cores. Slice thinly into equal slices. Sprinkle the slices with lemon juice to prevent browning.

5 Repeat with the pear: you can peel this if you like.

6 Place all the fruit, and any remaining lemon juice, in a serving bowl and strain the cold tea syrup over it.

7 Chill well for up to 2–4 hours before serving. Serve decorated with the mint sprigs.

RHUBARB FOOL

Serves 6
Preparation time: 15 minutes, plus chilling
Cooking time: 8–10 minutes

INGREDIENTS

1 lb 9 oz/700 g rhubarb, cut into 1 inch/2.5 cm lengths
generous 1 cup superfine sugar
grated rind and juice of 1 orange
1¼ cups heavy cream
2 tbsp grated bittersweet chocolate, to decorate

You will need a sharp knife, a cutting board, a medium pan, a wooden spoon, a grater, a hand whisk, a bowl, a metal spoon, and 6 glass serving dishes

METHOD

1 Put the rhubarb in a pan with the sugar and the orange juice.

2 Over a gentle heat, slowly bring to a boil, stirring well to make sure the sugar dissolves.

3 Reduce the heat and simmer very gently for about 5 minutes until the rhubarb is tender. Do not overcook because you need to retain a good color.

4 Remove from the heat and let cool. Taste for sweetness and add a little more sugar if necessary.

5 If the rhubarb is too liquid strain it, then place in a bowl, and beat it with a wooden spoon until smooth or process it in a blender if you like your fool absolutely smooth.

6 In a separate bowl, whip the cream until it is thick but not too dry. Using a metal spoon, fold in the cold rhubarb carefully, then add the orange rind. Only just combine the two—the fool looks more attractive if it has a marbled effect.

7 Spoon into the serving dishes, cover with plastic wrap, and chill well for up to 2 hours. Just before serving, decorate with the grated chocolate.

SUMMER PUDDING

This traditional pudding is made with slices of bread and summer fruits, hence the name. You can vary the fruits according to what you can buy at the time.

Serves 6
Preparation time: 15 minutes, plus chilling
Cooking time: 5 minutes

INGREDIENTS

1 lb 8 oz/675 g mixed soft fruits, such as red currants, black currants, raspberries, and blackberries
¾ cup superfine sugar
6–8 slices day-old white bread, crusts removed
¾ cup heavy cream, to serve

You will need a 3¾ cup bowl, a large pan, a wooden spoon, a bread knife, and a cutting board

METHOD

1 First prepare the fruit. Remove any stalks from the currants and blackberries—there is no need to wash them. Put the fruit in a large pan with the sugar.

2 Over low heat, very slowly bring to a boil, stirring carefully to make sure that the sugar has dissolved. Cook over low heat for only 2–3 minutes until the juices run, but the fruit still holds its shape.

3 Line the bowl with some of the slices of bread (cut them to shape so that the bread fits well). Spoon in the cooked fruit and juice, reserving a little of the juice for later.

4 Cover the surface with the remaining bread.

5 Place a saucer or small plate on top of the pudding. Use a large can of food or other weigh to weigh it down for at least 8 hours or overnight in the refrigerator.

6 Turn out the pudding and pour the reserved juice over it to color any white pieces of bread that may be showing.

7 Serve with the cream.

DESSERTS

Desserts are where American cooking comes into its own. Americans masters of the art of dessert making. Puddings were originally cook and made from flour. They were first steamed, and then baked when ovens became the norm. The "steamed pudding" as we know it now has made a revival and is usually made from a suet pudding mix or a creamed "cake" mix and can be cooked either by steaming (which gives a moist texture) or by baking (for a drier result). There are also some healthier puddings, which are not cooked—for example summer pudding (see page 207). Sweet dishes that are served hot include crisps, pies, tarts, milk puddings, and meringues. Lighter, cold desserts may contain fruit or cream and may be set with gelatin or frozen, such as mousses and soufflés, ice creams and sherbets, custards and trifles. Recipes for hot and cold desserts can be found in this section. But in the sections devoted to Eggs, Dairy Produce, and Fruit you will find other sweet dishes, which can be served at the end of a meal.

INGREDIENTS USED IN DESSERTS

Flour
All-purpose and self-rising flour are used. For buying and storage, see page 36.

Fats
Butter is usually used because of its good flavor and color, but sometimes other fats are used.

Sugar
Superfine sugar is used in the same way in desserts as it is in baking. Also syrup, honey, and different types of brown sugar are used in various ways.

Eggs
These are an important ingredient in desserts.

Cream
Light or heavy cream can be used in many desserts.

Other ingredients
Fruit, nuts, dried fruit, unsweetened cocoa powder, chocolate, gelatin, honey, syrup, and jelly all play an important part in preparing and cooking desserts.

EQUIPMENT

Bowls
Different sizes are needed, from individual dariole molds to 2½ cup and 5 cup bowls for steamed puddings and various molded desserts.

Ovenproof dishes
Oval or round ceramic dishes are useful for baked puddings and crisps.

Soufflé dishes
Individual ramekins are good for individual desserts and large, ovenproof dishes are useful for serving large mousses and soufflés and for baking sponge puddings.

Glass dishes
Individual sundae glasses and large glass bowls are good for serving smaller desserts and fruit salads. Large, heatproof glass dishes are good for baking crisps and other fruit desserts.

LEMON SURPRISE

Serves 4–6
Preparation time: 20 minutes
Cooking time: 45 minutes

INGREDIENTS

4 tbsp butter
grated rind and juice of 2 lemons
generous ½ cup superfine sugar
2 eggs, separated
½ cup self-raising flour
1 cup milk

You will need a wooden spoon, a grater, an electric hand mixer or a wooden spoon, 2 mixing bowls, a flexible spatula, a 3¾ cup ovenproof dish (a pie dish or a soufflé dish is best), a measuring cup, and a roasting pan

METHOD

1 Preheat the oven to 180°C/350°F/180°C. Using a little of the butter, grease an ovenproof dish.

2 In a mixing bowl, beat the remaining butter with the lemon rind and sugar until it is soft and creamy. Beat in the egg yolks one at a time.

3 Sift the flour and then fold it in alternately with the lemon juice and milk.

4 In a separate bowl, whisk the egg whites until stiff, then fold into the lemon mixture.

5 Pour the mixture into the prepared dish and place in a roasting pan half-filled with water. Transfer to the preheated oven and bake in the center for about 45 minutes until the dessert is golden brown and set on the top. Underneath the sponge topping there will be a lovely layer of lemon sauce, hence the surprise. Serve warm.

QUEEN OF PUDDINGS

This is a very traditional and popular pudding. Simply make it from bread crumbs, eggs, and milk, then top it with jelly and meringue—delicious!

Serves 4–6
Preparation time: 20 minutes, plus 15 minutes standing
Cooking time: 45 minutes

INGREDIENTS

2 tbsp butter
2½ cups milk
2 cups fresh white bread crumbs
generous ½ cup superfine sugar
grated rind of 1 lemon
3 eggs, separated
3 tbsp raspberry jelly, warmed
1 tsp golden granulated sugar

You will need a small pan, a wooden spoon, a grater, an electric hand mixer or a balloon whisk, a mixing bowl, a flexible spatula, and a 3¾ cup ovenproof dish (a pie dish or a soufflé dish is best) or 4 individual ovenproof dishes

METHOD

1 Using a little of the butter, grease an ovenproof dish.

2 Heat the remaining butter and the milk in a pan over medium heat and gently bring to a boil.

3 Remove from the heat and then stir in the bread crumbs, 1 tablespoon of the superfine sugar, and the lemon rind. Let stand and cool for 15 minutes, then beat in the egg yolks.

4 Preheat the oven to 350°F/180°C. Pour the mixture into the prepared dish and smooth the surface. Bake in the center of the preheated oven for about 30 minutes (20 minutes for individual puddings) until set. Spread over the jelly.

5 Whisk the egg whites in a mixing bowl until very thick, then gradually add the remaining superfine sugar. Continue, whisking, until all the superfine sugar is added.

6 Spoon the meringue mixture over the pudding and make sure the meringue covers it completely. Swirl the meringue into attractive peaks and sprinkle with the granulated sugar.

7 Bake again in the center of the oven at the same temperature for about 10–15 minutes until the meringue is golden brown. Serve while still warm.

BAKED ALASKA

A simple dessert, which looks spectacular yet is really easy to make; you can even prepare it ahead and freeze it.

Serves 8–10
Preparation time: 20 minutes, plus freezing
Cooking time: 4–5 minutes

INGREDIENTS

one 10 inch/25 cm sponge flan

2¼ cups double chocolate-chip ice cream, slightly softened

2¼ cups vanilla ice cream, slightly softened

1⅓ cups fresh raspberries

3 oz/85 g mint chocolates, chopped

4 egg whites

generous 1 cup superfine sugar

2 tsp golden granulated sugar

You will need an ice cream scoop or a spoon, a cook's knife, a cutting board, a mixing bowl, an electric hand mixer or a balloon whisk, a flexible spatula, and a large, ovenproof plate

METHOD

1 Place the sponge flan on an ovenproof plate and scoop spoonfuls of the ice cream onto it. Alternate the flavors and push the raspberries and the pieces of chocolate into the spaces; pile it up high into a mound. Put the plate into the freezer for 20 minutes so that the ice cream can firm up.

2 Preheat the oven to 425°F/220°C. Whisk the egg whites in a mixing bowl until very thick, then gradually add the superfine sugar. Continue until all the sugar is added.

3 Immediately spoon the meringue mixture over the ice cream. Make sure the meringue covers the ice cream completely and makes a seal with the flan base. Swirl the meringue into attractive peaks and then sprinkle with the granulated sugar.

4 Bake in the center of the preheated oven for about 4–5 minutes until the meringue is golden brown and the tips of the peaks are well colored. Serve immediately.

* Suitable for freezing. Prepare up to the end of step 3 and freeze for up to 2 days. Only keep it for 1–2 days because it is impossible to cover and will take up rather a lot of space in the freezer. When serving, remove from the freezer and allow about 15 minutes for the ice cream to soften a little before cooking.

STEAMED TOFFEE NUT DESSERT

Serves 6–8
Preparation time: 20 minutes
Cooking time: 1 1/2 hours

INGREDIENTS

2 tsp melted butter

Sauce
½ cup butter
⅔ cup light molasses sugar
⅔ cup heavy cream
12 whole pecan nuts

Base
½ cup butter, softened
½ cup light molasses sugar
2 eggs, lightly beaten
1½ cups self-rising flour
2 tbsp milk
½ cup pecan nuts, chopped
½ cup pecan nuts, to decorate

You will need a small pan, a wooden spoon, an electric hand mixer or a wooden spoon, a mixing bowl, a flexible spatula, a 5 cup heatproof bowl, some aluminum foil, a large, lidded pan, and a serving dish

METHOD

1 Use the melted butter to grease a heatproof bowl.

2 To make the sauce, place the butter, molasses sugar, and cream in a small pan. Bring to a boil over medium heat, stirring constantly. Lower the heat and simmer for 2 minutes until slightly thickened. Pour 2 tablespoons of the sauce into the prepared bowl and add 12 whole pecan nuts.

3 To make the base, beat together the butter and sugar in a mixing bowl until soft and creamy, then beat in the eggs a little at a time.

4 Fold in the flour carefully and then stir in the milk to make a soft pourable consistency. Fold in the chopped pecan nuts.

5 Turn the mixture into the heatproof bowl. Cover the surface with a disk of waxed paper or baking parchment and top with a pleated sheet of foil. Secure with some string or crimp the edges of the foil to make sure of a tight fit around the bowl.

6 Place the bowl in a large pan and half-fill the pan with boiling water. Cover the pan and bring back to a boil over medium heat. Reduce the heat to a slow simmer and steam for 1½ hours until risen and firm. Keep checking the water level and add more boiling water when necessary.

7 Remove the pan from the heat and lift out the bowl. Turn out the dessert onto a warm serving dish and decorate with pecan nuts. Reheat the remaining sauce over medium heat for 2–3 minutes. Serve the dessert immediately and pass the sauce separately.

CONTEMPORARY CHRISTMAS PUDDING

This is a wonderful pudding: it has no suet or added fat, and is deliciously rich and fruity. It could become a family tradition.

Serves 10–12
Preparation time: 30 minutes
Cooking time: 5 hours, then 2 hours to reheat

INGREDIENTS

4½ cups day-old whole-wheat bread crumbs
3⅝ cups mixed dried fruits
generous 1 cup no-soak dried apricots, roughly chopped
1 cup almonds slivered
2 cups crushed almond macaroons or amaretti
2 tsp apple pie spice
2 eating apples, cored and chopped
4 eggs
5 tbsp brandy
⅔ cup Marsala
grated rind and juice of 1 orange
2 tbsp coarse marmalade (see page 253)
2 tsp vegetable oil
sprig of holly, to decorate

To serve
thick cream, or brandy butter (see opposite)
2 tablespoons brandy (to flame the pudding), optional

You will need a blender (or grater), a large mixing bowl, a medium bowl, an electric hand mixer or a balloon whisk, a measuring cup, a flexible spatula, one 10 cup heatproof bowl (or two 5 cup heatproof bowls), some waxed paper and aluminum foil, and a large, lidded pan

METHOD

1 Prepare the bread crumbs by processing in a blender or grate the bread using a grater.

2 Put the bread crumbs, dried fruits, nuts, and crushed almond cookies into a mixing bowl, along with the apple pie spice and prepared apples.

3 Break the eggs into a separate bowl and beat well until frothy. Pour in the brandy and Marsala and add the orange rind and juice. Mix well. Stir in the marmalade.

4 Pour the liquid over the dry ingredients, stir well, then make a wish—to do this, get all the household together so that everyone can make a wish!

5 Cover the bowl with plastic wrap and let stand for at least 3 hours, or overnight is ideal.

6 Use the oil to grease the heatproof bowl, and spoon in the mixture. Cover with waxed paper or baking parchment and then with a layer of foil. Crimp the edges of the foil to make sure of a tight fit around the bowl.

7 Place the bowl in a pan. It is a good idea to make a long, folded piece of foil on which the bowl will stand in the pan—this makes it easier to lift out at the end of the cooking time. Half-fill the pan with boiling water, cover, and bring back to a boil over medium heat. Reduce the heat to a low simmer and steam for 5 hours. Keep checking the water level and add more boiling water when necessary.

8 Remove the pan from the heat and lift out the pudding. Remove the cooking paper and foil and replace with new pieces. Store in the refrigerator for up to 2 months until you want to serve it. To serve, steam for 2 hours (see step 7 above).

9 Now flame the pudding and decorate it with a sprig of holly. Serve with thick cream or brandy butter. To flame the pudding, heat 2 tablespoons of brandy in a small pan and pour over the hot pudding. Light and stand back—the flames will die out after 30–60 seconds.

BRANDY BUTTER

This rich butter makes the most delicious accompaniment to Christmas pudding and mince pies.

Serves 6–8
Preparation time: 10 minutes

INGREDIENTS

½ cup butter, softened
¾ cup soft brown sugar
4 tbsp brandy

You will need a bowl, a wooden spoon or an electric hand mixer, a flexible spatula, and a serving dish

METHOD

1 Beat the butter until pale and creamy—it will take 2 minutes if using an electric mixer and 4 minutes by hand. Add the sugar and continue to beat for a further 2 minutes until very light and fluffy. Gradually beat in the brandy.

2 Turn into a serving bowl and chill until required.

3 To store, cover with plastic wrap or put in a lidded plastic container and keep in the refrigerator for up to 2 weeks.

BROWN BREAD ICE CREAM

Serves 6
Preparation time: 15 minutes, plus freezing
Cooking time: 10 minutes

INGREDIENTS

2 cups day-old whole-wheat bread
1 tsp vegetable oil
generous ½ cup molasses sugar
2 cups heavy cream
2 tbsp superfine sugar
½ tsp vanilla extract
4–6 tbsp rum or brandy, to serve (optional)

You will need a blender (or grater), a cookie sheet, a mixing bowl, an electric hand mixer or a balloon whisk, a flexible spatula, and a lidded, rigid container or a loaf pan

METHOD

1 Preheat the oven to 400°F/200°C. Prepare the bread crumbs by processing them in a blender, or grate the bread using a grater.

2 Brush a cookie sheet with oil and sprinkle the bread crumbs over it. Sprinkle with the sugar.

3 Bake in the preheated oven for 8–10 minutes until the sugar caramelizes with the crumbs. Stir from time to time to prevent the crumbs sticking together.

4 When the crumbs are a good color, remove from the oven, break up with a fork, and let cool thoroughly.

5 In a separate bowl, whip the cream and sugar together lightly until just thickening. Fold in the vanilla extract. Carefully fold in the cold crumbs and turn into a rigid container. Cover and freeze until firm.

6 Before serving, allow the ice cream to soften slightly in the refrigerator for 1 hour. Spoon out onto individual serving plates or turn out the loaf shape and serve in slices. For extra flavor, pour a little rum or brandy over each serving.

* Suitable for freezing. This ice-cream will keep for 2 months in the freezer.

LEFT Brown Bread Ice Cream

EVE'S PUDDING

Serves 6–8
Preparation time: 30 minutes
Cooking time: 45 minutes

INGREDIENTS

1 lb 8 oz/675 g cooking apples
¾ cup raw brown sugar
¾ cup butter
scant 1 cup golden superfine sugar
3 eggs, beaten
1½ cups self-rising flour
½ cup ground almonds
3 tablespoons milk
1 tbsp sliced almonds
cream or custard, to serve

You will need a mixing bowl, a hand-held electric mixer or a wooden spoon, a flexible spatula, a deep pie dish or an oval gratin dish (about 7½ cup capacity), and a cookie sheet

METHOD

1 Preheat the oven to 350°F/180°C. Peel and core the apples and slice thinly into a large, ovenproof dish. Sprinkle with the raw brown sugar.

2 In a separate bowl, cream together the butter and superfine sugar until pale and fluffy, then beat in the eggs gradually. Fold in the flour and the ground almonds together with the milk. Spread the mixture evenly over the apples and sprinkle the sliced almonds on top.

3 Place the dish on a cookie sheet and bake in the center of the preheated oven for about 45 minutes, until the pudding is golden brown and well risen.

4 Serve hot with cream or custard.

Suitable for freezing. Prepare up to the end of step 3, cool well, then cover, and freeze for up to 3 months. To use, thaw and then reheat gently for 15–20 minutes at the same temperature.

QUICK CHOCOLATE MOUSSE

*This mousse is very rich and therefore needs to be served
in small portions.*

Serves 6
Preparation time: 15 minutes, plus chilling

INGREDIENTS

1¼ cups light cream

**7 oz/200 g good-quality bittersweet chocolate (should have
at least 52 percent cocoa solids)**

2 eggs, lightly beaten

2 tbsp Marsala

2 tbsp grated white chocolate, to decorate

You will need a small pan, a blender, a small bowl, a fork,
a flexible spatula, and 6 small ramekins or glass dishes

METHOD

1 Heat the cream in a pan over low heat for about
3–4 minutes until almost boiling.

2 Break up or chop the chocolate into small pieces and place
in a blender.

3 Pour the hot cream into the blender and then blend together
until smooth.

4 Pour in the eggs and blend again until well mixed. Add the
Marsala and give the mixture a final blend.

5 Pour into 6 ramekins or glass dishes and let cool. Cover
with plastic wrap and chill for about 2 hours. Serve
decorated with the grated white chocolate.

** Suitable for freezing. Make up to the end of step 5, but do not decorate
with the grated chocolate. Cover the dishes with plastic wrap and freeze
for up to 1 month. To serve, thaw in the refrigerator overnight and then
decorate with the grated white chocolate.*

PASTRY

*T*he range of traditional pastry is quite wide. You need to learn how to make pastry and it takes some practice. It is best to start with the simpler pastry and to progress to others when you have mastered the techniques. For this book, we are concentrating on making unsweetened pastry only, and the use of ready-made puff pastry and phyllo pastry. The ready-made varieties are increasing all the time and now come ready-rolled and in different shapes so that you do not even need a rolling pin.

TYPES OF PASTRY

Unsweetened

This is the basic pastry for everyday items, such as pies and quiches. It is very simple to make and can also be made with whole-wheat flour for a healthier version. It can also be bought ready-made, both fresh and frozen.

Rough Puff

This is also known as flaky pastry. It is simple to make when you want a raised, layered pastry. Use it to top savory pies.

Puff

This is layered during the making process and is very time consuming to make. In manufacturing, ready-made puff pastry is rolled and folded many times, resulting in many layers that allow the pastry to puff up on cooking. This gives a light, crisp-textured pastry.

Suet

This is pastry made using suet, to give a soft, spongy pastry. It is used for steamed puddings and dumplings.

Choux

Unlike all the other pastries, choux pastry is made by melting the fat in water and then adding it to the flour. It is used to make profiteroles and éclairs.

Phyllo

This Greek "strudel" pastry is widely available ready made. It consists of many wafer-thin sheets, which when assembled are brushed with butter and layered or rolled to make Greek dishes such as Baklava (a sweet pastry with honey and nuts) or German varieties of strudel. Phyllo pastry can be used for a variety of pastries and for pies.

INGREDIENTS

Flour

All-purpose white and whole-wheat flour can be used for unsweetened pastry. For puff pastry, white bread flour is used because the gluten content gives the dough more elasticity and helps the rising. For buying and storage, see page 36.

Fats

The type of fat used affects the texture and flavor of the pastry. Butter is the best fat for flavor and shortening is the best for texture. Traditionally, half butter and half lard were used for unsweetened pastry, but today people prefer to use either all butter or half butter and half vegetable shortening.

Sugar

Superfine sugar is often used to sprinkle over the top of pastry dishes before baking. This gives a crisp, crunchy appearance and texture.

Eggs

These are used only in the preparation of choux pastry, but they are also used as glazes for savory pastry. To make a glaze, use a whole egg and beat well. For a richer brown coloring, add a pinch of salt. Brush it over the pastry before cooking and again during cooking if a really rich crust is desired.

RULES FOR PASTRY MAKING

Cold temperature
Everything should be cold for pastry making, especially the hands. Use fat directly from the refrigerator and freshly drawn cold water.

Proportions
Measure everything accurately; the ratio of fat to flour is especially important.

Light touch
Rub the fat into the flour very carefully, using only the fingertips. Gather the pastry together gently, and handle it as little as possible. Do not knead. When rolling out, use a light touch with the rolling pin and do not stretch the pastry.

Relaxing
After mixing, leave the dough in the refrigerator for at least 30 minutes to reduce shrinkage. You can also repeat this once the pastry has been rolled if you have time.

Oven temperature
Always preheat the oven to the correct temperature (check your manufacturer's instructions to see how long it will take). Pastry needs a hot oven to set it into shape.

EQUIPMENT

Pie dishes
Pie dishes of different sizes, preferably metal, are necessary to produce good pies.

Loose-based quiche pans
These are ideal for quiches and sweet and savory tarts.

Muffin pan
This is necessary for jelly tarts and mince pies.

Cookie sheet
This is necessary for sausage rolls and other small items.

Rolling pin
This is an essential item.

Flour dredger
This makes life easier when rolling out pie dough.

BAKING BLIND

Pie shells are sometimes baked without a filling to make sure the base is crisp, especially if the filling needs little or no cooking.

1 Roll out the pastry to a size large enough to fill the base of the pan. It should overhang the pan by at least 2 inches/5 cm all around. Press it gently into the shape of the pan, then use a knife to trim off the edges.

2 Prick the base of the pastry all over with a fork. This will let any trapped air escape during baking. Cut out a piece of baking parchment or foil large enough to line the pie shell and overhang by 2 inches/5 cm all around.

3 Line the pie shell with the baking parchment, then fill it with ceramic baking beans, or dried beans or peas from your pantry.

4 Bake at 350°F/180°C for 10 minutes until the pastry is set and golden. Remove the beans and paper, then bake the empty pie shell for 5–10 minutes more. Let cool in the pan.

Whether you decide to use commercially made baking beans, or dried beans and peas from your pantry, they can be used over and over again.

SPINACH PHYLLO PIE

This pie is also good served cold—it makes a good dish for a picnic or for eating al fresco.

Serves 4–6
Preparation time: 20 minutes
Cooking time: 35–40 minutes

INGREDIENTS

9 oz/250 g fresh spinach
1 onion, peeled and finely chopped
1 tbsp olive oil
2 eggs
7 oz/200 g feta cheese, crumbled
1 tsp dried oregano
2 scallions, sliced (optional)
whole nutmeg, for grating
10 sheets phyllo pastry (about 6 oz/175 g)
4 tbsp butter, melted
salt and pepper
mixed salad, to serve

You will need a 9 inch/23 cm diameter pie pan, a cook's knife, a cutting board, a wooden spatula, a small bowl, a fork, a grater, a large pan, a pastry brush, and a cookie sheet

WINE SUGGESTION

A light Sauvignon, perhaps from New Zealand, would go well with this pie.

METHOD

1 Wash the spinach and remove any tough stalks. Dry well. Cook the onion and oil in a large pan over low heat for 1–2 minutes until soft but not colored. Add the spinach and cook for 1–2 minutes until wilted. Remove from the heat and cool. In a separate bowl, beat the eggs well and season (but remember the cheese is salty already). Add the eggs, cheese, oregano, scallions, if using, and a good grating of nutmeg.

2 Preheat the oven to 350°F/180°C. Lay one sheet of phyllo pastry in the dry pie pan and brush well with melted butter. Keep the phyllo pastry covered with a damp dish towel as you use it or it will dry out. Repeat using a further 3 sheets, arranging them around the pan and brushing them with butter, until the pan is fully covered.

3 Place the spinach filling in the dish and cover with 4 more sheets of pastry, brushing well with butter between each layer. Press the edges well together and trim the edges with a sharp knife.

4 Butter the top of the pie and scrunch up the two remaining sheets of pastry and arrange over the surface to give an attractive top. Brush with the remaining butter. Bake on a heated cookie sheet in the preheated oven for 35–40 minutes until the top is golden brown. Allow to stand for 10 minutes before serving in wedges accompanied by a mixed salad.

QUICHE LORRAINE

This quiche can be made without baking blind as long as you are going to eat it hot straight away; in this case bake at the hotter temperature for 30—40 minutes.

Serves 6–8
Preparation time: 20 minutes, plus chilling
Cooking time: 1 hour

INGREDIENTS

1½ cups all-purpose flour, plus extra for dusting

pinch of salt

6 tbsp butter (or use half butter and half vegetable shortening)

2–3 tbsp cold water, to mix

8 oz/225 g lardons, or bacon strips, snipped into small slices

1 onion, finely chopped

3 eggs

1¼ cups light cream

salt and pepper

You will need a 10 inch/25 cm diameter fluted quiche pan, a cook's knife, a cutting board, a skillet, a wooden spatula, a rolling pin, a flour dredger, a mixing bowl, a sheet of baking parchment, some baking beans, and a cookie sheet

WINE SUGGESTION
A white Alsace or an oaky Chardonnay would go well with this quiche.

METHOD

1 Sift the flour and salt into a bowl and gently rub in the butter until the mixture resembles bread crumbs. Sprinkle in the cold water and stir well using a round-bladed knife. Continue to mix until you have a smooth dough.

2 Wrap in plastic wrap and let rest in the refrigerator for 1–2 hours.

3 Preheat the oven to 400°F/200°C. Fry the bacon in a dry skillet until the fat runs. Add the onion and continue to cook for 5 minutes until the bacon is crispy and the onion soft and just turning golden.

4 On a lightly floured counter, roll out the dough into a round 2 inches/5 cm larger then the quiche pan. Fold the dough over the rolling pin and lift the dough over the pan. Ease the dough into the pan without stretching and press down lightly into the corners. Roll off the excess dough to neaten the pie shell. Prick the base of the pie shell and chill, uncovered, in the refrigerator for about 30 minutes.

5 Line the pie shell with baking parchment and fill with baking beans. Bake on a heated cookie sheet in the preheated oven for 10–15 minutes. This process is "baking blind." Remove the parchment and beans and return the pie shell to the oven for 10 minutes more until quite dry. Reduce the oven temperature to 350°F/180°C.

6 Beat the eggs and cream together in a bowl. Season well.

7 Put the bacon and onion into the pie shell and carefully pour in the egg mixture.

8 Put it on the cookie sheet and then bake in the oven for 30–35 minutes until set and golden brown; it will be quite puffed up. Serve immediately. Alternatively, to serve cold, let cool, cover with plastic wrap, and then store in the refrigerator for up to 48 hours until needed.

* Suitable for freezing. Cool first in a refrigerator for 2—4 hours, then open freeze on a cookie sheet. Remove from the freezer, discard the cookie sheet and wrap well in foil or a large plastic bag. To use, thaw at room temperature for 5—6 hours and warm through in the oven at 350°F/ 180°C for 20 minutes before serving.

STEAK AND MUSHROOM PIE

Serves 4–6
Preparation time: 30 minutes, plus standing
Cooking time: 2½ hours

INGREDIENTS

1 lb 9 oz/700 g braising steak, cut into 1½ inch/4 cm pieces
4 tbsp all-purpose flour
3 tbsp vegetable oil
1 onion, peeled and roughly chopped
1 garlic clove, peeled and finely chopped
4¾ cups sliced mushrooms
½ cup red wine
2 cups stock, store-bought or made from bouillon powder
1 bay leaf
14 oz/400 g puff pastry
1 egg, beaten
salt and pepper

You will need a large 10 cup flameproof casserole dish, a measuring cup, a rolling pin, a flour dredger, a pie funnel, a pastry brush, a slotted spoon, a sharp knife, and a 5 cup pie dish

METHOD

1 Preheat the oven to 325°F/170°C. Put the prepared meat with 2 tablespoons of the flour in a large plastic bag and season. Shake well until all the meat is well floured.

2 Heat the oil in a flameproof casserole dish over high heat and cook the meat until brown. Brown the meat in batches. Remove it from the dish with a slotted spoon and keep it warm.

WINE SUGGESTION
Try a red Tempranillo or Rioja from Spain with this.

3 Cook the onion and garlic in the casserole dish over medium heat for 2–3 minutes until softening and then add the mushrooms. Continue to cook for about 2 minutes, stirring constantly, until they start to wilt.

4 Carefully stir in the wine and scrape the base of the casserole to release all the sediment. Pour in the stock, stirring constantly, and bring to a boil; simmer for 2–3 minutes.

5 Add the bay leaf and return the meat to the casserole.

6 Cover and cook in the center of the preheated oven for 1½–2 hours until the meat is tender. Check for seasoning and adjust if necessary.

7 Remove from the oven, discard the bay leaf, and let cool in the refrigerator, preferably overnight (this allows the flavors to develop).

8 Preheat the oven to 400°F/200°C. Roll out the pastry on a lightly floured counter to about 2 inches/5 cm larger than the pie dish (use the inverted dish as a measure). Cut off a strip, ½ inch/1 cm wide, from around the edge. Moisten the rim of the dish with water and press the pastry strip onto it. Place a pie funnel in the center of the dish and spoon in the steak and mushroom filling. Do not overfill, and keep any extra gravy to serve separately.

9 Moisten the pastry collar with a little water and put on the pastry lid, taking care to fit it carefully around the pie funnel. Crimp the edges of the pastry firmly and glaze with the egg. You can use some leftover dough to make leaf shapes to garnish the pie; stick these on using the egg and glaze well with egg.

10 Place the pie on a cookie sheet and bake near the top of the preheated oven for about 30 minutes. If the pastry is getting too brown, cover it with foil and reduce the oven temperature to 350°F/180°C. The pie should be golden brown and the filling bubbling hot.

* Suitable for freezing. At the end of step 9, open freeze without covering until the pastry is firm, then wrap well in foil or a large, sealed plastic bag. Freeze for up to 3 months. To use, thaw overnight in a cool place and cook as above.

SAUSAGE ROLLS

These sausage rolls are delicious eaten straight from the oven but can be stored in an airtight container and reheated in the oven at 350°F/180°C for 10 minutes when needed.

Makes 18–24
Preparation time: 20 minutes
Cooking time: 20–25 minutes

INGREDIENTS

2 tbsp all-purpose flour, for dusting
1 lb/450 g puff pastry
1 lb/450 g good quality sausage meat or sausages (casings removed)
1 egg, beaten

You will need 2 heavy cookie sheets with a raised edge, a rolling pin, a flour dredger, a pastry brush, a sharp knife, a pair of scissors, and a cooling rack

1 Preheat the oven to 425°F/220°C. Sprinkle a counter or pastry board with a little of the flour and flour a rolling pin. Lightly roll out the pastry into a large rectangle, measuring about 18 inches x 9 inches/45 x 23 cm. Cut into two strips 18 inches/ 45 cm long and 4½ inches/12 cm wide.

2 Divide the sausage meat in half and roll into two long shapes the length of the pastry; use a little of the flour to help in the shaping.

3 Place the sausage meat on the pastry. Moisten the long edges of the pastry with a little water. Fold the pastry over and seal the two moist edges together. Press well down and use a sharp knife to trim the pastry to a good, firm edge. Make cuts horizontally into the sealed edge so that it will flake and rise well.

Suitable for freezing. Let cool, then open freeze on a cookie sheet, uncovered, for 1–1½ hours. Transfer to sealed rigid containers and freeze for up to 3 months. Reheat from frozen in an oven at 350°F/180°C for 10–15 minutes until warm.

4 Brush the pastry with egg, then cut into 9 or 12 smaller rolls per piece, whichever you like. Snip the tops of the rolls twice with scissors to give two attractive cuts and place on cookie sheets. Bake near the top of the oven for 20–25 minutes until well risen and golden brown (swap the cookie sheets over halfway through cooking). Remove from the oven and cool on a wire rack.

FAMILY APPLE PIE

Serves 6
Preparation time: 25 minutes, plus chilling
Cooking time: 30–35 minutes

INGREDIENTS

2 cups all-purpose flour, plus 2 tbsp, for dusting

pinch of salt

¼ cup butter

¼ cup vegetable shortening

2–3 tbsp cold water, to mix

1 lb 9 oz/700 g cooking apples, peeled, cored, and thinly sliced

generous ½ cup superfine sugar, plus 1 tsp, for sprinkling

1 tsp ground cinnamon

¼ nutmeg, freshly grated

scant ½ cup raisins

1 tbsp semolina

2 tsp milk

custard or ice cream, to serve

You will need a 9 inch/23 cm (top diameter) pie pan, a vegetable peeler, a sharp knife, a round-bladed knife, a rolling pin, a flour dredger, a mixing bowl, and a cookie sheet

METHOD

1 Place the flour and salt in a bowl. Gently rub in the butter and vegetable shortening until the mixture resembles bread crumbs. Sprinkle in the cold water and stir well using a round-bladed knife. Continue to mix until you have a smooth dough.

2 Wrap in plastic wrap and let rest in the refrigerator for 1–2 hours.

3 Preheat the oven to 375°F/190°C. In a mixing bowl, combine the apples, sugar, spices, raisins, and semolina.

4 Divide the dough into two, one piece slightly larger than the other. On a lightly floured counter, roll out the larger piece of dough into a round just larger than the pie pan, and use it to line the ungreased pan. Press the down down well and make sure no air is trapped.

5 Put the fruit filling into the pie shell.

6 Roll out the remaining dough to a round just larger then the top of the pan. Moisten the dough around the rim of the pan with water, and lay the rolled out dough on top. Press down well around the rim to seal, and cut any excess pastry away. Crimp the edges of the dough with your fingers or use a fork.

7 Glaze with a little milk and sprinkle with sugar.

8 Put the pan on a cookie sheet and bake near the top of the preheated oven for 30–35 minutes until golden brown. Serve while still hot with lots of custard or some ice-cream.

* Suitable for freezing. Open freeze, uncovered, on a cookie sheet for 2 hours when cooked and chilled, then wrap well in foil or a large plastic bag. Freeze for up to 3 months. To use, thaw at room temperature for 4–5 hours and warm through in the oven at 375°F/190°C for 20 minutes before serving.

MINCE PIES

These pies make a delicious, quick dessert.

Makes 24
Preparation time: 40–45 minutes, plus chilling
Cooking time: 25 minutes

INGREDIENTS

3 cups all-purpose flour
½ tsp salt
6 tbsp butter
6 tbsp vegetable shortening
3–4 tbsp cold water, to mix
1–1¼ lb/450–550 g mincemeat
2 tbsp brandy
4 tbsp milk
2 tbsp superfine sugar
thick cream or brandy butter (see page 215), to serve

You will need a muffin pan with 12 patty pans, two fluted cutters (one 3 inches/7.5 cm and one 2½ inches/6 cm), a mixing bowl, a round-bladed knife, a rolling pin, a flour dredger, a pastry brush, a fork, a metal spatula, and a cooling rack

METHOD

1 Sift the flour and salt into a bowl and gently rub in the butter and vegetable shortening until the mixture resembles bread crumbs. Sprinkle in the cold water and stir well using a round-bladed knife. Continue to mix until you have a smooth dough.

2 Wrap in plastic wrap and let rest in the refrigerator for 1–2 hours.

3 Preheat the oven to 400°F/200°C. Divide the dough into two, one piece slightly larger then the other. Roll the larger piece out as thinly as possible on a lightly floured counter and stamp out rounds using the larger cutter. Gather together the trimmings, re-roll, and cut out until you have 24 round.

4 Carefully place the dough rounds in the ungreased patty pans and press down gently.

5 In a separate bowl, mix the mincemeat with the brandy and spoon a good teaspoonful into each pie.

6 Roll out the remaining dough and stamp out more rounds, using the smaller cutter this time. Gather the trimmings, re-roll, and cut out until you have 24 rounds.

7 Brush the edges of these rounds with water and place them, damp side down, on top of the pies, pressing gently around the edges to seal the top and bottom rounds together.

8 Glaze the top of the mince pies with milk and sprinkle with a little sugar.

9 Bake near the top of the preheated oven (if you are cooking two pans together, change positions on the shelves at half-time) for 20–25 minutes, until lightly golden brown.

10 Remove the pans from the oven and carefully remove the pies with a metal spatula. Transfer them to a cooling rack for about 1 hour. When cool, store in an airtight container for about a week. To serve, warm through gently in an oven at 350°F/180°C for 10 minutes, and serve sprinkled with a little more sugar and some thick cream or brandy butter.

* Suitable for freezing. Open freeze, uncovered, on a cookie sheet for 1½–2 hours, then transfer to rigid sealed containers. Freeze for up to 3 months. To serve, reheat in an oven at 350°F/180°C for 10 minutes.

TREACLE TART

Serves 6
Preparation time: 25 minutes, plus resting time
Cooking time: 25 minutes

INGREDIENTS

1½ cups all-purpose flour, plus extra for dusting
a pinch of salt
6 tbsp butter
2–3 tbsp cold water
1 cup light corn syrup
2 cups fresh white or whole-wheat bread crumbs
4 tbsp heavy cream
2 tbsp milk, for glazing (optional)
cold light cream, to serve

You will need an 8 inch/20 cm quiche pan or metal pie dish, a mixing bowl, a rolling pin, a flour dredger, a small pan, a round-bladed knife, a wooden spoon, and a pastry brush

METHOD

1 Make the pastry by placing the flour and salt in a mixing bowl and rubbing in the butter until the mixture resembles bread crumbs. Sprinkle in 2–3 tablespoons of cold water and stir into the flour using a round-bladed knife. Cut through the mixture until it starts to cling together. Using a floured hand bring the mixture together in the center of the bowl and form a smooth ball. Handle very carefully because pastry needs a delicate hand. Put the dough in a plastic bag and rest in the refrigerator for 30 minutes.

2 Meanwhile, warm the syrup gently in the pan until it is runny. Add the bread crumbs and cream and stir well. Set aside for about 15 minutes for the bread crumbs to swell.

3 Preheat the oven to 375°F/190°C. On a lightly floured counter, roll out the chilled dough into a round large enough to line a quiche pan. Press it gently into the ungreased pan and cut off any excess.

4 Pour the syrup filling into the pie shell. Roll out the remaining dough trimmings to make a lattice decoration, lay it on top of the tart, and glaze with the milk, if using, or otherwise leave it plain.

5 Place the tart on a cookie sheet and bake in the center of the preheated oven for about 25 minutes until the pastry is golden brown. The filling should still be soft as it sets.

6 Remove from the oven and let stand for 5 minutes. Remove the quiche pan and serve while still warm, with some cold light cream.

* Suitable for freezing. Open freeze, uncovered, on a cookie sheet for 1–1½ hours and then wrap well with foil or a large sealed plastic bag. To use, thaw at room temperature for 3–4 hours, then warm in an oven at 350°F/180°C for 10–15 minutes before serving.

PEAR TARTE TATIN

Serves 6
Preparation time: 30 minutes
Cooking time: 20 minutes

INGREDIENTS

6 tbsp butter
generous ½ cup superfine sugar
6 pears, peeled, halved, and cored
flour, for dusting
8 oz/225 g ready-made puff pastry
heavy cream, to serve (optional)

You will need a 10 inch/25 cm heavy ovenproof skillet, a wooden spoon, a sharp knife, a cutting board, a vegetable peeler, a rolling pin, a flour dredger, a large, deep serving dish, and a pair of thick potholders

METHOD

1 Preheat the oven to 400°F/200°C. Melt the butter and sugar in an ovenproof skillet over medium heat. Stir carefully for 5 minutes until it turns to a light caramel color. Take care because it gets very hot.

2 Remove the pan from the heat, place on a heatproof surface, and arrange the pears, cut side up, in the caramel. Place one half in the center and surround it with the others.

3 On a lightly floured counter, roll out the dough to a round, slightly larger than the skillet, and place it on top of the pears. Tuck the edges down into the skillet.

4 Bake near the top of the preheated oven for 20–25 minutes until the pastry is well risen and golden brown.

5 Remove from the oven and let cool for 2 minutes.

6 Invert the tart onto a serving dish that is larger than the skillet and has enough depth to take any juices that may run out. Remember that this is very hot so take care with this maneuver and use a pair of thick potholders.

7 Serve warm, with heavy cream if using.

BAKING

*T*he term "baking" covers the method of making cakes and cookies with a flour base (breadmaking is covered in a separate section). It also refers to the method of cooking in the oven, although some biscuits are cooked on a griddle pan.

INGREDIENTS
The ingredients used in baking include:

Flour
All-purpose white flour, self-rising flour (contains baking powder as a raising agent), whole-wheat flour, multigrain flour (a mixture of brown and rye flours and malted grains), and brown flour (contains 85 percent of the grain). For buying and storing flour, see page 36.

Raising agents
Baking soda is a raising agent which, when mixed with an acid, produces carbon dioxide to raise cakes and biscuits. Baking powder is a mixture of baking soda and tartaric acid which, when moistened, also produces carbon dioxide.

Sugar
Superfine, granulated, confectioners', soft light- and dark-brown, light and dark molasses, and raw brown sugar should all be used according to recipe instructions. For buying and storage, see page 37.

Eggs
For more information on eggs, see pages 72–75.

Fats
Oils, butter, and shortening are used in baking. For more information on fats, please see pages 38 and 91.

Nuts
For more information on nuts, please see page 43.

Dried fruits
For more information on dried fruits, please see page 42.

METHODS
In cake and cookie making four methods are used:

Creaming method
This is where the fat and sugar are creamed together, using either a wooden spoon or an electric mixer. For an example of the creaming method, see the Sponge Layer Cake recipe on pages 232–3). The eggs are then added and the flour folded in. Cakes made by this method keep well owing to the amount of fat in the mixture.

Whisking method
This is when the eggs and sugar are first whisked together to form a fat/sugar foam. This technique entraps the air, which, when heated in the oven, expands and raises the cake. The flour is then carefully folded into the egg and sugar mixture. These cakes are often called fatless sponge cakes and do not keep as well as creamed cakes.

Rubbing-in method
These cakes and cookies are less rich and the fat content is usually below half that of the flour. The fat is incorporated by rubbing it into the flour using the fingertips until the mixture resembles bread crumbs. This method is used for biscuits, shortbread, rock cakes, and teabreads.

Melting method
This is the method used to make moist, heavy cakes like gingerbread and parkin, and cookies such as flapjacks. The fat and sugar, together with any other ingredients, are heated until all are dissolved before the addition of the eggs, flour, raising agent, and any spices. These cakes keep well owing to their high fat and sugar content; wrap them well in plastic wrap to maintain their moist texture.

EQUIPMENT

Here is a list of the main items you will need for baking. Other baking equipment is mentioned in the equipment section (see pages 28–29).

Cookie sheet

A good-quality cookie sheet is essential to cook cookies and small cakes.

Layer pans

A pair of layer pans is useful for sponge cakes.

Deep, round pan

This kind of pan is needed to cook a Christmas cake or other rich fruit cake.

Medium-sized square pan

This is good for gingerbreads (see pages 28–29 for further advice regarding baking pans).

Baking parchment (or silicone paper)

This is more reliable than waxed paper and can be used for meringues as well.

Muffin pan

This will be needed if you want to make small cakes.

SPONGE LAYER CAKE

Sponge layer cakes are delicious when freshly baked. However, you can store any remaining in an airtight container for up to one week.

Serves 8–10 slices
Preparation time: 25 minutes, plus cooling
Cooking time: 30 minutes

INGREDIENTS

¾ cup sweet butter, softened at room temperature
scant 1 cup superfine sugar
3 eggs, beaten
1½ cups self-rising flour

To serve
3 tbsp jelly or lemon curd
1 tbsp superfine or confectioners' sugar

You will need two 8 inch/20 cm layer pans, greased, and bases lined with waxed paper or baking parchment, a hand-held electric mixer or a wooden spoon, a mixing bowl, a flexible spatula or a metal spoon, and a cooling rack

1 Preheat the oven to 350°F/180°C. Put the butter and superfine sugar in a mixing bowl and cream together until the mixture is pale, light, and fluffy. Cream for 1–2 minutes if using a hand-held mixer, or 5–6 minutes by hand. Add the eggs, a little at a time, beating well after each addition.

2 Sift the flour and carefully add it to the mixture, folding it in with a metal spoon or a spatula.

3 Divide the mixture between the two prepared layer pans and smooth over with the spatula. Bake on the same shelf in the center of the preheated oven for 25–30 minutes until well risen, golden brown, and beginning to shrink from the sides of the pans. Remove from the oven and let stand for 1 minute. Use a spatula to loosen the cakes from the edge of the pans.

4 Turn the cakes out onto a clean dish towel and remove the papers. Invert the cakes onto a cooling tray (this prevents the cooling tray from marking the top of the cakes). Leave for 30–45 minutes in a cool place to cool completely. Sandwich together with jelly or lemon curd, and sprinkle with the sugar.

* Suitable for freezing. Open freeze, uncovered, on a cookie sheet for 1 hour. Transfer to a sealed freezer bag, or freeze in a rigid plastic container. Freeze for up to 3 months. To use, thaw at room temperature for about 4 hours.

CHRISTMAS CAKE

This delicious cake is a wonderful treat during the festive season. Try to use natural colored candied cherries if possible. They are available from many healthfood stores.

Makes 20–24 portions
Preparation time: 45 minutes, plus 15 minutes
marzipan and 25 minutes icing
Cooking time: 2–2½ hours

INGREDIENTS

¾ cup sweet butter, softened
¾ cup dark molasses sugar
3 eggs, beaten well
2 cups all-purpose flour
1 tsp baking powder
2 tsp apple pie spice
1⅔ cups golden raisins
1⅔ cups raisins
scant ½ cup candied cherries, roughly chopped
generous ½ cup candied mixed peel, finely chopped
scant ½ cup no-soak dried apricots, roughly chopped
scant ½ cup almonds, chopped
grated rind of 1 lemon
grated rind of I orange
½ cup sherry or brandy

Decoration
1 lb 10 oz/750 g marzipan
3 tbsp apricot jelly
3 egg whites
5¾ cups confectioners' sugar

You will need an 8 inch/20 cm round cake pan, baking parchment, a mixing bowl, an electric hand mixer, a strainer, a flexible metal spatula, a grater, some aluminum foil and waxed paper, a metal skewer, 10½ inch/26 cm silver cake board, a wooden spoon, a pastry brush, a small pan, a piece of string, and a cook's knife

METHOD

1   4

TO DECORATE THE CAKE

9   13

1 Prepare the pan carefully, by lining with a double thickness of baking parchment.

2 Cream the butter and sugar together in a mixing bowl until creamy and fluffy. Add the eggs, a little at a time, beating well between each addition.

3 In a separate bowl, sift together the flour, baking powder, and apple pie spice, then carefully fold into the egg mixture using a metal spoon or a spatula.

4 Add all the dried fruit, the nuts, and the grated rind, and fold in together with the sherry or brandy until everything is well mixed. (If you have time, you could soak the fruit in the sherry or brandy overnight). The mixture should be a soft consistency, which will drop easily from a spoon.

5 Preheat the oven to 325°F/160°C. Turn the mixture into the prepared pan, use a metal spatula to smooth the top, then cook in the center of the preheated oven for about 2 hours until the cake is firm in the center. Test by inserting a skewer into the middle: if it comes out clean it is done. Check the cake from time to time and if it is getting too brown, cover it with a piece of aluminum foil. Remove from the oven and let cool in the pan for 1–1½ hours. You can feed the cake with a little more brandy at this stage to make sure it is moist. Prick the surface all over and pour on 2–3 tablespoons brandy.

6 Remove the cake from the pan, wrap it in waxed paper, and then store it in an airtight container in a cool place for up to 2 days.

7 Divide the marzipan into three equal-size pieces. Roll out one piece into a round large enough to cover the top of the cake.

8 Roll out the remaining marzipan to a rectangle, twice the depth of the cake and half the circumference (measure this with a piece of string). Cut the rectangle in half so you have two pieces that will fit around the cake.

9 Warm the jelly in a pan over low heat for 1–2 minutes, then brush the edges of the cake with it. Position the cake on its edge and roll it onto the marzipan, then press firmly. Repeat with the other piece and smooth over the joins. Trim any rough edges.

10 Brush the underside of the cake with the remaining jelly (this way you have a smoother surface). Place the round of marzipan over the top and smooth the edges. At this stage it is a good idea to allow the marzipan to dry in a cool place for up to 1 week, but if there is not time, continue with the frosting.

11 Make the frosting by placing the egg whites in a large bowl and adding the confectioners' sugar a little at a time, beating well until the frosting is very thick and will stand up in peaks.

12 Use 1 tablespoon of the frosting to secure the cake to a cakeboard.

13 For a simple finish, spread the remaining frosting over the cake and swirl it around so that you have attractive peaks all over the sides and top. You can leave the cake just as it is or arrange decorations of your choice over the top. Store in an airtight container for up to 2 months.

CARROT CAKE

Makes 16 pieces
Preparation time: 30 minutes
Cooking time: 40–50 minutes

INGREDIENTS

2 eggs
¾ cup molasses sugar
scant 1 cup sunflower oil
generous 1⅛ cups coarsely grated carrots
2 cups whole-wheat flour
1 tsp baking soda
2 tsp ground cinnamon
whole nutmeg, grated (about 1 tsp)
1 cup roughly chopped walnuts

Topping
½ cup half-fat cream cheese
4 tbsp butter, softened
¾ cup confectioners' sugar
1 tsp grated lemon rind
1 tsp grated orange rind

You will need a grater, a mixing bowl, a wooden spoon, a cook's knife, a strainer, a cutting board, a 9 inch/23 cm square cake pan (lined with baking parchment), and a cooling rack

METHOD

1 Preheat the oven to 375°F/190°C. In a mixing bowl, beat the eggs until well blended and add the sugar and oil. Mix well. Add the grated carrot.

2 Sift in the flour, baking soda, and spices, then add the walnuts. Mix everything together until well incorporated.

3 Spread the mixture into the prepared cake pan and bake in the center of the preheated oven for 40–50 minutes until the cake is nicely risen, firm to the touch, and has begun to shrink away slightly from the edge of the pan.

4 Remove from the oven and let cool in the pan until just warm, then turn out onto a cooling rack.

5 To make the topping, put all the ingredients into a mixing bowl and beat together for 2–3 minutes until really smooth.

6 When the cake is completely cold, spread with the topping, smooth over with a fork, and leave to firm up a little before cutting into 16 portions. Store in an airtight container in a cool place for up to 1 week.

* Suitable for freezing. Open freeze, uncovered, on a baking sheet for 1½ hours until the top is firm, then transfer to a rigid container and freeze for up to 3 months. To use, allow to thaw at room temperature for at least 3–4 hours.

BANANA CHOCOLATE CHIP COOKIES

Makes about 18 cookies
Preparation time: 15 minutes
Cooking time: 15–20 minutes

INGREDIENTS

generous ½ cup sweet butter
5 tbsp raw brown sugar
2 tbsp granulated sugar
1 large egg
½ tsp vanilla extract
1 small, ripe banana, mashed
1½ cups all-purpose flour
¼ tsp baking soda
pinch of salt
2 tbsp milk
4 oz/115 g good-quality bittersweet chocolate (with at least 50 percent cocoa solids), roughly chopped
½ cup chopped walnuts

You will need a mixing bowl, a hand-held electric mixer or a wooden spoon, a cook's knife, a cutting board, metal spoon or metal spatula, 2 or 3 solid cookie sheets (lined with baking parchment), and a cooling rack

METHOD

1 Preheat the oven to 375°F/190°C. In a mixing bowl, cream the butter and sugars together until the mixture is pale in color and light and fluffy.

2 In a separate bowl, beat the egg and vanilla extract together.

3 Add the egg mixture to the butter mixture, a little at a time, beating well between each addition.

4 Finally, beat in the mashed banana until the mixture is completely smooth.

5 In a separate bowl, sift together the flour, baking soda, and salt and add to the mixture, carefully folding it in with a metal spoon or a metal spatula. Stir in 2 tablespoons of milk, then fold in the chocolate and walnuts.

6 Drop dessertspoons of the mixture onto the lined cookie sheets, spaced well apart (about 6 per sheet). (If you only have one cookie sheet, you will need to do this in batches.)

7 Bake in the preheated oven for 15–20 minutes until lightly golden. Remove from the oven and let firm up slightly before placing on a cooling rack to cool completely.

8 Repeat with the remaining mixture if necessary.

9 Store in an airtight container in a cool place for up to 1 week.

Suitable for freezing. Open freeze, uncovered, on a cookie sheet for about 1 hour, then transfer to rigid containers, and freeze for up to 3 months. To use, thaw at room temperature for 3–4 hours or warm in an oven at 350°F/180°C for 10 minutes.

CHOCOLATE BROWNIES

Makes 12–16 pieces
Preparation time: 20 minutes
Cooking time: 25–30 minutes

INGREDIENTS

140 g/5 oz good-quality bittersweet chocolate (with at least 52 percent cocoa solids)

⅔ cup sweet butter

3 eggs

scant 1 cup superfine sugar

1 cup all-purpose flour

1 tsp baking powder

pinch of salt

1 tsp vanilla extract

½ cup chopped walnuts

crème fraîche or ice cream, to serve

You will need a heatproof bowl, a small pan, a mixing bowl, an electric hand mixer, a strainer, a flexible metal spatula, a 10 inch/25 cm square pan (lined with baking parchment), and a cooling rack

METHOD

1 Preheat the oven to 350°F/180°C. Melt the chocolate and butter together in a heatproof bowl over a pan of just simmering water, then remove from the heat, and let cool for 5 minutes.

2 In a mixing bowl, whisk together the eggs and sugar until thick and creamy.

3 In a separate bowl, sift together the flour, baking powder, and salt, then fold into the egg mixture. Add the vanilla. Carefully fold in the cooled chocolate mixture and the chopped nuts.

4 Turn the mixture into the pan and bake in the preheated oven for 25–30 minutes. Do not overcook. The top will be crusty, but the center should be slightly sticky.

5 Remove from the oven and then immediately cut into 12–16 pieces (depending on preference), but let cool for a while in the pan. Remove from the pan and peel off the paper before transferring to a cooling rack.

6 Serve warm for dessert with crème fraîche or ice cream, or let cool completely and store in an airtight container for up to 1 week, to eat as a snack.

* Suitable for freezing. Open freeze, uncovered, on a baking sheet for 1 hour, then transfer to a rigid container and freeze for up to 3 months. To use, allow to thaw at room temperature for at least 3–4 hours.

BISCUITS

Makes 10–12
Preparation time: 10 minutes
Cooking time: 10–12 minutes

INGREDIENTS

2 cups self-rising flour, plus extra for dusting
½ tsp salt
1 tsp baking powder
2 tbsp superfine sugar
¼ cups butter, plus extra for greasing
generous ⅓ cup mixed dried fruit
⅔ cup milk
3 tbsp milk, to glaze

To serve
strawberry jelly
thick cream

You will need a solid, greased cookie sheet, a mixing bowl, a measuring cup, a round-bladed knife, a flour dredger, a 2½ inch/6 cm pastry cutter, a pastry brush, and a cooling rack

METHOD

1 Preheat the oven to 425°F/220°C. Sift together the flour, salt, baking powder, and sugar into a bowl. Rub in the butter and add the fruit. Stir in the milk, using a round-bladed knife, and make into a soft dough.

2 Turn the mixture onto a floured surface and lightly flatten the dough until it is of an even thickness, about 1 cm/½ inch. Do not be heavy handed—biscuits need a light touch.

3 Using a pastry cutter, stamp out the biscuits and place on the prepared cookie sheet. Glaze with a little milk.

4 Bake in the preheated oven for 10–12 minutes until golden and well risen.

5 Remove from the oven and cool on a wire rack. Serve freshly baked, with strawberry jam and thick cream. Serve them warm, if possible, but certainly on the same day.

Variation

To make cheese biscuits, omit the sugar and fruit and replace with ½ cup finely grated cheese (Cheddar or brick) and 1 teaspoon of any mustard. Sprinkle with 1 tablespoon of finely grated Parmesan cheese before baking.

* Suitable for freezing. Freeze in a rigid plastic container, or open freeze, uncovered, on a cookie sheet for 1–1½ hours and then transfer to a well-sealed freezer bag. Freeze for up to 3 months. To use, thaw at room temperature for 3–4 hours. Reheat in an oven at 350°F/180°C for 10 minutes from thawed or 15–20 minutes from frozen.

SHORTBREAD

Makes 8 pieces
Preparation time: 15 minutes
Cooking time: 40–50 minutes

INGREDIENTS

1 cup all-purpose flour, plus 1 tbsp for dusting
⅓ cup fine semolina
pinch of salt
4 tbsp superfine sugar
½ cup butter
2 tsp golden superfine sugar, for dredging

You will need a mixing bowl, a rolling pin, a flour dredger, an 8 inch/20 cm layer pan lined with baking parchment or an 8 inch/20 cm fluted quiche pan, and a cooling rack

METHOD

1 Preheat the oven to 150ºC/300ºF/150ºC. In a mixing bowl, mix the flour with all the semolina, salt, and sugar.

2 Cut the butter into small pieces and rub it into the dry ingredients. Continue to work at the mixture until it forms a soft dough.

3 Gently roll out the dough into a round on a lightly floured counter and then place it carefully in the pan. Lightly press it into the pan and prick all over with a fork.

4 Bake in the center of the preheated oven for 1 hour to 1 hour 10 minutes until the shortbread is firm and pale golden.

5 Remove from the oven and mark into 8 wedges with a knife. Let cool in the pan for about 1 hour. Dredge with the sugar. Cut into wedges following the markings made earlier, then transfer to a cooling rack for another 30 minutes to cool completely Store in an airtight container in a cool place for up to 1 week until needed.

* Suitable for freezing. Open freeze, uncovered, on a cookie sheet for 1 hour, then transfer to a rigid container, and freeze for up to 3 months. To use, thaw at room temperature for 2–3 hours.

FLAPJACKS

Makes 21 pieces
Preparation time: 10–15 minutes
Cooking time: 30–35 minutes

INGREDIENTS

1 cup butter
1 cup light molasses sugar
generous ½ cup light corn syrup
4½ cups rolled oats

You will need an 8 x 12 inch/20 x 30 cm deep baking pan, baking parchment, a large pan, a wooden spoon, and a sharp knife

METHOD

1 Preheat the oven to 180°C/350°F/180°C. Line the pan with the baking parchment.

2 Put the butter, sugar, and syrup into a pan and heat over low heat for 2–3 minutes until melted. Mix in the rolled oats and stir well.

3 Pour the mixture into the prepared pan, press down well, and bake in the center of the preheated oven for 30–35 minutes until golden brown but still moist and slightly soft when pressed.

4 Remove from the oven and let cool for 5 minutes. Cut into about 21 squares and let cool completely for about 30 minutes in the pan.

5 Carefully remove the flapjacks from the pan and store in an airtight container in a cool place for up to 3–4 days.

* Suitable for freezing. Pack carefully into a rigid container and freeze for up to 3 months. To use, thaw at room temperature for at least 2–3 hours.

BREAD

There are times in our lives when we want to make a special effort and really treat our family and friends to some very special home cooking. Breadmaking is probably the epitome of this: it is very simple and very therapeutic to make, and results in something very special.

Once you have confidence, the timing can be controlled by you and can be fitted into any schedule; it does not have to be made, risen, kneaded, risen again, and baked all on the same occasion. First mixing and rising can be done as quickly or as slowly as you wish; in a warm place or even in the refrigerator overnight. There is nothing better to greet your family or guests than the smell of home baked bread and nothing more that can make any house feel more like home.

The use of active dry yeast has contributed to the simplicity of breadmaking—no longer do you have to cream the yeast and sugar together and wait for the dough to start rising. The yeast is simply added to the flour and mixed in. A ¼ oz/7 g envelope is usually enough to raise 4 cups of white bread flour. To use dry yeast, sprinkle the dried granules into a little lukewarm water and add a little sugar, stir well, and leave to act. Exact quantities and times depend on the recipe. It is ready when the surface is covered with froth. Note that with whole-wheat flour and rich recipes (those containing eggs and fruit) the amount of yeast needs to be increased.

There is also a better selection of flours available for breadmaking—organic, plain white bread, multigrain, and whole-wheat flour to enable you to bake good-quality, well-flavored loaves. Always make sure you buy bread flour for breadmaking because it has a high gluten content and becomes elastic, letting the dough rise to give a good loaf.

MAKING BREAD

You can make bread simply by mixing it by hand in a mixing bowl, turning out onto a floured counter, and kneading well before shaping. Otherwise you can use a free-standing mixer, which takes all the heavy work out of kneading. Some people will say that this takes all the fun and enthusiasm out of making bread, but for those with weak hands or arthritis it is a very good way to make the dough. The newer, popular way to make bread is to use an electronic breadmaker; this allows you to put all the ingredients into the machine and the machine

does all the work—the mixing, kneading, rising, and baking all in one go. The downside of these machines, apart from the cost, is that you get a uniform loaf every time and that shape is not ideal. Making your own dough allows you greater individuality in terms of size and shape.

RULES FOR BREADMAKING

There are a few rules concerned with breadmaking, as follows. Everything needs to be warm; it is a good idea to warm the bowl and the flour so that the rising time will be shorter. Do take care how hot the ingredients become because if they are above 86°F/30°C, the yeast will be killed and the bread will not rise. The answer is to make sure everything is lukewarm, that is, comfortable to touch and feeling just warm.

Kneading is essential: this is how the gluten is developed to give structure to the bread. To knead properly by hand you need to use the heel of your hand and push the dough down onto the surface and away from you—almost a rolling action. Once you get into the rhythm you will enjoy the sensation and it is a good method of ridding yourself of any tension you might have.

Bread is always baked at a high temperature in order to kill the yeast. In breadmaking, it is always better to overcook rather than undercook because undercooking results in a rather mealy flavor. If the bottom of the loaf is not cooked sufficiently when tested, you can replace the loaf in the oven without its pan to crisp up the base.

This section contains a few simple recipes for basic breadmaking: a basic white loaf, seeded whole-wheat bread, fruit and nut rolls (which are ideal to serve with soup), focaccia, and pizzas (which are easily made).

OPPOSITE FROM TOP: Whole-wheat bread, fruit bread, rye bread with sunflower seeds, whole-grain rye bread, fruited soda bread.

BASIC WHITE BREAD

Although we know that whole-wheat bread is supposed to be healthier for us, there are times when a good loaf of white bread suits the occasion, especially for toast.

Makes 1 large loaf
Preparation time: 20 minutes, plus rising
Cooking time: 25–30 minutes

INGREDIENTS

4 cups white bread flour, plus 2 tbsp for dusting

1 tsp salt

one ¼ oz/7 g envelope active dry yeast

1 tbsp vegetable oil or melted butter, plus 1 tsp for greasing

1¼ cups lukewarm water

You will need a large mixing bowl, a wooden spoon, a measuring cup, a flour dredger, a 2 lb/900 g loaf pan, and a cooling rack

METHOD

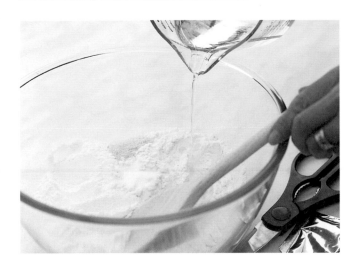

1 Mix the flour, salt, and yeast together in a mixing bowl. Add the oil and water and stir well to form a soft dough.

2 Turn the dough out onto a lightly floured board and knead well by hand for 5–7 minutes. Alternatively, use a free-standing electric mixer for this and knead the dough with the dough hook for 4–5 minutes. The dough should have a smooth appearance and feel elastic.

3 Return the dough to the bowl, cover with plastic wrap, and let rise in a warm place for 1 hour. When it has doubled in size, turn it out onto a floured board and knead again for 30 seconds; this is known as "punching down." Knead it until smooth.

5 Preheat the oven to 425°F/220°C. Bake in the center of the preheated oven for 25–30 minutes until firm and golden brown. Test that the loaf is cooked by tapping it on the base—it should sound hollow. Cool on a cooling rack for 30 minutes. Store in an airtight container in a cool place for 3–4 days.

4 Shape the dough into a rectangle the length of the pan and three times the width. Grease the pan well, fold the dough into three lengthwise, and put it in the pan with the join underneath for a well-shaped loaf. Cover and let rise in a warm place for 30 minutes until it has risen well above the pan.

Suitable for freezing. When thoroughly cooled, wrap in a plastic bag, seal well, and freeze for up to 3 months. To use, thaw at room temperature for 4–5 hours before using.

FOCACCIA

Focaccia is delicious with any Italian food, but particularly with antipasti, soups, and salads.

Makes 1 loaf
Preparation time: 15 minutes, plus rising
Cooking time: 20–25 minutes

INGREDIENTS

4 cups white bread flour, plus 2 tbsp for dusting
1½ tsp active dry yeast
½ tsp salt
5 tbsp good-quality Italian extra-virgin olive oil
1¼ cups lukewarm water
1 tsp olive oil, for greasing
2 tbsp coarse sea salt

You will need a large mixing bowl, a wooden spoon, a measuring cup, a flour dredger, a cookie sheet, and a cooling rack.

METHOD

1 Combine the flour, yeast, and salt in a mixing bowl.

2 Pour in 3 tablespoons of the extra-virgin olive oil and add the lukewarm water. Mix well with a wooden spoon or your hands until you have a soft dough.

3 Turn the dough out onto a lightly floured counter and knead for 8–10 minutes until very smooth.

4 Place the dough in a bowl, cover with a clean cloth, and let rise in a warm place for 45 minutes–1 hour until doubled in size.

5 Turn the dough out onto a lightly floured counter and knead gently, taking care not to knock out all the air.

6 Grease a cookie sheet with the olive oil. Gently roll out the dough until it is ¾ inch/2 cm thick and about 12 inches/30 cm in diameter: it does not need to be a perfect circle—a slightly rounded rectangle is good.

7 Place the dough on the cookie sheet, cover with a clean dish towel or a piece of greased plastic wrap, and let rise again in a warm place for 20–30 minutes. With the handle of a wooden spoon, make holes about 2 inches/5 cm apart all over the surface of the dough.

8 Drizzle with the remaining oil and sprinkle with the sea salt.

9 Preheat the oven to 400°F/200°C. Bake in the center of the preheated oven for 20–25 minutes until well risen and golden brown. Transfer to a cooling rack for a few minutes, but serve the bread while still warm. Store in an airtight container in a cool place for 2–3 days or in a sealed plastic bag in the refrigerator for 4–5 days.

Variations

• Add an extra 2 tablespoons olive oil and 2 tablespoons chopped fresh herbs, such as basil, rosemary, or thyme before cooking.

• Fold 4 oz/115 g prosciutto and 4 oz/115 g mozzarella into the dough before the second rising to give a savory snack loaf.

• Sprinkle fried onion rings and garlic over the loaf before cooking. Use 1 onion and 1 garlic clove.

• Add 2 oz/55 g sun-dried tomatoes and 2 oz/55 g chopped olives before the final rising, or just sprinkled on top, for a wonderful Mediterranean flavor.

Suitable for freezing. Let cool thoroughly and wrap well in a plastic bag, then seal well, and freeze for up to 3 months. To use, thaw at room temperature for 2–3 hours and warm gently before serving.

HAZELNUT AND RAISIN ROLLS

These are delicious served with cheese. The fruit just adds a little sweetness and makes an ideal accompaniment to strong varieties of cheese such as Stilton and Gorgonzola.

Makes 16–20 rolls
Preparation time: 20 minutes, plus rising
Cooking time: 15 minutes

INGREDIENTS

4 cups whole-wheat flour, plus 3 tbsp for dusting
2 cups white bread flour
1 tsp salt
two ½ oz/7 g envelopes active dry yeast
3 tbsp olive oil or hazelnut oil
2 cups lukewarm water
1 cup coarsely chopped hazelnuts
¾ cup raisins

You will need a large mixing bowl, a wooden spoon, a measuring cup, a flour dredger, 2 cookie sheets, and a cooling rack

METHOD

1 In a mixing bowl, combine the flours, salt, and yeast. Add 2 tablespoons of the oil and all the warm water and stir well to form a soft dough.

2 Turn the dough out onto a lightly floured board and knead well for 5–7 minutes. The dough should have a smooth appearance and feel elastic. Add the nuts and raisins and mix well.

3 Return the dough to the bowl, cover with a clean cloth or with some plastic wrap, and leave in a warm place for 1–1½ hours to rise.

4 When the dough has doubled in size, turn it out onto a lightly floured board and knead again for 1 minute.

5 Divide the dough into 20–24 even pieces and shape into good rounds. Grease the cookie sheets well with the remaining oil. Place the rolls on the sheets, leaving enough space between them to allow for expansion while they rise.

6 Cover again and let rise again for about 30 minutes, until the rolls are risen and have doubled in size.

7 Preheat the oven to 400°F/200°C. Bake in the preheated oven for about 15 minutes, swapping their positions halfway through. The buns should be golden brown and their bases should sound hollow when tapped.

8 Cool on a cooling rack and eat on the same day, or store for 2–3 days in a sealed container in the refrigerator.

*Suitable for freezing. When thoroughly cooled, place in a plastic bag or rigid box. Seal well and freeze for up to 3 months. To use, remove as many rolls as you need from the freezer and reheat in an oven at 350°F/ 180°C for 10–15 minutes before serving.

PIZZA

Serves 2
Preparation time: 15 minutes, plus rising
Cooking time: 20–25 minutes

INGREDIENTS

2 cups white bread flour or whole-wheat bread flour, plus 2 tbsp for dusting

2 tsp active dry yeast

½ tsp salt

1 tbsp olive oil, plus 1 tsp for greasing

¾ cup lukewarm water

Topping
14 oz/400 g canned chopped tomatoes, drained well

1 red onion, peeled, sliced, and cooked in 1 tbsp olive oil for 5–10 minutes

1 tsp chopped fresh oregano

4 slices salami, halved

5 oz/140 g mozzarella cheese, sliced

⅔ cup freshly grated Parmesan cheese

salt and pepper

You will need a large mixing bowl, a wooden spoon, a measuring cup, a flour dredger, and a cookie sheet

METHOD

1 In a mixing bowl, mix together the flour, yeast, and salt.

2 Pour in 1 tablespoon of the oil and all the warm water. Mix well with a wooden spoon or your hands until you have a soft dough. If you are using whole-wheat flour, you may need a little more water.

3 Turn the dough out onto a lightly floured counter and knead for 8–10 minutes until very smooth and elastic.

4 Grease a cookie sheet with oil. Gently roll out the dough into a round about 12 inches/30 cm in diameter and place it on the cookie sheet. Let rise while you make the topping.

5 Spread the tomatoes and onion on top of the pizza. Add the oregano, season well, and arrange the salami slices around the edge. Place the mozzarella on top and sprinkle with the Parmesan.

6 Preheat the oven to 425°F/220°C. Leave for 10–15 minutes more until the edges of the pizza are beginning to rise.

7 Bake in the center of the preheated oven for 20–25 minutes until golden brown. Serve immediately.

Variations

• Sun-dried tomatoes and chopped olives can be added, with a few torn basil leaves.

• Roasted bell peppers can be sliced and added on top of the tomatoes; omit the salami and add a few sliced green olives.

• Drain a can of tuna and flake the fish onto the tomato, onion, and oregano base (omit the salami). Add the cheese and top with 4 sliced anchovy fillets and some black olives.

• Sauté 1⅓ cups white mushrooms with a crushed clove of garlic in 1 tbsp olive oil, spread over the tomatoes, and cover with 4 slices of prosciutto; top with the cheese before cooking.

* Suitable for freezing. Let cool thoroughly and wrap well in a plastic bag, then seal well, and freeze for up to 3 months. To use, thaw at room temperature for 3–4 hours and heat in an oven at 425°F/220°C for 10–15 minutes before serving..

WALNUT AND SEED BREAD

If you are making bread, it always seems sensible to make more than one loaf. The extra effort involved in making three loaves instead of one is negligible. And, after all, if you are have the oven switched on it is more economical to utilize the whole space.

Makes 1 large and 2 small loaves
Preparation time: 20 minutes, plus rising
Cooking time: 25–30 minutes

INGREDIENTS

4 cups whole-wheat flour
4 cups multigrain flour
1 cup white bread flour
2 tbsp sesame seeds
2 tbsp sunflower seeds
2 tbsp poppy seeds
1 cup chopped walnuts
2 tsp salt
two ½ oz/7 g envelopes active dry yeast
2 tbsp olive oil or walnut oil
3 cups lukewarm water
1 tbsp melted butter or oil, for greasing

You will need a large mixing bowl, a wooden spoon, a measuring cup, a flour dredger, a 2 lb/900 g loaf pan and two 1 lb/450 g loaf pans or alternatively two 2 lb/900 g loaf pans, and a cooling rack

METHOD

1 In a mixing bowl, combine the flours, seeds, nuts, salt, and yeast. Add 2 tablespoons of oil and all the lukewarm water and stir well to form a soft dough.

2 Turn the dough out onto a lightly floured board and knead well for 5–7 minutes. The dough should have a smooth appearance and feel elastic.

3 Return the dough to the bowl, cover with a clean dish towel or plastic wrap, and leave in a warm place for 1–1½ hours to rise.

4 When the dough has doubled in size, turn it out onto a lightly floured board and knead again for 1 minute.

5 Divide the dough in half. Shape one piece into a rectangle the length of the pan and three times the width. Grease the pans well with melted butter or oil. Fold the dough into three lengthwise. Place in a large pan with the join underneath for a well-shaped loaf. Repeat with the other piece, divided in half for two small loaves, if you like.

6 Cover and let rise again in a warm place for about 30 minutes, until the bread is well risen above the pans.

7 Preheat the oven to 450°F/230°C. Bake in the center of the preheated oven, with the larger pan toward the back, for 25–30 minutes. If the loaves are getting too brown, reduce the temperature to 425°F/220°C. To test that the bread is cooked, tap the loaf on the base—it should sound hollow.

8 Cool on a cooling rack for 30 minutes to 1 hour; this enables the steam to escape and prevents a soggy loaf. When cool, seal in a plastic bag and keep in the refrigerator for up to 1 week.

*Suitable for freezing. When thoroughly cooled, wrap in a plastic bag, then seal well, and freeze for up to 3 months. To use, thaw at room temperature for 4–5 hours. It is always nice to warm the loaf before serving, so heat in an oven at 350°F/180°C for 10–15 minutes.

PRESERVING

Preserving was carried out over the centuries to make sure that there was always a good supply of food when the weather became inclement and to make use of all the fruit and vegetables when there was a glut. Nowadays, methods have changed as technology has improved—we no longer salt our meat or fish, or bottle fruit, because freezing has superseded these methods.

Although we no longer use all the preserving methods our ancestors used, the making of jams, marmalades, and chutneys has stayed with us. They produce not only useful commodities, they also give us pleasure to make and provide us with lovely gifts for friends and neighbors who may not have the time or the inclination to make their own. And great satisfaction is to be had from looking at a row of neatly labeled jars of preserves in the pantry.

Homemade chutneys are a delicious accompaniment to cold meats, cheese, and salads and for adding to sandwiches; you cannot have too much. You can use almost any fruit or vegetable together with lots of sugar, vinegar, and spices to produce a well-flavored chutney.

Making marmalade is a good way to spend half a day when the days are very short and cold; an ideal time to stand near a warm stove preparing a great pan of bubbling, sweet, pungent Temple orange marmalade—something to look forward to during January when the fruit comes into the shops. You do not need any special equipment: a very large pan is all that is needed. However, a long-handled wooden spoon to avoid any burns caused by splashing is useful, and safe.

I would also recommend a jelly funnel; this enables you to fill the jars quickly and gives a cleaner result, which will save the time of wiping the jars.

Do not buy special jars—collect them throughout the year and ask friends and neighbors to keep them for you. I try to keep all sorts of jars throughout the year, particularly those special jars you may be given for Christmas; it does not really matter about the size. In fact, it is nice to have a variety of sizes to give as presents. Jars with lids are particularly useful for chutneys: basic cellophane covers are not good enough because they let the chutney dry out.

SPICY TOMATO CHUTNEY

1 Heat 3 tbsp sesame oil in a preserving pan. Add 10 oz/300 g chopped onions, 2 red chiles (seeded and chopped), and 1 chopped bulb of garlic. Cook over low heat for 4–5 minutes. Add 2 lb/1 kg tomatoes (peeled, seeded, and chopped). Cook for 15 minutes.

2 In a separate pan, dissolve ½ cup brown sugar in 1 cup distilled spice vinegar over low heat, then pour it into the tomato mixture. Bring to a boil, then simmer for 40–45 minutes, stirring frequently, until thickened. Remove the pan from the heat.

3 Make sure the jars have been warmed in an oven at 350°F/180°C for 10 minutes first. Using a jelly funnel, ladle the hot chutney into the jars carefully. Top with waxed paper discs and cover with a layer of cellophane to prevent the lids from corroding. Screw on the lids, wipe the jars, and cool. Label with contents and date. Store in a cool, dry, dark place for up to 2 years. Once opened, refrigerate and use within 3 months.

RIPE TOMATO CHUTNEY

I have made this chutney very successfully using canned tomatoes (cheap supermarket brands work well and are very economical). They are very useful when fresh tomatoes are expensive and out of season.

Makes 8 lb/3.6 kg
Preparation time: 45 minutes, plus potting
Cooking time: 2–3 hours

INGREDIENTS

6 lb/2.7 kg tomatoes

1 lb/450 g onions, peeled and finely chopped

2½ cups distilled spice vinegar

½ tsp paprika

pinch of cayenne pepper

3 tbsp salt

3½ cups granulated sugar

You will need a large pan, a colander, a bowl, a wooden spoon, eight 1 lb/450 g jam jars with lids, a ladle, a jelly funnel, waxed paper discs, cellophane covers, and labels

METHOD

1 Remove the skins of the tomatoes by dipping in boiling water for 1–2 minutes and then covering in cold water. This will make the skins easier to remove and is kinder to the hands.

2 Cut the tomatoes into quarters and remove the seeds. Roughly chop the flesh.

3 Put the tomatoes and onions in a pan and cook over medium heat without a lid for 1–2 hours until a thick pulp is obtained. The cooking time will depend on the type of tomatoes used and the size of the pan.

4 Add half the vinegar, the spices, and salt and simmer for about 20 minutes until thick.

5 In a separate bowl, dissolve the sugar in the remaining vinegar and add to the pan. Cook for 40–45 minutes until a good, thick consistency is achieved. The liquid should have all been absorbed, but the chutney should still be moist and not dry. ladle into jars while still hot.

6 Make sure the jars have been warmed in an oven at 350°F/180°C for 10 minutes and then fill them carefully using a ladle and a jelly funnel. Top with the waxed discs and cover with a layer of cellophane to prevent the lids corroding. Screw on the lids. Wipe the jars clean and let cool. Label with the type of chutney and the date.

7 Chutney is better if it is stored before use to develop its flavor. Label and store in a cool, dry, dark place for up to 2 years before use. Once opened, keep in the refrigerator and use within 3 months.

TEMPLE ORANGE MARMALADE

*This recipe is adapted from a very old cookbook, but it is
the best I have used. Only Temple oranges are suitable.*

Makes 10 lb/4.5 kg
Preparation time: 3 hours, plus potting
Cooking time: 20–30 minutes

INGREDIENTS

3 lb/1.3 kg unpeeled Temple oranges, washed
9½–12½ pints/2.5–3.5 litres boiling water
13¾ cups granulated or preserving sugar
juice of 2 lemons

You will need a large preserving pan or a large pan, a large
heatproof casserole dish, a colander, a strainer, a measuring
cup, a wooden spoon, a sugar thermometer or a saucer, ten 1
lb/450 g jam jars with lids, a ladle, a slotted spoon, a jelly
funnel, waxed paper disks, and labels

METHOD

1 Put the whole fruit in the casserole dish and cover with the
boiling water. Bring to a boil, cover, and simmer gently for
2 hours, or cook in an oven at 300°F/150°C for 2 hours.

2 Remove the pan from the stove or oven. Using a slotted
spoon, carefully lift out the fruit from the water and put it
into a colander. Let cool.

3 When cool enough to handle, cut the fruit in half, separating
the flesh and seeds from the peel. Use a sharp knife and a
fork to cut the orange peel into strips to the size you like—thin
strips or chunky depending on your preference.

4 Add the seeds and flesh to the cooking water in the
casserole, return it to the stove, and bring back to a boil.
Boil briskly for 5 minutes with the lid off. This helps to set the
marmalade.

5 Strain this liquid through a strainer and press the pulp
through using a wooden spoon.

6 Place the sliced peel and the strained liquid in a preserving
pan and add the sugar.

7 Place the pan over gentle heat and stir well for 4–5 minutes
until the sugar is dissolved. Turn up the heat and boil rapidly
for 20–30 minutes until the marmalade has reached setting
point. Test that it is setting by using a sugar thermometer (if you
have one). When it reads 221°F/105 °C it is a good setting
point. Alternatively, use the saucer test: drop a small spoonful of
marmalade onto a cold saucer, chill to cool it, then push it with
a finger. If it forms a wrinkled skin, it is ready. If not, boil for a
further 5 minutes and repeat the test.

8 Remove the pan from the heat and cool for 10 minutes.
Skim any scum off the surface with a tablespoon.

9 Warm the jars in an oven at 350°F/180°C for 10 minutes,
then fill them carefully using a ladle and a jelly funnel. Top
with waxed discs and screw on the lids. Wipe the jars clean and
let cool. Label with the type of marmalade and the date and
store in a cool, dry place for up to 2 years. Once opened, keep
in the refrigerator and use within 3 months.

INDEX

INDEX

INDEX